CW00545465

Select Medii

THOMAS TRAHERNE was born in about 1637, in the city of Hereford. He entered Brasenose College, Oxford on 1 March 1653, and became B.A. in 1656, M.A. in 1661 and B.D. in 1669. In December 1657 he was admitted to the living of Credenhill in Herefordshire as a Commonwealth conformist, but after the Restoration he received episcopal ordination on 20 October 1660, and subscribed to the Act of Uniformity. He held the living of Credenhill until his death, but by early 1674 he had become a domestic chaplain to Sir Orlando Bridgeman, former Lord Keeper of the Great Seal. He died in Bridgeman's house at Teddington, Middlesex, shortly after having made his will on about 27 September 1674. He was buried in Teddington on 10 October 1674 under the reading-desk in the church.

Traherne published *Roman Forgeries* (1673) and *Christian Ethicks* (1675), but he became known in the twentieth century through a remarkable series of manuscript discoveries, among them his *Select Meditations* in 1964 and *Commentaries of Heaven* in 1982. In late 1996 a manuscript was found containing an unknown poem by Traherne of over 1800 lines, written entirely in his own hand, entitled *The Ceremonial Law*. In early 1997 a further manuscript was identified, containing five prose works: two untitled pieces now known as *Inducements to Retiredness* and *Love*, and three works with the titles *A Sober View of Dr Twisse his Considerations*, *Seeds of Eternity*, and *The Kingdom of God*. Although the number of Traherne's original manuscripts which have survived is already almost without precedent for any seventeenth-century author, it is quite possible that yet more may come to light.

JULIA J. SMITH read English at Somerville College, Oxford. She has held a research fellowship at the University of Newcastle, and has taught for the Open University. She is now an independent scholar, with a particular interest in seventeenth-century literature, and has published extensively on Thomas Traherne, his manuscripts and his biography.

Fyfield*Books* aim to make available some of the great classics of British and European literature in clear, affordable formats, and to restore often neglected writers to their place in literary tradition.

Fyfield*Books* take their name from the Fyfield elm in Matthew Arnold's 'Scholar Gypsy' and 'Thyrsis'. The tree stood not far from the village where the series was originally devised in 1971.

> *Roam on! The light we sought is shining still.*
> *Dost thou ask proof? Our tree yet crowns the hill,*
> *Our Scholar travels yet the loved hill-side*

from 'Thyrsis'

THOMAS TRAHERNE

Select Meditations

Edited with an introduction by
JULIA J. SMITH

CARCANET

in association with
The Dean and Chapter of Hereford

First published in Great Britain in 1997 by
Carcanet Press Limited
Alliance House
Cross Street
Manchester M2 7AQ

This edition published in association with The Dean and Chapter of Hereford

Edition, introduction and notes copyright © Julia J. Smith 1997, 2009
Preface copyright © Louis L. Martz 1997, 2009

The right of Julia J. Smith to be identified as the editor of this work has been
asserted by her in accordance with the Copyright, Designs and Patents Act
of 1988
All rights reserved

A CIP catalogue record for this book is available from the British Library
ISBN 978 1 84777 071 4

The publisher acknowledges financial assistance from Arts Council England

Printed and bound in England by SRP Ltd, Exeter

Contents

PREFACE

It is a great pleasure to see the *Select Meditations* of Traherne published at last with such a carefully edited text and such an illuminating commentary. I say 'at last' because it has now been more than thirty years since the day in 1964 when my friend and colleague, James Osborn, asked me to come over to his office in the Beinecke Library to examine an anonymous manuscript that he had just purchased for the large collection of manuscripts that he and his wife were gathering with a view toward an ultimate gift to Yale. He thought the manuscript might have something to do with Traherne, and he was asking me to consider this intuition because he knew that I had been spending a large part of the preceding year in studying Traherne's *Centuries*. He handed me the manuscript with a quizzical smile, making no suggestion about possible authorship. I sat down and sampled the work from beginning to end, and after perhaps a half hour, Osborn declares that I *levitated*, crying out, 'This can only be something written by Thomas Traherne!' 'Why are you so sure?' he asked. I answered that, first of all, I had come upon the meditation (III.29) about the vision of the world as it appeared to 'the little Stranger': 'As sweet every thing as paradice could make it'. It seemed like a version of several well-known passages in the *Centuries*. Furthermore, the peculiar breathless style, with its strange spelling and idiosyncratic punctuation – or lack of punctuation – struck me as being exactly the characteristics of the manuscript of the *Centuries* that I had been studying in the Bodleian, while working on *The Paradise Within* (1964). The handwriting of the manuscript, however, presented a more difficult problem, since it was utterly different from the cursive hand that Traherne used for the *Centuries*, and we reached no firm conclusion about it. The galley-proofs for my book arrived only a few days after Osborn called me in to look at his new acquisition; and so I was able to add to the page-proofs a five-page account of the new manuscript.

James Osborn had planned to edit the manuscript himself and had made preliminary arrangements for publication. But his health was failing, and he could barely manage to complete his posthumously published essay, 'Thomas Traherne: Revelations in Meditation', before his death in 1976. Sometime during his last months he said to me, 'Now promise that you will see that the Traherne is published'. I knew that he wanted me to complete the editing, and I thought for some years that I would do this, as soon as other scholarly obligations to Thomas More and John Milton would permit me. But as these obligations were being cleared away, the news came of the discovery of yet another Traherne manuscript, the massive *Commentaries of Heaven*, now in the British Library. No one could hope to edit the *Select Meditations* without mastering this new manuscript. And so I was delighted and relieved to learn of Julia Smith's interest in Traherne, for she was able to study the new manuscript as soon as it became available. She has mastered not only this latest manuscript, but all the other manuscripts, published writings, and documentary materials related to Traherne. James Osborn would be pleased to see his manuscript at last in print, edited with scholarly skill and critical perception.

Louis L. Martz
Yale University

to of whose Blessednesse also is Implanted in Man. So y^t
He enjoyeth both God & His own.

30.

The Similitude of His power is planted within,
of His Wisdom and liberty, as well as comprehension. For
a Creature wch can enjoy all things is indued with powrs infinity
Greater y^n y^t of makeing and Enjoying worlds. could He make
worlds and not enjoy y^m it would be childish weaknesse: could
He make & Enjoy y^m it would be infinitly lesse y^n y^t powr
of Enjoying all things. God being Infinitly Greater y^n worlds
Tho all possible Should be made. This Dismonstration we
haue cited, heretofore: but it is not felt, Nor yet prized as it
ought to be. Men Dream onely of what they haue, & are no
Ravished, Nor Awaked out Slumber according to ye Merrit
of Soe Divine a caus. were they well aware of ye Things we
are Speaking, They would Sing Hallelujahs forevermore.

31

In ye Blessednesse of God there is not only ye Enjoyment of Creature, but ye Manifestation of Glory. w^{ch}
nevertheless are Coincident, for ye World is his treasure
only for ye sake of his glory. His Goodnesse being infinit,
desires to be received, & to becom an Object of infinit
Delight to all Spectators. wch to be, is indeed to be Gle-
rious. That he may be this Object of Delight he made
ye World, & for this End only is it usefull to him.

32

Man is made to appear in Glory as well as to inherit all
Treasure. And therefore is Endued with liberty of will as
well as comprehension. He is Glorious in Abilitie in respect
of life powre and Intelligence. Glorious in respect of Height
Exaltation Treasure. Glorious in Attendants in respects of
Angels & Men. But God would haue Him Glorious
in Himselfe in respect of His own Actions Works & operations.
He would haue Him voluntary as God is, wise, Holy, in all
his Enjoyments, that He might be most Blessed in being ~
Glorious.

33

Select Meditations, II.30-32, by permission of the J. M. and M.-L. Osborn
Collection, Beinecke Rare Book and Manuscript Library, Yale University.

INTRODUCTION

Select Meditations proclaims Traherne's desire to be infinitely 'Communicativ', and with it his perception that the most private religious devotion takes place before an audience of God, angels and men. It acknowledges his own need not only 'To talk of His wisdom Goodness and power, to speak of his Lov, and to Adore His GodHead', but also 'to have living Auditors while we sing his praises' (II.45), a need which is mirrored both in the interplay of private and public themes in *Select Meditations* and in the collaborative production of the manuscript which contains it.

Traherne's desire for living auditors received new possibilities of fulfilment when in 1964 the manuscript was offered for sale in a Birmingham bookseller's catalogue, described as 'Select Meditations. Four Centuries', and was acquired and identified as Traherne's by the American collector James Osborn.[1] The manuscript, in a small calf-bound octavo volume measuring only 5¾" x 3¾", is quite badly mutilated; most of the first Century of *Select Meditations* is missing, and a number of other pages have been cut or torn out. Nothing is known of its whereabouts since Traherne's death in 1674, and the only clue to its history is an inscrutable note written in pencil inside its front cover which reads 'bought near montgomery Possibly Henry III'. Contrary to Osborn's belief, the small, neat italic hand in which the manuscript is primarily written is not that of Traherne himself, but Traherne's authorship is demonstrated both by the work's content, including the poem 'All musick sawces Feasts Delights and Pleasures' (IV.60) later to be published in his *Christian Ethicks* (1675), and by the evidence of the manuscript that Traherne himself supervised its production.

It is important that *Select Meditations* is interpreted within the context of the manuscript, and what this can tell us about how Traherne saw the role of his own writing. In spite of the apparently deeply private nature of its self-criticism, and Traherne's frank analysis of the shortcomings of his own character, 'Too easy and complying a Nature. Speaking too much and too Long in the Best Things' (III.65), its end is not fulfilled in spontaneous self-expression. The text of *Select Meditations* is a copy, and Traherne did not choose to make this copy of his intimate reflections for himself. The manuscript in fact contains two other hands besides that of Traherne, and also a number of shorter works, of some of which he may not be the author, so that it cannot be seen as the private possession of an individual writer, but as in some degree the construct of a group. All of these factors impinge on both the privacy of the content of *Select Meditations*, and paradoxically on the prominence of the author of the work whose individuality and idiosyncrasy powerfully stamp it.

Select Meditations is the first work in the Osborn manuscript. Most of the text is written by someone who was clearly an amanuensis copying from an earlier draft; the text contains all the kinds of mistakes associated with scribal copying, leaves blanks for words or even parts of words which cannot be read, and shows a hesitancy over Latin quotations. The copyist does not seem to have been a professional scribe, and was perhaps a friend, a pupil, or a member of Traherne's family. The spelling is generally characteristic of Traherne's own, as are some of the peculiarities of punctuation and capitalization. Traherne himself was clearly in control, and from time to time read over what had been written, checking the work of his amanuensis and making numerous small alterations and corrections, although he by no means succeeded in eliminating all the mistakes, or filling in all the blanks. On two occasions he completed a meditation himself, and on one occasion wrote out a whole meditation. This can be seen in the frontispiece, where meditation II.31 is written entirely in Traherne's hand, while 30 and 32 are copied by the amanuensis. After meditation III.51 Traherne seems to have stopped checking the scribe's work, and there are no further occurrences of his hand. The copy may be unfinished, as it stops at meditation IV.68, and is followed in the manuscript by nine blank pages. One of the meditations (III.90) also contains an addition in the hand of a third person. Following the nine blank pages at the end of *Select Meditations*, this same hand has written 'A Prayer for Ash wednesday' and 'A Meditation', neither of which sounds as though it was composed by Traherne. Then after another thirteen blank pages, the hand which wrote the bulk of *Select Meditations* has copied two treatises, the first 'treating of the Soul' and the second 'of Love to God and man', which end the volume. Traherne probably is the author of these treatises, and intriguingly 'of the Soul' seems to have been written in response to a request by someone else, since it begins, 'I am willing to gratifie your desires in treating of the Soul: not out of any vain Humor to appear abroad; but from a native desire that the Glory of God may be seen with many eys' (manuscript, p. 246).

There are many unanswered questions about the production of the manuscript. We do not know why or for whom the copy of *Select Meditations*, and the compilation of which it forms a part, were made; whose hands appear in it; or whose pressing questions about the nature of the soul needed to be answered. But this pattern of collaborative production is in fact typical of the Traherne manuscripts. Although most of the other manuscripts differ from *Select Meditations* in that they are primarily written in Traherne's own hand, almost all of them contain sections or additions in the hands of other people too, who are generally, but not invariably, copying out text at Traherne's direction.[2] Writing, even of the most private kind, does not seem to have been a solitary activity for Traherne, and the picture which emerges from the Osborn manuscript confirms his description of himself in 'A Thanksgiving and Prayer for the NATION' as 'a sociable Creature ... A lover of company' (ll. 215-17), even where literary composition was concerned.

That so little of Traherne's work was published in print during his lifetime should not obscure his clear desire to be read. He perhaps did not have 'any vain Humor to appear abroad', but as his recently discovered *Commentaries of Heaven*, an alphabetical celebration of felicity, makes clear, he did want to

> signalize our name
> With some thing that may after Times enflame
> With Love to thee![3]

The manuscript of *Select Meditations*, in contrast with *Commentaries*, bears no sign of having been intended for publication. Its immediate context of communication is not posterity but friendship, possibly the friends whom Traherne apostrophizes in meditation II.38: 'O my T. G.

O my S. H. O my Brother! ye wise and Holy Sages!' Its constant recurrence to the reciprocal role of friends who might, as 'living Auditors',
'Enflame each other with more High Resentments of Joy and
Gratitude' (II.45) may perhaps explain what prompted Traherne to
have a copy made of a work, the origins of which were not didactic
but introspective.[4]

Select Meditations is generally agreed to be a comparatively early
work, written when Traherne was in his twenties, and this is
supported by both its public and private themes. Many references to
the political situation in England seem to date its composition
(though not necessarily the manuscript copy) shortly after the
Restoration of Charles II in 1660. The king had clearly returned, as we
see from prayers such as 'Soften our Kings Heart, Teach our Senators
Wisdom' (I.82), but the memory of turmoils which preceded the
Restoration is fresh, and Traherne's anxiety about the precarious
settlement of the national church and the 'Disobedient Hereticks'
(III.23), the Protestant nonconformists who opposed it, suggests a
date not long after 1660. The words 'As long as our Nation continueth
in peace' (I.86) also make it likely that the work was composed before
the declaration of war on the Dutch in March 1665.[5] Stylistically, too,
Select Meditations gives the impression of an early work; both its
command of language and its portrayal of the role of the speaker are
more tentative, less assured than the *Centuries* or the *Christian Ethicks*.
Although *Select Meditations* contains many passages of great beauty
and originality, and provides a unique insight into Traherne's character, its literary quality is uneven.

That *Select Meditations*, like the later *Centuries*, is organized in
groups of one hundred has led a number of critics to speculate on
whether there is a deliberate relationship between them, and whether
Select Meditations was perhaps an earlier version of the *Centuries*. In
fact, however, as Osborn noted when the manuscript was first discovered, none of the meditations is identical with any in the *Centuries*,
and parallels, other than in the recurrence of characteristic ideas and
images common to all Traherne's works, are not particularly close.[6]
The distinctiveness of Traherne's use of this organizing structure
should not be overestimated; it is not uncommon in other seventeenth-century works, such as Francis Quarles's *Enchiridion* (1641)
from which Traherne could have imitated it.[7] *Select Meditations* has as

much in common with Traherne's *Christian Ethicks*, particularly in its analysis of the virtues in the Fourth Century, as it does with *Centuries*.[8]

The combination in *Select Meditations* of devotional, autobiographical, political and theological themes might at first make it appear simply a disparate collection of Traherne's thoughts, as he ranges from confessions of anxiety about his own failings, through theological enquiry into the relationship between the persons of the Trinity, to reflections on the nature of kingship, and the problems confronting the ecclesiastical settlement of Restoration England, and the work has been contrasted with the *Centuries* as 'written without any special thematic center'.[9] But all of these themes can be seen as unified by the way in which they bear on Traherne's exploration of his own vocation as a minister, and his recognition of the extent to which such a vocation in the 1660s was as inseparable from the making of political choices as it was from the self-scrutiny which he had been taught by his Puritan education. Indeed, the very distinction between the public and private spheres seemed to Traherne at this date to be a political issue. In one meditation he reflects on two parties of Christians, those who were preoccupied with 'what belongeth to the privat Goverment of their Single person', and those 'more ... publick Souls' who 'consider well What Maketh for External peace' in the government of churches, a characterization perhaps of the principles ruling decisions whether or not to conform. Both in this passage and in *Select Meditations* as a whole, Traherne himself rejects this as a choice, praying 'O make me Comprehensiv of all thy Gloryes' and rejoicing in both 'External Goverments' and 'Hidden Thoughts' (I.87).

Select Meditations contains many reflections on Traherne's sense of vocation, and on the responsibility of 'my work of calling others' (III.67), engendered both by the pressure of his vision of felicity, and by educational privilege. Although at Oxford Traherne had notoriously not found 'a Tutor that did professely Teach Felicity' (*Centuries*, III.37), his vocation had none the less been nurtured there, and having been 'nourished at universities in Beautifull Streets and famous colledges', he saw himself as 'sent thither From God Almighty the maker of Heaven and Earth, to teach Immortal Souls the way to Heaven' (*Select Meditations*, III.83). This was a work 'more Sublime then any Employment that Adam had in Eden' (II.15), but Traherne was very well aware of the gap between the ideal and the reality for the country clergyman in his parish. *Select Meditations* wrestles with the extent to which both his own weaknesses and those of others obstructed his attempts to teach the art of felicity. He reflects at length on the difficulties of living with a congregation: 'not to follow their Opinion, not to be Provoked by their censure, not to approve ones selfe to them, not to give them occation of evill Speech, not to be swayed by their example, are Difficult Things' (IV.52). In spite of the fact that *Select Meditations* exalts the 'Sweetness of conversation upon wise Foundations' (II.44) by which friends can lead one another to God, Traherne seems to have been doubtful about the ability of his congregation to engage in this process of mutual sanctification. A sequence of meditations in praise of friendship concludes,

> And when I enter into Houses, let me remember the Glory I saw in the feilds and the Blessedness of thy Kingdom! it is imposible at once to be present with Men and Thee my God, unless we oppose and Greive at their Thoughts. (II.100)

We know that Traherne's churchwardens in his parish of Credenhill in 1667 thought well of him, 'a good Preacher of gods word and a very devout liver',[10] but in moments of self-doubt Traherne was not immune from feeling undervalued. After listing the many ways in which he is assisted in calling people to God, 'by Miracles, by the word of God, by Sacraments Heroes Martirs Examples', he concludes, 'All which meanes of God if men Despise, I cannot but expect that they should Despise me' (II.16). This sense of struggle with a recalcitrant congregation has largely dropped out of Traherne's later writings, but so too has the sense of there being a congregation.

Extensive self-examination in *Select Meditations*, in which Traherne shows much more affinity with Restoration nonconformists than with the established church to which he declared his allegiance, necessarily involved the confession of many failings and the uncovering of many weaknesses in Traherne himself. *Select Meditations* is distinctive amongst Traherne's works both for its emphasis on his own sin, and for the sketch of his character which emerges from the enumeration of his faults. Some of these confessions are couched in general terms, although the very generalities seem striking when we hear them in Traherne's voice: 'O work in me, for I Loath my Selfe, and confess I am

a Rebel. my Heart is Rotten, and Daily Backsliding. But yet well as I
can I offer it up unto Thee' (III.100). But he also reflects much more
deeply on the particular faults of his own character, stressing repeatedly the difficulty which he finds in moderating his speech: 'Since
Thou hast Given me a Tongue; Tho I am an Eternal Sphere in
Communion with Thee, Teach me to use it moderately Prudently
Seasonably to thy Glory' (II.100). In discussing the virtue of prudence
he comments, 'I am exceeding Dull in Appr[e]hending this vertue'
(IV.57). He instructs himself, 'Be more Silent. Less apt to mingle with
other mens words' (III.15), and fortifies himself to resist the influence
of other people's conversation: 'I will be more silent when they talk of
vanitie' (III.2). The most extended character sketch, found in a series
of autobiographical meditations in the Third Century, picks up the
same theme: 'Too much openness and proneness to Speak are my
Diseas. Too easy and complying a Nature. Speaking too much and too
Long in the Best Things' (III.65). The image of Traherne as an invet-
erate talker is one which we can easily believe from our knowledge of
all his works, and it is also the image conveyed to us by the anonymous acquaintance who after Traherne's death described him as so
full of his 'notions' of felicity that 'those that would converse with
him, were forced to endure some discourse upon these subjects,
whether they had any sense of Religion, or not'. What *Select
Meditations* adds to this picture of evangelical enthusiasm is
Traherne's simpler delight in conversation for its own sake, 'A lover of
company; a delighter in equals'.[11] In spite of his confession that he was
too prone to speak, he was very reluctant to concede that it was intrin-
sically a sin. In Heaven, he reflected, 'it is the Joy of all to be
Communicativ and He most Happy that is Infinitly So' (III.65).
Meditation III.65, however, shows him struggling not merely with the
private fault of loquacity, but with the more public issue of communication. The passage reflects Traherne's engagement with Restoration
debate both about the nature of language and its relationship to
reality, and about the appropriate literary presentation of the self. It is
interesting that those whom Traherne records as criticizing him 'for
Speaking in the Singular number, and Saying I', probably did so
because they associated this trait with enthusiasm and dissent.

Select Meditations also contains spiritual autobiography of a kind
more familiar from the *Centuries*, in which Traherne looks back to his

childhood and traces some of the experiences which have led him to his present knowledge of felicity. Some passages in the Third Century of *Select Meditations* in particular evoke the language of the better known Third Century, such as this recreation of childhood vision.

> Gods kingdom, His subjects and Laws are Divine Things, when I Look upon them in the Light of the Citty wherein I Lived. I remember the time when its Gates were Amiable, its streets Beautifull, its Inhabitants immortall, its Temple Glorious, its Inward Roomes and chambers Innocent and all Misterious, Soe they appeared to the little Stranger, when I first came into the world. As sweet every thing as paradice could make it. For I saw them all in the light of Heaven. (III.29)[12]

But in the later work the didactic use made of the experience is rather different from that which we find in *Select Meditations*. In *Centuries* Traherne is offering his own spiritual development as a way of teaching certain truths about the way to blessedness: 'They are unattainable by Book, and therfore I will teach them by Experience' (III.1). This kind of autobiography has an intentionally symbolic value, which the account of similar experiences in *Select Meditations* perhaps does not have. Stanley Stewart rightly stresses the lack of particularity in the autobiography of the *Centuries*;[13] but in the earlier work Traherne is trying to understand how the actual events of his own history have led him to the present point of 'my work of calling others'. In one of the most striking meditations of the work Traherne remembers as formative, not as typical, a vision which 'so wholy Ravished and Transported my spirit, that for a fortnight after I could Scarsly Think or speak or write of any other Thing' (IV.3). Rather than wishing to recreate a spiritual state of the past, he looks to a develop-ment beyond it:

> Surmount therefore O my Soul thy fathers hous, by way of Eminence Enclude thy family, exceed the Citty wherein thou wast born, fill the Ages, Salute the Angels, Inherit kingdoms. (I.92)

There is a constant sense of onward movement in spiritual pilgrimage in his recollections of the past. Thus, having reflected that 'In my

Close Retirements I was some years as if no Body but I had been in the world', he continues, 'When I came a-mong men I found them to be Superaded Treasures' (III.69). His present knowledge can satisfy his soul as nothing in his past experience could do, and yet his past experience has created the very need which that knowledge answers. Having turned from the 'Drie and Empty Theames' of the schools, from heathen poets, from markets, taverns and roaring boys, 'O what a Glorious thing is that Kingdom which in the Temple I behold! How doth it overflow with Living waters to Refresh a Droughty Soul. whence ever I come I find it' (III.30). This last sentence contains an important reassurance for Traherne because the question, not wholly resolved, of whence he had come to his present calling is one of the preoccupations of *Select Meditations*.

It is not a question, however, which can be answered entirely in terms of the personal spiritual experience which I have discussed so far. It has to be seen too, as *Select Meditations* does see it, in the context of the turmoils in church and state of the mid-seventeenth century. Traherne's position as incumbent of Credenhill during the 1660s is inescapably a political issue, and was the result of what were in part political decisions. Traherne, like most of the younger generation of clergy at the Restoration, had been a Commonwealth conformist. He had been at Oxford in the 1650s, at Brasenose College, whose Principal had been recommended by Cromwell for his 'zeale for Reformation', and in December 1657 was admitted by the Commissioners for the Approbation of Public Preachers to the living of Credenhill, supported by some eminent Puritan preachers. Five of the six ministers who provided certificates for him were ejected from their livings after 1660. Traherne at the Restoration was confronted with the same decisions as they were: whether or not to receive episcopal ordination; whether or not to give 'unfeigned assent and consent' to the revised Book of Common Prayer in 1662. The decisions he took, in view of his Commonwealth conformity, could not have been foregone conclusions. In fact he promptly sought episcopal ordination in October 1660, long before it became clear that there would have been any obligation on him to do so, but even this did not make his acceptance of the revised Book of Common Prayer inevitable. He could hardly have attached great importance to the Prayer Book: shortly after the Restoration he is not likely to have been very familiar with it, since its use had been proscribed since 1644/5, when he was about seven. And there were quite a few Puritan clergy ejected in 1662 who had, like Traherne, received episcopal ordination in the early months of the Restoration. However, Traherne conformed, and his subscription to the Act of Uniformity made in August 1662 still survives.[14] How difficult Traherne found it to make these decisions, or whether he was left with any sense of betrayal of those of his former colleagues who now became persecuted as nonconformists, we do not know. But it must have been at about the time that these decisions were taken, or perhaps just afterwards, that *Select Meditations* was written.[15]

As *Select Meditations* makes clear, Traherne's conformity was prompted not by a commitment to the particular ceremonies and discipline which the Act of Uniformity laid down, but a passionate espousal of the concept of a national church, 'when they Move by Consent like an united Army': 'How Ravishing is their Beauty, How Sweet their Order! It is O my God as if the Nation had but one Soul' (I.85). He attacks the 'wickedness of Ignorant Zealots! who contemn thy mercies and Despise the union the Beautifull union of my Nationall church' (I.85), and interestingly rejects the private consciences of those who could not conform: 'And for every Trifle and for evry Scruple must ye all Abandon her and Lay her wast! O prodigious and unreasonable men!' (III.25). Traherne himself, in spite of his perception of the weakness of the national church and the insincerity of the king who was its head, still thought it the source of 'union, Peace, and External Flourishing' (III.23). Like many of his contemporaries he saw nonconformity as being as much a threat to civil stability as to true religion, and his own liturgical preferences in *Select Meditations* do not clearly differentiate him from moderate nonconformists at the Restoration. It is the Lord's Prayer, not the Book of Common Prayer, which is the 'Liturgie of His church and pattern of Devotion' (III.58b). *Select Meditations* contains only a very occasional echo of the Prayer Book liturgy, and quotations from the Psalms, as indeed in later works, are almost invariably taken from the Authorized Version.[16]

Traherne's sense of vocation was implicated in these public events not only in the way in which it was tested by the requirements of religious conformity, but also by the role which Traherne hoped that he could play at a time of crisis in the nation's political and spiritual life.

xx

In common with many other religious writers of all persuasions, Traherne regards the upheavals of seventeenth-century politics as a divine judgement on the sins of the nation.[17] Like many preachers, too, he lamented that England was not spiritually chastened by the 'Great Judgments which have so latly happened' (II.42), nor adequately thankful for God's redemption of the nation in the Restoration, 'advancing his people, Bringing them out of Egypt into the land of Canaan' (II.80). *Select Meditations* joins his voice, in words based on Jeremiah, to the widespread denunciation of national sin: 'The prophets and the preists are corrupted them selves, from them prophaness is gon forth among the People. They know not me Saith the Lord, they understand not my wayes nor the Operation of my hands. Shall I not be Avenged of such a Nation as this!' (I.85). This public theme is linked to more personal meditations by Traherne's casting himself as an intercessor on behalf of the nation, as he was to do again in 'A Thanksgiving and Prayer for the NATION':[18] 'I beseech Thee to hear my Daylie prayers. Save this Nation, Spare its People, let me O Lord rejoyce in the felicity of thy chosen' (I.82). His part is

to Lament the crimes
Which here appear
To wash the Times
With Teares (I.89),

but he finds himself severely tested by this duty: 'O my God I Could be Quickly weary Quickly weary both of Repenting and Interceding. But thy Lov is the encourager of mine' (I.84).

Traherne's response to national crisis is determined by a biblical model, just as it is couched in biblical language. The extensive political comment of *Select Meditations* may be obscured for the modern reader by the fact that it largely operates through scriptural quotation and allusion, a ubiquitous idiom for interpreting current affairs which could have both the theological advantage of confirming the identification of seventeenth-century England with the chosen nation, and the political advantage of being a means of evading censorship. *Select Meditations* reads contemporary events in the light of biblical events: Traherne can hope that God will save England because 'He that is Conversant with the Ancient Prophets shall See Him Contending,

wooing and pursuing an Incorigible Nation many 100. years: before
He Destroyes them' (I.84). The books of the Bible most frequently
quoted in *Select Meditations*, usually from memory and rather inaccu-
rately, are Psalms and the prophets Isaiah and Jeremiah, all well established as politically relevant, and quotations from them are clustered
most densely in meditations which reflect on the state of the nation.
Traherne's tendency to shift 'freely between his own voice and that of
the Scriptures' has often been noted, but in *Select Meditations* this is
more than a stylistic issue.[19] As England re-enacts the history of Israel,
Traherne defines for himself the role of an Old Testament prophet, in
his denunciation of the nation's sin, in the apocalyptic vision of the
poem 'Thy Turtle Doves O Lord to Dragons turn!' (II.17), and in the
appropriation of prophetic language.[20] This sense of prophetic vocation was to continue and develop; in 'A Thanksgiving and Prayer for
the NATION' (*c.* 1667), Traherne prays ambitiously and explicitly,

$$\text{Make me a } \left\{ \begin{array}{l} \textit{Moses,} \\ \textit{Nehemiah,} \\ \textit{Ezra, David} \end{array} \right\} \text{ to thee \& them.}$$

(ll. 51-53)

The very detailed way in which *Select Meditations* engages with
contemporary political issues makes it paradoxically one of
Traherne's most public works. But this should not be taken to imply,
as is sometimes supposed, that Traherne's later writing withdraws
from this external world to dependence on an inner one; as Nabil
Matar rightly argues, 'all his writings testify to his concern with
national affairs'.[21] This interest is no less present at the end of
Traherne's life, in the ironic criticisms made of the Court in
Commentaries of Heaven and in its systematic reflections on sources of
authority, than it is in *Select Meditations*. What I think did change was
the conviction expressed by *Select Meditations* that Traherne's own
ministry could encompass both the public and the private spheres.

Many other themes in *Select Meditations* reflect the challenges and
preoccupations of Restoration England. Traherne discusses the very
pertinent issue of the source and nature of the king's authority and the
'Tinsell vanities' of ceremonial which surround it (III.10). He affirms
Arminian views on the nature of free will to a degree which must
have laid him open, like the Latitudinarians, to accusations of

Socinianism: we are 'infinitly free to Act and doe' (IV.28). He explores
the idea of the best of all possible worlds in a way which anticipates
Leibniz (II.1-3 and III.90-93). His 'Instructions Teaching us how to Liv
the Life of Happieness' (III.31) begin with the social context of virtue,
a reminder that it is contemporary civilization which restores 'the
world to the Beauty of Paradice', and for which we must be thankful.
At the same time, however, *Select Meditations* never forgets the spiritual reality which lies behind the contemporary in all its manifesta-
tions. Some of its finest meditations are an invitation to look beyond
the visible to the invisible, and beyond the present to providential
history, for 'without the Sence of Invisible Things no Thing visible can
be enjoyed' (III.84). It is this sense which transforms a little church
from 'an heap of Stones' into a celebration of divine goodness (III.83);
illuminates the ground where Troy stood with 'the Remembrance of
Priamus and its Ancient Glory' (IV.30); and transcends a weak and
dissolute monarch with an image of triumphant spiritual kingship: 'If
I live truely in the Divine Image I shall appear among kings a Greater
king. For to be a King like God is a thing more Divine then to Reign
like a Man, unless that Man Reign Like a God' (III.15). *Select
Meditations* is characterized as much by a refusal to separate the spiritual and the temporal as to separate the public and the private.

Select Meditations, both in its themes and in its existence as part of a
collaboratively produced manuscript, displays that desire for inclu-
siveness which is so very characteristic of Traherne's thought. Just as
Commentaries of Heaven, on a vastly greater scale, was to be dedicated
to demonstrating that 'ALL THINGS' rightly understood could be
seen as 'Objects of Happiness', so this early work, in more personal
terms, struggles to place the variety of spiritual, social, political and
intellectual experience in relation to 'my work of calling others'
(III.67). The result remained, in both works, fragmentary, and *Select
Meditations* fully recognizes the extent to which this was the inevitable
result of human weakness, Traherne's own, his congregation's, the
nation's. Even friendship, which is both a powerful theme of the work
and the probable context of the manuscript's production, has its limitations. Traherne's need for 'Intelligent Friends and Heavenly
Companions',[22] is confronted with defect and imperfection:

But O that I might be compleate in all Things! I would yeeld unto my freind joy and consolations after the similitude of God: But then my freind must be clothed with his similitude and be Able to resent, as He resenteth. We are imperfect here upon Earth, but our Imperfections shall be blown a way. (II.97)

But Traherne continued to yearn for a state in which he might be infinitely communicative, sharing with all a vision of felicity completely apprehended. Such a felicity would break down the distinctions between temporal and spiritual, public and private, the self and others, enabling Traherne to fulfil his expressed aim of seeing all people as 'his enlarged Selfe' (II.79).

A NOTE ON THE TEXT

The text is based on the unpublished manuscript of *Select Meditations* in the Osborn Collection, Beinecke Rare Book and Manuscript Library, Yale University, which is the only extant version of the work. The manuscript is not Traherne's autograph, but a copy made by an amanuensis who was working from another written text under Traherne's supervision, and it contains occasional passages and many small alterations in Traherne's own hand.

This edition is intended for the general reader. But it is also a critical edition of a previously unpublished manuscript, which has to record the editorial judgements on which the text is based, and which cannot refer the reader elsewhere for textual information. My aims in balancing these considerations have been to produce an uncluttered text which is pleasurable to read and which does not present the reader with unnecessary obstacles; to convey to the reader the character of a manuscript which has close associations with its author; and to provide a scholarly and accurate text with a complete record of verbal emendation.

The edition contains only *Select Meditations*, and not the prayers and short treatises found at the end of the Osborn manuscript (see Introduction, pp. xi-xii). The complete text of *Select Meditations* is given, except where the manuscript is badly mutilated. I have printed as much of damaged meditations as makes sense, but have omitted incomplete sentences and fragments. All such omissions are recorded in the notes. Mutilation of the manuscript also means that some meditations are missing from the numerical sequence, and others were apparently omitted by the scribe. Wherever the numerical sequence is not complete, the reason is given in the notes.

A number of faded words and letters in the first few pages of the manuscript can be read only under ultraviolet light.

The original spelling and capitalization of the manuscript are preserved. The manuscript is neatly written and easily legible, but as with Traherne's own hand it is sometimes difficult to distinguish between upper and lower-case letters where this is simply a question of size. Nor can one assume, again as with autograph Traherne manuscripts, that either sentences or proper names begin with capitals, and occasionally capital forms are used in the middle of words. Decisions on 's' in particular often have to be arbitrary.

'u' is transcribed as 'v' when used as a consonant.

Standard abbreviations, including the ampersand, superscriptions and contractions, have been expanded, as has Traherne's characteristic use of 'H.' for 'Holy'. 'y^n', which could stand for 'then' or 'than', is always transcribed as 'then', the form preferred by Traherne in autograph manuscripts, and by the scribe of *Select Meditations*.

The punctuation of the manuscript is more problematic. While it broadly follows a system of its own, it is highly idiosyncratic by seventeenth-century as well as by twentieth-century standards, one of its most conspicuous features being the marking off of subordinate clauses, or phrases within a list, with full stops, while the ends of sentences are often unpunctuated. This can be very bewildering to the reader, and so I have modified the punctuation to some extent. While alterations are necessarily quite numerous, I have made them as conservatively as is consistent with clarifying the sense: the punctuation has not been modernized, but altered in a way which harmonizes with usages found elsewhere in the manuscript. Peculiarities which do not confuse the sense remain; to eliminate them entirely would destroy the structure and prose rhythms of the meditations. In an edition for the general reader it has not been possible to list alterations to the punctuation in the notes, and with this in mind I have refrained from making modifications which are too actively interpretative.

The double hyphen has been replaced with a single hyphen throughout, except where it marked a word-break at the end of a line, where it has been omitted.

All verbal emendations are recorded. These are mainly associated with characteristic scribal errors. The editorial addition of omitted words or letters is marked in the text with square brackets, and is not otherwise annotated. Emendations of other kinds are recorded in the notes. Blanks left by the scribe are enclosed in square brackets with the appropriate number of spaces, and are commented on in the notes.

A number of leaves of the manuscript, especially in the First Century, have suffered slight damage to the page edge. Letters lost in this way are supplied in square brackets, and the reason given in the notes. The only exception to this practice is in 1.82 and 1.84 where almost every line has lost one or more letters; in order to avoid cluttering the page too heavily with square brackets I have, for these meditations only, listed the editorial additions in the notes instead.

Occasional catch-words at the bottom of pages have been omitted without comment.

Where the scribe has made deletions or additions in the manuscript, these corrections are adopted without comment unless their sense is unclear. All corrections and additions in Traherne's own hand are recorded in the notes, so that the reader can see the nature of his supervision.

ACKNOWLEDGEMENTS

My thanks are primarily due to Louis Martz for generously allowing me to edit a work with which he himself has been so closely associated, and for the pleasure of discussing it with him; and to the Curator of the J. M. and M.-L. Osborn Collection, Beinecke Rare Book and Manuscript Library, Yale University, for permission to publish the edition and a facsimile of a page of the manuscript.

I am grateful to Somerville College, Oxford, for an award from the Alice Horsman Travelling Fund which contributed to my visit to Yale to work on the manuscript, and to Peter Beal, John Carey, and Anne Ridler for their support and encouragement. I also thank Christopher Palmer for more than can be enumerated.

81

When I retire first I seem to com in my selfe to a centre, in that centre I find Eternitie and all its Riches. By leavi[ng] things as they Stand without, I find them within in a richer Manner. They are all in Thee, and Thou art there: O my God I flie unto Thee.

82

Haveing made me Lord and Heir of the world, Reedeemed me by the Blood of thy Son, Exalted me to thy Throne by thy Holy laws, Received me to liv in Communion with thee, made me a Temple of all Eternity, A Son of God so Great and High, for whose Sake thou hast prepared all Things: I beseech Thee to hear my Daylie prayers. Save this Nation, Spare thy People, let me O Lord rejoyce in the felicity of thy chosen, and be glad with thine Inheritance. Remember I beseech Thee How much thou lovest me, Who lovest me so much, as if me a-lone. yea more O Lord, for as much as by loving others, Thou Raisest them to be my freinds and Treasures. O remember how all Thy Lov Terminates in me: How I am made thy Bride, the End of all Things, A lover of all Things and in that like Thee. An Active ey, an Infinit Sphere in which thou Dwellest forevermore. They are not purses and Trunks of Jewels that I regard, but God and kingdoms. O let thy Glory Abide a-mong us, Thy praises in our Assemblies. let Thy citties prosper, our vilages flourish, our children Grow up in fear of thy Name, like Oliv plants about thy Table. Soften our Kings Heart, Teach our Senators Wisdom, Heal the Abominable, cleans the Profane, giv our young Men and Maydens Knowledg, let our people walk in the light of thy Countenance, O Let the Ministers Mourn for the profanes of our Streets, And giv not Thy Turtle Dove the Beloved of thy Soul into the Enemies Hand. O Lord they will not regard the Glory of thy kingdom, nor mind the Hidden Riches of thy Benefits. They all are gon a way and refuse to return. They would not make Mention of Ihy loving kindness nor understand the Excellency of thy Holy laws nor be enflamd with thy lov nor sing praises unto Thee, yet O Lord pardon us, and make us not a Desolation, nor an Astonishment in the Earth. for Thy Tender Mercys sake which have been ever of old be favorable unto us, and Continue thy presence in the midst of us. [   ] our Cittyes O my God, and make me a Blessing in all the land. [   ] will I prayse Thee while I have any Being.

83

I com unto Thee the father of Lights, the creator of Heaven and lover of Mankind, the Infinite lover of every soul. O what Incredible Things hast thou don for Men! Made every Soul almost a God, Like God unto Thee. For Thou art in us as we in Thee. every Soul is an Infinit Centre, A Temple of Heaven and Earth, a Sun Shining upon all Thy creatures. A joy and Blessing to men and Angels, a possessor of them. Each one thy Darling, Each one a lone more Blessed in Thee, and more Beloved then if Himselfe were made a Dietie. His Body a lone is Greater then the World because men and Angels minister unto it; O let us not become as Dung for the Streets. Profane Not O lord the Throne of Thy Glory. Dash not to peeces thy Beautifull vessels. Abhor not thy Darlings! O how Destructiv is every Sin, which maketh God to Despise his I-mages! to Abhor his freinds, and forsake his Bride in the Day of Indignation. Yea to cast her out of his sight and Trample under feet So many Thousand Thousand Souls as Mire in the Streets! O the Desolation of Such precious creatures! each one So Wonderfull! each a king: each one Greater and Higher then the rest, each one the End and comprehensive of all, and yet Destroyd! O my God becaus they will regard [not] the operation of thy hands, therefore wilt thou Destroy them and not Build them up. But O remember thy Ancient loving kindness: and what Things thou Didst Design us at first to be. O Thou that makest every one thy Image, and givest thy Selfe wholy to every Soul! Thou all Wise and Gracious Lawgiver, Thou Prudent Governer of all the World, Thou King of Ages, pitty thy Sons, forget not thy foote stool. Through many Generations thou hast been Gracious in vain, in vain hast thou called, and Stretched out thy Hands all the Day long to a Rebellious people. but now O God, Turn us a gaine, cause thy face to Shine, and we Shall be Saved. O let the Bowels of thy Compassion yern, and be melted over us¹

84

God tendereth his Saints as the Apple of his Eye. but he is terrible in his Anger against all his Enemies, becaus by How much the Greater his Goodness was, So much the Greater his Provocation is. Because he knows the Good things He Intends, He Deferreth them long and is many Ages before he is weary of Repenting. I admire and Tremble at the Height and Depth of his Infinite patience: I Adore the Riches of his long Suffering, extended unto Kingdoms from Generation to Generation. He that is Conversant with the Ancient Prophets shall See Him Contending, wooing and pursuing an Incorigible Nation many 100. years: before He Destroyes them, And tho he know all Ages to be alike from the Begining of the World, pervers and obstinat, yet is not Discouraged to forbear, and Intreat, but by his prophets and ministers endeavoureth to Melt them, Refine them, Gain them. I have (Saith He) Spoken by the Prophets, Multiplied visions, used Similituds, which Tho He ever seeth to be in vain, yet He proceedeth still to use them and by such meanes Endeavoreth to perswade them. The Ox knoweth his owner and the Ass his Masters crib. but Israell doth not know, my people doth not consider. His voyce Daylie Sounds in the Temple, His preachers cry a-loud but non regard it. They call us to Repentance for all Abominations, And cry out to the Heavens and silent Earth as more Sencible then we. They call us again to the knowledg of God. but He hath brought up children and they have Rebelled against Him. They will not know Him that Nourisheth them, nor feel the Nature joy and Glory of His Image in them Selves, Nor See the Heavens that Splended crib, nor understand His Lov who Established the Earth, and created it for them. The Seas, The sun, the clouds the corn the wine and oyl, all Minister and Serv in vain. Neither is their owner Seen, nor our father known: And that which Glorifieth more every Soul is more Despised. O my God I Could be Quickly weary Quickly weary both of Repenting and Interceding. But thy Lov is the encourager of mine, the Soul and strength that Animates mine. Becaus thou

lovest them with an Infinit Love therefore art thou So long before thou
art weary. O pardon my weakness, who am made in thine Image.
Make me Great in patience and compassion and Lov to Thee. Tho
they have been and are Rebellious against Thee and will be, yet let me
Continually Intercede for them. As they are thy Garden, Jowols,
Peculiar Treasures, So they are mine, Members of My Body as they are
of Thine, more Dear to me, more Beautifull then Eden. O lay it not
wast, Bereav us not O lord. Remember How thy Name is praised in
our Temples, And How our children are taught the Knowledg of thy
Son. Tho the whole Nation will Not Come in, yet like waters that
sqweez in by Drops one of a family and two of a Tribe Return unto
Thee. In every one of which Thou hast a nother Selfe, an Infinite
Treasure, a freind, an IMAGE.

85

The prophets and the preists are corrupted them selves, from them
prophaness is gon forth among the People. They know not me Saith
the Lord, they understand not my wayes nor the Operation of my
hands. Shall I not be Avenged of such a Nation as this! O How thou
Lovest them. Becaus thou wouldst not have all thy labor in vain, Thou
hitherto sparest. O my God Thou Rem[em]berest the cost, which thou
hast been at in planting them. Besids the Heaven and the Earth which
the Heathen enjoy, Thou hast brought in the Gospel of thy Son into
our land, Converted our Kings Senators and Nobles, Exalted thy
name, Established thy word and worship by Laws, Builded thy Selfe
Temples, and Apoynt[ed] Revenues for thy church and Ministers,
Greatly are the Bishops [of] our Saviour Dignified, and our Cittys
Beautified with those thy most Glorious and Beautifull Houses. wear
all this to be Done againe Thou knowest the Sweat and Bloud wherewith it was Atcheived. But O the wickedness of Ignorant Zealots! who
contemn thy mercies and Despise the union the Beautifull union of
my Nationall church! every way thou art provoked to Anger, by Open
profaness and Spirituall wickedness. And by the Ignorance of both,
Despising thy mercies O lord when our citties and Teritories are
united by Laws in the fear of thy Name: and are at one accord in
Calling upon Thee; when they Move by Consent like an united Army.
How Ravishing is their Beauty, How Sweet their Order! It is O my

God as if the Nation had but one Soul. In all which while thy Glory Reigneth, She is made thy Throne; one Throne and Temple unto Thee. Be not wroth very Sore O Lord, neither remember Iniquity forever. Thy Holy Citties are a wilderness, Zion is a wilderness, Jerusalem a Desolati[on], our Holy and our Beautifull house where our fathers praised Thee is burnt up with fire and all our pleasant Things are layd wast. Wilt thou Refrain thy Selfe for these Things O Lord, wilt thou ho[ld] thy peace and afflict us very Sore: O profane not the Throne of thy Glory! let not the Heathen Trample it under foot! Much Less let Christians Defile it with their Bloud!

86

Once more O Lord I will Speak unto Thee, be not Angry, Tho I am but Dust and Ashes! As long as our Nation continueth in peace, under the wings of Magistrates and christian Laws thy people in peace may celebrat Thee: In Publick courts, in Solemn Assemblies, even thy Hidden ones, thy saint may come unto Thee; flourish a mong the Tares, Sit at thy Table, a mong Thornes Spring up as the Lillies, Among Hipocrites rejoyce in the Light of thy Countenance, Sincerly prais Thee! In her peace We inherit peace; Extend peace unto her like a River, and thy Tender mercies Like an Overflowing Streame!

87

Narrow Souls seldom Consider all thy Glories. Even Ants can see the splendor of this world, the Glory of the Heavens, Gr[ass] Trees, and flowers, the Brightnes of the Sun, and Beauty of the Day. Bli[nd] men Seldom See them. But Things Invisible they cannot See, Immortall Souls, thy Lov, thy laws, Affections, vertues. O how Happy am I that See them. some men see Imortall Souls, but the Eternal Glor[y] of thy Holy Laws, and the Riches of thy kingdom in all Ages they Doe not understand. Even So Some Discern what belongeth to the privat Goverment of their Single person; Sincerity meekenes forgivene[s] of Injuryes, Joy in the Holy Ghost, prayer unto thee. Is it not Sufficient to tast of these Things? No, No! Large Draughts and continual feeding in these pastures, with universal Lov, and pure resignation are ever requisite. So are Humility, pruden[t]

Circumspection into External Things, Obedience unto Lawes: and
what not; if Reverance unto Magistrates! Some are wise in Secular
Conveniences, and consider well What Maketh for External peace.
Thcoe are the more Learned and publick Souls. others understand the
Happienes of thy Lov in the Interior Man, but mind not the union
prosperity Stability and flourishing of thy churches. These are
Ignorant and more Devout. O make me Comprehensiv of all thy
Gloryes. and Let me See External Goverments and the Beauty of
Temples, in a land consecrated by her laws unto Thee: But see more
over all those Hidden Thoughts, flowing Streames, Concealed Mines,
of melting Sweet affections, Sacred Pleasures, Tears and prayers,
which in Holy Communion belong unto Thee. Ants are Industrious
and profitable to them selves, but Spoyl the Gardens in which they are
working, while they mind them Selves. It is not Sufficient to be
Devout, unless thou art modest and very Humble. He that will be
medling with Goverments and Laws, hath very Great Need to be
Exceeding wise. Who ever Thou art that Desirest to be perfect, Thou
must not be Blind on either Side. but See to the Peace and Quiet of thy
people, and at the Same Time regard the Purity of an Inward Life.

88

What ever it is for which God regardeth it, with wonderfull Zeal
He ever regardeth the peace of a kingdom. and when He is provoked
by their Abominations to Anger, He proceedeth warily and Slowly to
Disolve it. Somthing Amiable He beholdeth in it which He is Loath to
Destroy. But those Sons of Core See not the Beautyes which He
beholdeth. And therefore being Blind can Throw away the peace and
welfare of a Nation upon every Trifle. Invade her Liberties, Lay wast
her laws, Rejoyce in her Confusion, contemn her Magistrates, Trample
her Peace and flourishing Estate, Like Mire in the Streets: and think
Nothing but a Shadow and a Dream Destroyed: Because all the
Reallity of Happieness and woe consists in the Inward and Spiritual
Estate, of the Soul with God. But doth not God know as well as you, O
ye Sons of fire, that Delight in hast, what are the Beauties of Inward
Holiness? yet doth He Regard the external flourishing of Setled kingdoms. And after many Hundred years forbearance even when there is
no Remedy, with Greife and Compunction goeth a bout to Destroy

them. And is Scarcly willing even after all provocations, and Contempts of His Majestie yet to do it. Certainly did ye understand what Things He values in the Secret of a Kingdoms peace; you would have one Jewell of Infinite Esteem, more in your Treasure, a Treasurie it selfe in His Holy Kingdom.

89

1

If after all Endeavors made
Tears Shed in vain
Lament the Trade
of filthiness and Sin:
He that doth pure in midst of Sin remain,
It Shall be well with Him.

2

Tho Bodies [   ] Defild with Gore,
And Staind the Land,
Tho waves doe roar
Tho mountains Tossed flie
Tho raging waves above their Tops do Stand

3

His Holy joyes Shall never Die
An Inward flood
Doth from on High
His soul within revive
And rais Him up to that Transcendant Good
That keeps Him Still alive.

4

Yet ought he to Lament the crimes
Which here appear
To wash the Times
With Teares, which not in vain,
Tho vain Shall be; A Jewell every Tear
Shall be. While He doth reign.

90

Drie Barren Arguments whereby we Strive,
The joy to Shew which makes a Soul revive;
Inferior are to all the Streames of Bliss,
Nor can its Treasures be Declard by this.
Joyes, Triumphs! Raptures! Elas he must sing,
Hosannas, Praises! Hallelujahs Bring
That will advance and magnifie his Bliss
To shew the Truth and joy that in it is.
He Sacrifices, Incense, Flame must Speak,
And all the Silence of the Heaven break,
With Songs more Heavenly: that will worthy be
To Speak the joyes of True Felicity.
Angelick Raptures, and Transported Senc
Scarce Shadow forth its Smallest Influenc
From all the Coasts of Heaven and Earth it Comes,
Transcends the Beames of Twenty Thousand Suns:
Gold! Amber! wine and oyl! Perfumes!
Crowns! Scepters! Thrones! Bright Temples! kingly Roomes!
All these are little parts of Holy Bliss
Kings! Angels! Souls! Even God a Treasure is.
Can He be Quiet, or in peace Confute,
Can He be Idle, or at all Dispute,
Sees Ages, Kingdoms, Heaven, Earth his Gain!
Can He be cold that over all doth Reign!
O King of Kings no other Thing but Thee
Can I confer with. O Felicitie!
Thou Dost Transport me! Extasies Dispence
Scarce halfe a Grain of thy Sweet Influence.
He Soaring must a bove the Heavens flie
As Angels do, that would true Bliss Descrie.
Leav Earthly Dross untoucht, Complaints and Greifes,
Beneath his feet, Leav all its weak Releifs.
Storms are the Triumph of his Holy Art,
While He doth Light to all the World Impart.
He Glitters, Shines, Transcendant is to kings
Beholds their crowns as mean Inferior Things

Doth lightly touch their joys, and cleeping flie
From them to joyes that Shine above the Skie.
Can He be Quiet that Doth all Enjoy,
Even kings and kingdoms in a Better way
Then kings them selves! O! O my Soul! Divine,
Divine the way, whereby all are Thine!
Can He that is the Image, Bride and Freind
Of God Himselfe, of Heaven and Earth the End
Can He that is Exalted by the Laws
Of peace and Bliss, Even to the utmost claus
Of Holy joy, and Prais, Do less then fill
With Flame, fire, Rapture, Melodie and Skill,
The vaults of Heaven and Earth! In every Thing
I will a world of praises to my king
Infuse and Sacrifice! an High Preist be
In every Part of all Eternitie.
In every Creature, Centre, Sphere and Thing,
I will Appear, and Alters Rear! a king!
A Preist! an Angel be! And every where,
Beyond the Bounds even of the utmost Sphere,
Again an Angel, king, and Preist appear.

91

O my God so perfect is the Glory of thy Divine Image that my understanding is not only a sphere like Thee of Infinite Extent: an Ey without walls, All unlimited and Endless Sight, nor a Sun only to Shine on all the kingdoms, and Things in kingdoms, that are or move within its Living Temple: nor is it only an Incomprehensible Misterye, present every where, yet finite and confined, filling Nothing; but is like Jesus Christ, my Elder Brother, by whom it is Restored to its first power, an[d] again Called to be a Son of God, by Him who Bringeth int[o] His Eternall Glory. Infinitly more Happy in pleasing Thee, then in be[ing] pleased. Is it possible for God to make a Sun That Shall b[e] wholy seen in many kingdoms: and at once Shine over many Nations, and raise fruits and Trees and flowers in every coast: w[hich] Nevertheles did service to one in its first creation, and is now but a Minister made to serve us; and Shall it not be possible to create a Soul to do more then so. Infinity of Extent is the least perfection in the Soul of Man! It is able to be wise Holy Righteous Devine and Blessed. O my Soul these words are too Sublime to be understood! Such fruits can a Soul render unto God, Such joys occation in the Soul of Angels, Exhibit Such peircing Transporting GODLIKE Beauties in it Selfe, That all the Spices Treasures feasts sweet perfumes and kingdoms in the world are a Bubble and a Shadow in comparison. If Thou canst not beleive this, remember, that all the Spices Stars and perfumes were made for this: and this that it might be Wise Holy and Divine, the Sovereign End and crown of them.

92

The Same causes that moved God to Delight in his own works mov Him to Delight in their Similitude. whatever maketh Acts of mercy Goodness and Lov in Him to be Delightfull; maketh them So to Him in us. If therefore our Holiness be Such to Him, as His to Himselfe, where will our pleasures rest or who Shall fathom the Depths of Holiness! Therefore hath he made Affections Goodness wisdom Holines Infinite, becaus they are infinitly Sweet and profitable, if not to Him, to Angels and Men. O my God Since thy Goodness is So Great that thou Infinitly delightest in our Happieness, in being Sweet and profitable to us, they are Sweet to Thee. nor will the Beauties of felicity ever be Displayed, till these are reaveled. Wise and Holy must man be to all the Creatures in Heaven and Earth. And as he is an Ey to see, So must he be seen of all Ages. Surmount therefore O my Soul thy fathers hous, by way of Eminence Enclude thy family, exceed the Citty wherein thou wast born, fill the Ages, Salute the Angels, Inherit kingdoms, penetrat the Earth, Encompass Heaven, Reign, Triumph, prais, Adore, O Life and Lov, Sing forever. See the churches throughout the world, let the souls and affections of all Ages be wings and streams to Elavat and Carry Thee. feare and be Enlarged. flie a way, Ascend in the Incense of all their Devotions, Mingle with their Praises, be united to them, Enflamed with them, Ravished with their Beauty, Transported with their melodie, Transformed with their Lov. All these are the Materials of Bliss, but no more compared with Bliss it selfe, then Ink and letters with the Strength of Laws.

Nor have I any leasure;
To Speak or Think but of Celestial pleasure.

93

A Broken and a contrite Heart is made up of knowledge Sorrow
and Lov: knowledge of our primitiv felicitie in Eden, Sorrow for our
fall, Lov to God so Gratious and Redeeming. know ledg of our
Happiness in being Redeemed, Sorrow for sin against our Redeemer,
Lov to God yet Continuing favorable and Gracious. knowledg of the
Joys prepared for us, Sorrow for our unworthyness in living beneath
them, Lov to God for his Goodness Magnified and Exalted over us.
one Broken Sigh, or Contrite Groan is more Acceptable to God, then
Thousands of Rams, and ten Thousand Rivers of oyl, and maketh
more pleasant musick in his Eares, then all the fained musick of the
Spheres. Which because it is so He Botleth up our Tears. for they
Abide in the places wherever because they are pearls, Dissolved pearl,
Tho not vanishing; which he reserveth in Store for the Holy Angels.
Neither is this Metaphorical, He really Bottleth all our Teares. For they
Abide in the places where they fall, and in those Moments wherei[n]
they were Shed, are Treasured up for all Beholders. are not all the
parts of all Eternitie present at once to God; are not all their contents
present in them, Is not all Eternity present [to] our understanding: if
not in us! How then shall it otherwise be, but that Gods Eternitie is a
Bottle like the Heavens Wherein the Tears of Penitents Glitter like the
Stars; Scattered at a Distance, yet all before us! O my God since I know
my selfe the Joy of Angels in Repenting, the very knowledge of that
Shall encreas my Tears, Sweeten my Sorrow, Alleviat yet Augment
and compleat my Repentance. Were it not for the Sun no vapors
would arise, Light immitted rarifies and prepares them. Light Emitted
makes them Transpire. Light Refl[e]cted Elivates in Counion. Light
immitted, Emitted, and reflected as they all ascend refines and carries
them. without Light there would be no vapors; without which vapors
recondensing into clouds, there would be no Rain, no fruits, no
flowers. clouds of Penitence ma[y] seem to overwhelme and oppress
the Face, but not appear till first raised by the Sun of Righteousness
Shining on the Earth which is Mans Heart. Light immitted is Glory
Seen, which melts and Soften[s], Light Emitted is Lov returned, which

Transpires as Sighs and bears us upwards, light reflected is the means
of Grace Shining [on] the Soul, and cooperating with the Spirit, which
works within us With Sighs and Groans unutterable. without which
sighs There can be no clouds Tears fruits or flowers. Since Therefore
Repentance is a work of the Light, and Sin can never be Hated but In
the open day, since those clouds on the face of Happienes Beautifie the
Heavens, fructifie the Earth, and make it flourish, Since the world is
the better for some Rainy Days, and Sinners Tears are Dissolved pearl
that Shine for-ever, I will not be without some o[f] those, but Esteeme
Repentance Disguised Happieness. And wonder at God for making
every Thing a part of Eternal Blessedness.

94

Eternity is a Sphere into which we Enter, all whose parts are at once
Standing round a bout us. How else could all its parts before, and
after, be objects present to the understanding. Eternitie in the Dark is
an Object upon the Earth, Therefore Seems an Empty Space prepared
before us. But is with God an Eternal Day, whose Evening and
morning and noon are present: and in every part also the Things with
which they are filled. Eternitie that was before the creation may seem
the Morning wherin all Things began [t]o Bud and flourish, Eternity
after the world is Ended may seem the evening, wherein all are at Rest
in Heavenly Peace and receiv the fruits of their Labors. Eternity now
as it Surrounds the world, may Seem the Noon and Heat of the Day,
wherin all things are growing and creatures labouring: but indeed all
These are at once in God, changeable in them selves and succeeding
each other, but standing there and A-biding for ever. Otherwise the
Eternity before the world would be indeed the Evening, for the
evening and the morning were the first Day, or the Empty Darknes
and Space of time wherein God was without the Emanations of his
Goodness in the works of his Hands, and Things were not. The
Eternity of the world, the womb of the Morning in which it began, All
Things then having their Birth and spring: The Eternity which is to
Endure when Time is Done, the High Noon of Meridian Glory. But Oh
wonderfull is the Eternal God who is Himselfe his own Eternity! How
Glorious is the world which wheather it be the Morning or noon of
His kingdom we cannot tell! How Happy are we that Liv in a world

so Glorious, where Eternity is on every Side a Standing Object of Divine Enjoyments for evermore!

95

So wonderfull is the Incomprehensibility of the Divine Essence, that the world was with God from all Eternity. It was not, and yet was. It was not in it selfe, for it had a Begining Some 5000 years agoe: yet was in God. for he being his own Eternity, must of Necessity include it. for out of Eternity nothing can be nor can any Thing at all begin to be within it. Begin in it selfe every Thing may, and must except God. But the very moment in which every Thing Begins is included in Eternity, and Tho other moments were a Great while before it, and many Succeed it, it is a Standing object, which can never possibly remove from Its place. Tis we are Successiv, Eternity is not so. Trees in a walk are past by, Tho them Selves stand still. And to him that runs seem to run Backward. The moments Stand, we mov by, and cry the Time passeth away. As we go forward the time passeth and seems to go behind us: But cannot move or Stir. what infinite liberty is there in His Kingdom!

100

Words are but feeble Barren Things,
Worlds, Hearts, Arts, praises to the king of kings.

He onely Blessed is that praises Sings,
That sees with Angels Eys, Soares on the wings.

SELECT MEDITATIONS
THE SECOND CENTURY

1

Haveing made me the Image of God Himselfe, and Given me Dominion over the works of His Hands; He maketh Laws, Wherein he teacheth me to lead the Best of all possible lives, and commandeth all creatures in Heaven and Earth, to regard me with Reverance care and Lov as they do Him.

2

The best of all possible lives is that wherein the best of al[l] possible things are after the Similitud of God enjoyed. And becaus his laws require me to lead this Glorious Life, both they them Selves are the best of all possible laws, and by them I know that he loveth me Infinitly.

3

The best of all possible things are God, His essence, Attr[i]butes, works, counsels, Laws, wayes, And whatsoever else is include[d] in these. Angels, men, Thought and affections. The best of all possible manners to which any thing created can possibly attain is the Similitude of God. And the world is an Hous wherin I am placed in communion with God So to enjoy them.

4

Angels and men if they live in His similitude keep his laws, and Lov me as themselves: if they do not they incurr his Indignatio[n] and fall from the Glory in which they were created. All other creatur[e]s by

Indispensible Necessity are made to serv me. Nor can they at all
Swerv from his ordinance, till I become Rebellious in sinning against
him.

5

By being endued with power to keep his laws I am advanced to his
Throne; and to do that which above all Things in Heaven and Earth
He desireth: and therein I am made His Bride to Delight Him. For
haveing made the world that I should enjoy it, and in it Him, He
cheifly desireth that I should doe that, which is the End for which He
made the world, and me His Image. Nor is the Creation of many
worlds So pleasing unto Him, as that I Should keep his laws in the
world He hath made, and live in His Similitude.

6

By falling into Sin I revolted from His Love and Defaced His Glory.
Neither could I by any other means be Redeemd from Hell but by the
Incarnation of His Son, by whose Death I am restored to Glory.

7

Being restored to glory, I may again live in the Similitude of God:
and as all his works are made more rich by the Death of His Son, Soe
are all works more Ardently Desired, being the end now as well of my
Redemption, as of my first creation. whereby he is made more
precious to me, and I to Him. So that at this day the Heavens and the
earth are not onely like Adams Eden but the Stage and Theatre of my
Saviours passion. And He for undergoing Such Things for me a
Greater Treasure Then all beside.

8

Haveing restored me so to enjoy his Glory, if I do it not, my Sin is
Greater then it was before: and Therefore have I need to take Greater
Care then Adam in Eden.

9

The Sons of men being made Greater Treasures then Heaven and earth are more to be beloved: and his Bounty in giving them more to be esteemed, Howbeit they have made it Difficult, by withdrawing their love from Him and me, and by Swerving from His Image.

10

His Compassion Nevertheless to me and them, should move me to imitate his tender pitty. Now pitty Embalms Love, and makes it more vigorous, Especially to such Divin and Noble creatures.

11

By corrupting them selves and turning after vanity they have Blinded the world and me in like manner. Thick Darkness covereth the Nations, and Gross Darkness the people. which is cheifly contracted by their Inventing and following other Treasures, for by magnifiing Riches of their own Devising, they have Covered the Treasures of Innocent Eden, forgotten the Delights of God, Buried in oblivion them selves and the world; Eclipsed the clear and open Joys of True Felicity.

12

Nevertheless even vanities them selves may be made Enjoyments, when by courage and wisdom we over come them.

13

Victory and Triumph are now Added to our former Delights. Benefits arising even from Sin it Selfe. but Such is the power of prevayling Custom, and Such the Darkness which those clouds and Snares have induced upon the Earth, that none, or but very few can clearly see them.

14

In being a Son of God like Jesus Christ, in forgiving Sinners, and living contrary to their Inferior customs, I shall recover Glory more Great then before: Those very Things that increas the Difficulty, Increas my Happieness when they are over com. So that a way of conquering be layd open, All Things shall work togeather for Good to Him that is faithfull. For He Shall not only be mor[e] Approved by How much the Greater his oppositions are: but by How much the Rubbish is, in this world of chaffe, be soe much the more Orient in the Eys of God like a Singular Jewel. Nor is this Meditation quickly to be over. For by how much the more Desolate the world is left by Revolting Sinners, by how much the Greater the Number is of owls and Dragons that Defile it with their manners, by How much the more is an inEstimable man in the Midst of Dragons; that being wise and Holy walketh with God in the Enjoyments of His works. Their thoughts are fled, they have left it Desolate and made the world a wildernes by neglecting to Consider the wisdom and power of Him that made it. And therefore doth his soul more Earnestly Desire one to Contemplat the Glory and Goodness that he hath placed in it.

15

God hath use now for an Holy man, which maketh Him more precious then the Golden wedge of Ophir, use for him Greater then what Angels are Admitted to, more Sublime then any Employment that Adam had in Eden, namely the calling of those wonderfull ones to their Ancient possessions, to the Enjoyment of God, to their Inheritance of the world, to the Recovery of their Blessedness, and to the Similitude of God in the possession of Greater Things then Adam Enjoyd. Hell from beneath, and the joy of their returne, Highly Magnifie and Advance their office.

16

We are mightily assisted by the Ancient Revelations of God in Ages, by Temples Ministers Magistrates and Saboths, by Miracles, by the word of God, by Sacraments Heroes Martirs Examples, Holy

Kings Sages and philosophers, All which meanes of God if men
Despise, I cannot but expect that they should Despise me. but Tho
they be not Gather'd I shall be Glorified. And therefore I Admire at
God[s] Goodness in giving me all these Ayds, yet not Diminishing a
Tittle of my Rewards. But I Stand amazed at the Bound of any fall for
at the first it was Greater then the fall of lucifer, as we may see by the
Greatnes of our Instauration.

17

1

Thy Turtle Doves O Lord to Dragons turn!
 Lay wast thine Heritage, and make
 The world a cave: wherin they mourn!
Whoe Should the Glory of thy Throne partake.
 Seas weep in Briny Tears,
 leaves Tremble on the Trees with fears,
 The Starrs do Twinkle as if all in Doubt,
 Wheather were best; to shine, or els goe out.
 The Heavens fledd
 The Earth is Dead
Thy turtle Doves to Owls and Dragons turn

2

like Dolefull Dragons in the wilderness
 Surrounded all with poyson, They
 Blast thine Abode and Blessedness
That Lovly Queen of GOD in prisons Lay.
 Green Grass is parcht, the flowers
 wither! The Heavens Languish in their Powers!
 The Mountaines are burnt up! the Rivers Dry!
 Tears onely flow in Rivers from mine Eye
 All these are fled
 They Dread, They Dread,
Those Dolefull Dragons in the wilderness.

3

Fled? whither O my Soul! O Fled from Men
    Fled from their Thoughts! Among the Blind
    The world is Gone, turnd to a Den;
In it we owls and Madmen onely find.
      A Salvage wilderness
Cares [   ] Drought, Thornes, Briars, all Distress!
Dayes turnd to Night, the Setting Sun gon Down
At noon! Doggs on the wall Surround the Town
        Tho made to Reign,
        They all complain.
Fled! whither O my Soul! O fled from Men!

4

His Image in themselves laid in a Grave,
    Is Dead and Buried! The Treasure
    Which they lik Dragons in them have
Unknown's unknown! They feel not any pleasure,
      But Snuffe! Snuffe up the wind
And wallow in their filth like Adders Blind
Their Skins Like Dragons clad with Golden Ore
Shine Brightly, overcast with Greenish Gore.
        Their Scales Display
        A poysond Day.
His Image in them's laid within a Grave!

5

O that from pomps, from fals and fained pleasures,
    From poysond splendor I might them
    Recall! And from Infected Treasure
Turning their Skins into a Diadem.
      To thee O lord would I
And to thy Goodness Brighter then the skie
In all the Heavens Shining, them Reclame,
And Shew the Glory of thy Holy Name.
        O Lord Revive
        And them retrive
From Dragons pomps from Fals and filthy pleasures

6

Then Shall thy Turtle Dove a gaine return
A filthy Dragon No More be
Her face Shall Like an Angel burn,
And She a cherub In Her Lov to Thee
Another Glory then
In wholesome Sort Shall Deck the Sons of men
Noe poysond verdure but the purest Gold
I on Thy Turtle Shall with joy Behold
Angelique Life
Throughout her Skin
Shall clad thy wife and mak her Shine within.

18

O my God would She See thy Goodness! How should her soul be Ravished! thy Goodness and thy Wisdom seen, would make thy Bride, of Heaven and Earth a Queen! She would then Inherit her Ancient Glory. Thy Blessedness would Delight the Earth, And the Sons of Men be advanced to Communion with Thee in their Happines! O my Soul! Bloud, Life, Breath, Estate, if I knew How to expend them So as to be Effectual; would all be too Little, Even with my understanding and Liberty to releive them. Trades, Taverns, Markets, Houses, Moneys, coache[s], clothes, Dragons, Lace, Bury their Happienes: and are become no[w] a funeral Solemnitye. Like Snares and clouds they cover the face of Nature, that Darken and oppress at the Same time. My Lovly Heritag is a Rebell unto me, and a Devouring Lyon. Tho in Aphorisms plainer then the Sun their Glory be made to appear, and Divine Wisdom Shine unto them: They will Do that which proceedeth out of their own mouth, to heap up Gold, and Liv in pleasure of their own DiviSing. nor Shall any thing turn them out their way; to perswade them that they are Angels, or that they might liv in Heaven. in the land of uprightness will they Deal unjustly, and will Not behold the Majesty of the Lord.

19

The Heavens Declare the Righteousness of the Lord and all the people See his Glory. yet what they see they regard not, and therefore perish. They know not what place, what Realm, what kingdom they are in. They know not them Selves, nor who it is that walketh among them. Their High estate, the Glory wherin they walk, God here with us, and the Kingdom of Heaven here on Earth, they n[o] more perceiv then crawling vipers. Apostat Devils are in a Happier estate then we, if we Rebel against Him. But no Sence will they ever have, Nor any other more High and Divine Apprehensions!

20

It is a misery to bewayl, But a Blessed mans missery a Step to Happienes, to lament the Corruption of a Degenarate and unrighteous world. How much more is it to Thirst and love and bear, and long to reClaime! this is my portion under the sun, and my task with God, wherein I am to Labor under as fellow workman. O Blessed be the Eternal King for my Glorious Employment!

21

Could I call them back but to the fruition of Heaven and Earth, It would Recompence my paines: All the Earth would resound His praises, His Goodness Wisdome and power being seen would make all rejoyce! Then the Heavens would appear most Beautifull, and the Earth Blessed. All the Nations Sing praises unto God, and the Earth yeeld Its increas. God, Even our own God, would give us his Blessing. But I have Higher Delights, and Infinit Treasures, Greater and more Excellent to reveal, wherin God would appear.

22

O His Lov! His wisdom is Glorified in ten Thousand things Greater then the world, which His Goodness hath made even in the world, more then Millions of worlds our Treasurs, For the Sake of which the world was Erected. The very Thoughts them Selves in the Bosom of Men, His wayes, our Souls! But these are too Near or High to be Beleeved. Sabaths, Temples, kings alsoe are Neglected! as if No Delight or Beauty were in them! An Island of Divels! Drown'd in perdition, that will not understand, till Hell openeth her mouth and Swalloweth them! All the Glory round a bout them maketh them worse. They are Infinitly Beloved! O How they Reign in His Bosom! How He longeth for them and Desireth them! yet they will not See. no man Regardeth.

23

They may Liv in His Image, Not towards the world and Sin onely, but towards Himselfe. and be the Darlings and Delights of God. See all his Blessedness and Eternitie their own. O How Infinitly High hath he Exalted them! He hath made them Compleatly to Enjoy them selves.

24

To enjoy ones Selfe compleatly is a word full of Infinite misterye. which no creature can do, Nor at all understand, which cannot Search into the Heights and Depths and Abysses of Eternity, and haveing Searched all the Borders of Eternity, See plainly that it is impossible that a creature more Glorious then Himselfe could be made. for till then there can be noe rest nor Absolute complacency, much less any Compleat or perfect joy. For he that would enjoy Himselfe, must first of all be content with his being, and then Infinitly Delight in it.

25

No man can Infinitly Delight in his Being that sees not his Being at least Infinite, nor offer up to God a Sacr[i]fice of Complacency, that Doth not Infinitly Delight in Himself. For he that Doth not Delight Infinitly in Himselfe can never Delight Infinitly in God. For He Delighteth in God because God hath made him to enjoy Infinite Blessedness, and to Delight in Himselfe Infinitly because he is [a] Creature Meet to enjoy Infinite Blessedness.

26

A creature that can enjoy Infinite Blessedness has unlimited comprehensions for all Eternity: and very clear and distinctive powers to penetrate the Bowels of every centre: in every poynt of which He findeth a Diety, yet one God in the whole Sphere. And is Himselfe a God to God. that is a Delight, an Image magnified and Exalted to the utmost Height: I have Said ye are Gods, bu[t] ye Shall Dye like men, and fall like one of the princes.

27

The Reason why man is a Feeble worm is because He DeSpiseth His understanding, and lives onely by His Fleshly Body: wou[ld] He live by His understanding He Should Soone perceiv Himselfe an infinite creature. All Sight, and Love: the Nature of which are both Infini[t]. All! all! all the souls in Heaven and earth Shall Dwell in Him. and He in them, and they in God, and God in Him, and He in God forevermo[re]: they limmit not each other.

28

God is such that there may be the Similitude of Himself, and the soul is such that it is the similitude in extent, Duration, Essence, value. In Extent because it is a Temple of his omnipreSence, in Duration becaus It is like Him Immortall. in Essence becaus it is a Spirit, limiting Nothing, Excluding Nothing, Life and Love. in value. And if any contemn and Despise these: He Sleighteth God. Dishonoureth his maker. For greater perfections cannot be.

29

He that can enjoy all things hath Infinite cause to Delight in Himselfe. Becaus the Treasures of God are Infinite. And God wholy in every thing to be enjoyed. The Similitude of whose Blessedness also is Implanted in Man. So that He enjoyeth both God, and His own.

30

The Similitude of His power is Implanted within, of His wisdom and liberty, as well as comprehension. For that Creature which can enjoy all things is Endued with powrs infinitly Greater then that of makeing and Enjoying worlds. could He make worlds and not enjoy them it would be childish weakness: could He make and Enjoy them, it would be infinitly less then that power of Enjoying all things. God being Infinitly Greater then worlds, Tho all possible should be maile This Demonstration we have cited, heretofore: but it is not felt, nor yet prized as it ought to be. men Dream onely of what they here, and are not Ravished, nor Awaked out [of] Slumber according to the merit of Soe Divine a caus. were they well aware of the Things we are Speaking, They would Sing Hallelujahs forevermore.

31

In the Blessedness of God there is not only the Enjoyment of Treasure, but the Manifestation of Glory. which nevertheless are coincident, for the World is his treasure only for the sake of his Glory. His Goodness being infinit, desires to be received, and to becom an Object of infinit Delight to all Spectators. Which to be, is indeed to be Glorious. That he may be this Object of Delight, he made the World, and for this End only is it usefull to him.

32

Man is made to appear in Glory, as well as to inherit all Treasure. And therefore is Endued with Liberty of will as well as comprehension. He is Glorious in Abilitie in respect of Life power and Intelligence. Glorious in Estate in respect of Height Exaltation Treasure, Glorious in Attendants in respects of Angels and Men. But God would have Him Glorious in Himselfe in respect of His own Actions works and operations. He would have Him voluntary as God is, wise, Holy, in all his Enjoyments, that He might be most Blessed in being Glorious.

33

God is more Blessed in Being a Treasure then in haveing all. Nay all are His Treasures onely for This, that he may be a Treasure. the Delight, wherwith He loveth to be Enjoyed is that, the satisfaction wherof he intended when he made all.

34

O my God how infinite art thou in Goodness! How I in unworthyness! I loath and abhor my Selfe; who have Sinned a[gainst] the Light
of thy countenance! The works of Darkness have Blinded mine Eys.
And Since my Baptisme, and Since my Repentance I have Greiveously
Sinned. Insomuch that all the creatures in Heaven and Earth may rise
up against me. Especialy thy Saints may justly Abhor me! I admire O
Lord the exceeding Multitude of thy Tender Mercies. that thou
sufferes[t] me to flourish in any of their affections, that I am not cast, as
an Abominable Branch out of the Kingdome. O my God I Greive and
am ashamed that I must make such a Confession. but my Guilt is
Great, blot it I beseech Thee out of the Book of thy Remembrance. And
wheras I have Deserved utter Darkness, O let my Soul be Humbled
within me, and thine Infinite Mercies be exalted over me. Spare me O
Lord and b[e] Reconciled to me, and my Love Shall be more Enflamed
unto Thee! O Let the Sun of Righteousness arise upon me! O Let hi[s]
Bloud Sprinkle me! Let the Holy Ghost O Lord overshadow me, that I
may conceive of Thee Such Glorious Things, as may be worthy of thy
Blessedness and Eternal Majesty, and the Grea[t] joy of thy Church and
people. O let a Sinners Lips out of the Depth of Hell praise Thee. Guilt
is Hell. and the Blindness wherby a Sinner is Divided from Thee, a
Mist Like the Blackness of Eternal Darkness! O Let this confession
stan[d] here as a Token How I loath and abhor my selfe! I have
deserved to be vile in mine own eys, And I abhor my Selfe in Dust and
Ashes. But Thou O Lord remember a contrite and broken Heart, and
How Thou hast promised to Dwell within it. Let this Blot which
appeareth a-mong my joyes, Shew thy mercy and their Beauty more! O
manifest thy Selfe, and Dwell within me! Giv me care to Sin no more!
By sin I am Divided from Thee my God, and onely by thy Grace can be
restored againe to the Light of thy Countenance. Nor can I ever Shew
forth the Glory of thy Lov, but in the Light of thy presence, where all
the fullness of joy appeareth! O Lord my God I rejo[y]ce in Thee!

35

O my God How am I to Admire and Adore Thee forever more, that
am called to live in the similitude of thy Blessedness and in thy

Blessedness. Thou hast So obliged me in makeing me Like Thee, that
Thy Blessednes is more then mine, becaus my Blessed[ness] is made
Like thine. For as Thou art, so am I forevermore. The Light of thy
Kingdom, the Joy of thy Saints, a Temple of thy Glory, and the End of
all Things. O my God I Tremble at my Ignorance! And acknowledg
my selfe a prodigie by reason of my sin. Shall I be as Gall and Shame,
to them before whose faces I ought to be a King Amiable in Holiness
Joy and Glory. O let me never sin more! never be Remiss, never careless! if the Displeasure of my freind be such Greife unto me, O what is
thine if it is not, O what will it! I beseech Thee keep me, O keep me
that I may Sin no more!

36

As a prisoner returning from the pitt, as a Malefactor Saved from
the cross, yea as a Devill taken out of Hell, I return O Lord to the Glory
of thy kingdom. For my crime hath been wors then Satans. Having
Sinned more, O more, much more in Sinning against my ReDeemers
Lov! How Sweet then will the Glory be to which I am restored, and
How Delightfull his Lov, by whom I was Redeemed. O prince of peace
who sittest at the Right Hand of God in the Glory of the father I Adore
Thee. and Desire to Dye for Thee, or to Liv to please Thee. Thy Lov, O
thy Lov is Better then Heaven! It is indeed the very only Sun and Soul
of Heaven.

37

To be as Jesus christ is, Surrounded with all the Glory of God, King
of Heaven and earth, Environed with the world, crowned with the
Glory of His fathers Lov, clothed with His Righteousness, as an Heir
of Eternity, in the midst of all his own possessions the object of Delight
to Angels and men, Natures Darling and Beloved of God. To appear in
all this Glory and to be So Beloved of every soul, so Accepted honored
prized and magnified. O the Rapture and extasie Satisfaction and the
joy to Abide with every Single Soul, as a person clothed with all this
Glory yet our Individuall and Eternall freind. to See but one Raysed
up of God and clothed with all this Glory for our Sakes. Oh How
Transporting. but to see all others raised up for his Sake, that as a king

more High he might be more Glorious, and a more Blessed and Delightfull freind, O the Rapture and TranscenDent Lov that this begetteth. But to see every one thus supream and thy Selfe Heir of their Delight! O the wisdom! O the Beauty! O the praises! O the Joy! wherewith that Kingdom must be Replenished! yet is all this nothing in comparison to the Joy We take in Him, whose Goodness is the Basis of this Blessedness; and whose wisdome the fountain of this Glory.

38

And cannot I here on earth so Lov my freinds! O my T. G. O my S. H. O my Brother! ye wise and Holy Sages! that see a little, and understand your Glory. ye are Treasures unto me Greater then the world! ye who are exalted in the Glory of the father, and of his son Jesus christ, by the Lov and ministery of all Angels and all Ages, and by the Subserviant Ministery of all the world, which Served you in Each of them: O how am I superabundantly exalted in your exaltation! Keep your selves O my freinds, in the Light of Gods countenance, in the midland Territories of his Holy Kingdom, and be sencible of his Lov, and Delight in his Glory.

39

O what pleasure doth he take to see you Reigning. first to see a creature made by Himselfe So Highly exalted. 2^{ly} To See a creature so Highly exalted magnifieing Him. 3^{ly} to see a creature whom He So Loveth so perfectly Blessed. 4^{ly} To see a creature so Beautifull in all its Enjoyments. yea 5^{ly} How sweet is it in Him to communicate his Blessedness in such a manne[r] and to see that creature made a Blessedness so to all, And Himselfe sovereign and Supreme over all, by their Supremacies over each other Infinitly Exalted!

40

But after all to be Beloved is the Greatest Happieness. All This Glory and all these Treasures, being but the Appendencies, and the ornaments of that person that is our Bride or Freind, prepared all for the Sake of Lov, to commend and Sweeten it more unto us. But How

Great must His Lov be, who not onely created the Heavens and the earth for one, but becaus a Lover is the sweetest thing, and Himselfe the most Glorious Lover, created the most Glorious Image of Himselfe to giv us and made many Millions of Angels Cherubims and Men to Honor and Attend that Image, that Like a God He might be Lov unto us! Nay How Glorious and full of Wisdom is that work, that maketh every one of Those Attendants So Glorious a Sovereign that being after his Similitude the supreme of all, He Should Still be an Attendant to that Single Image who was our First Freind, and yet Himselfe the principal Lover and all the Residue His Attendants! every one being So the Sun in Heaven among the plannets! Yet is all this Atcheived by Lov, for God is Lov. And all this shews his Lov unto my Soul. Yea it Shews indeed that for which I intirely Lov Him, that He is Infinite Lov to every Soul!

42

Blessed be the Eternal God for shewing me the Treasures of Felicity! O what could this world be, but a silent chaos, a Dull and Empty wilderness, were [it] not for the Invisible Things of His Eternal Kingdom! When all other Comforts fail, when the Sword hath wasted our land, when our Cittys are Destroyd, when our Assemblies are Fled, when nothing is near but woefull Solitariness, the Soul that can Liv in Communion with Him shall Sing His praises: And be to it selfe a Temple of Delights, and Assemblies and Treasures! yet will the Face of His Happieness be Disguised, with Lamentations for his people: Silent venerations of Gods Justice that hath made him naked, an Awfull Dread of his High Majestie and Great Judgments which have so latly happened, will be his food.

43

Then will the Beauties of Divine Laws be seen, which now are Hidden in their own Splendor. The Happienes of Living a-mong such Heavenly Joys. The Glory of Loving and Doing Good, the sweetness of companions, so near at Hand; the Delectable Excellency of being a Delight, a Treasure, a Blessing. O my Soul why should they not now, even now be Treasures; since their Removall will make them so to appear. now Spend thy Life in Thankfullness for them, Least thy Ingratitude make Thee to Spend it in Tears!

44

It is a pleasant thing to enjoy Heaven and Earth, but much more pleasant to Lov a man, that is possessor of it. The Sweetness of conversation upon wise Foundations, being an Elevation of the Soul above the Spheres. To see a nother Contented with his Being, Contemplating the Glory of Heaven and Earth, Adoring God, and Living in the Temple of this world a Divine and Beautifull Life, a celestiall joy to the Holy Angels.

45

To talk of His wisdom Goodness and power, to speak of his Lov, and to Adore His GodHead, to shew our complacency and the pleasure we take in our Eternall freind, to have living Auditors while we sing his praises, and to Enflame each other with more High Resentments of Joy and Gratitude, to a God Invisible: These are Joys Transcendant unto Sence, and that would turn the world into a very Heaven. Heavenly Joys, but therefore unknown, because Exterminated our Borders. at Least Seldom, if ever Acted.

46

Blessed is the Man that Delighteth in His Law, that Meditateth therein Day and Night. He shall be Like the Tree planted by the Rivers of waters, his Leaf shall not wither, He Bringeth Forth His Fruit in its season, what soever he Doth Shall prosper. Why? These Laws are the Rivers, the streams whereof refresh the Citty of our God: Meditation in them, is a planting, by them; the soul is brought near to the Brink of this River by Meditating their Excellencies. Through the S[c]ent therof He shall bud forth, and flourish. what so ever He doth Shall prosper, becaus they are His counsellors, Shew him Delights and teach Him to manage his Affayrs with Discretion.

47

What Excellencies are in the laws of God, or why they Command us such a Duty, is a Disquisition meet for the understanding of Angels, a Great part of whose Celestiall pleasures flow in the River of Gods Laws, which are not onely Kept but Delighted in in Heaven. A seaventh part of their Eternal joys consisteth in the complacency of their soul therin.

48

For the Laws of God either Glorifie or colour all their Lives, as Guids or Ingredients in all their affections, And Extend their Influence to all Objects throughout all Eternity, either Sweetning their affections and Heig[h]tening their Enjoyments, or else Debateing them, and makeing them Displeasant. That therfore the Laws of God are Eternal Lights Directing them all to live in His Similitude, to God Angels and Men, Kingdoms Ages Heaven Earth &c: This is at Least a seventh part, if not the comprehensiv of all their Joys. which the Blindness of men hindereth them upon Earth from Seeing and enjoying.

49

It was a marvellous Question, and the very Asking of which satisfied my soul with abundant Delight, becaus it touched the Ground of my Nature, Which plato moved: a Question worthy of so Divine a Philosopher, Whether Things were Holy becaus they were commanded or therefore Commanded becaus they were Holy.

50

The Heathen Answered not his own Question: for it was too Deep for his Intelligence. Ability to mov it was sufficient for Him, in us to Answer it. Nor is it sufficient to Answer it, but Delight in the Answer. And See the Necessity and Benefit of Doing it.

51

He that would rest with Complacency in God, must among other causes Delight in Him for his Holy Laws. Take pleasure in Him, extoll and prays him, for the Beauty of his will, as He is the Sovereign Lawgiver of Heaven and Earth: And He that will do this must not onely Submit to His Laws because of His Dominion: but Subscrib to His Laws, as the onely Laws which his Soul Could desire, and prais His Dominion for the excellency of them. Because of them the most pleased person in Heaven and Earth.

52

If we respect God the Author of them, Things are Therefore Commanded becaus they are Holy: If creature[s] that are to Obey, Things are therefore Holy becaus they are commanded. For Gods Authority is So Divine, and we are So profoundly Subject by our obligation to His soveraign Dominion that we are bound to Obey whatever He Commandeth. Yet God in his Dominion is so Divine, that is so Good as well as Great, that had we the first Disposal of his Laws, we Could not have more pleased our selves then he hath don. He commandeth onely the most Excellent Things.

53

Those Things are most Excellent that are most Agreeable with the Nature of God. Tho the Nature of God being Goodness and Lov, those Things are most agreeable to his nature wherein Goodness is Satisfied and Lov Delighted. Those Thing[s] are most Excellent that are most Expedient for the Happieness of his creatures: becaus Goodness and Lov Delighteth in makeing His creatures Happy.

54

Becaus Goodness is Satisfied and Love Delighted in the Happiness of His creatures, Those Things are in them selves Holy that make us Happy. And those alone hath he Commanded by his Laws. There being a concurrance of all Interest to make us Obedient.

55

Since Gods Goodness and our Happieness are Individually one, Gods Goodness is our Happieness. And those things most Holy that are Agreeable unto both, Him and us

56

Those Things are most Holy which are most Agreeable with Gods Glory. Whose Glory is that he is Infinit Lov.

57

Those Things are most Holy that are the Greatest Similitude of his Eternall Nature. Since therfore God is Lov he commandeth Lov: which being the first Begotten of his Goodness, the most Conduciv to our Happiness, the Similitude of His Essence, and the onely thing conformable to His Glory, is the most Holy, absolute Best and most necessary, so that no Laws could possibly be made but those which are the Laws of Lov. The Best Laws being most Inevitable.

58

Who would not keep those Laws, to which we are obliged by Infinit obligations, which are them Selves the Greatest and which command Things most Agreeable to God and us? who would Not Sing and Rejoyce in their unity? who would not Exult and be Ravished with joy to See Gods Goodness and our Happieness so Individu[a]lly united! His Glory love and Blessedness conspire to make us Blessed.

59

Becaus His Image is most Holy, He made His Image. in which alone all the rest of His works are Sanctified, by which aLone He is Glorified, to which aLone His Laws are Natural, and for the sake of which He created All Things. which is then Holy when like Him it Loveth all, and Delighteth to be Beloved.

60

The Blessedness of God consisteth in this, that He is Infinite Lov. for by lov He enjoyeth all His works, by Lov He delighteth in all our Happieness, by love He is the Treasure of all His Hosts: in being Lov He is most Beautifull, and ever Meet to be Delighted in. For being Lov he is praised by His Holy Angels and by all his Hosts in the Heaven of Heavens.

61

By being Lov a Lone, was it possible that He should be wise. for the greatest wisdom, is to be the End of all, of which He is the Author; to Glorifie Himselfe and enrich others; to enjoy the Treasures which He gives away; to satisfie Himselfe and exalt us; to Knit our Happieness all in one; to enrich Himselfe by Giving His Treasures; to possess all in such a manner, as to be the joy of all. And all this He Atcheiveth, or is by Lov aLone.

62

That Lov is a Necessary and eternal Being is Infini[t]ly the Joy of God and Angels: the exultation and Delight of Men, the Jubilee and the Glory of all his Creatures.

64

How Happy hast Thou made me O God in making me to Lov! A Divine and spirituall Lover is a wonderfull Great and unknown Creature. A strang Being here upon Earth. An Image of the Diety in the wilderness. A Disguised prince walking InCognito among forrein people. unknown, unseen, Incredible. Exceeding Great yet very little, Exceeding Rich yet very poor, Exceeding High yet very Low, Exceeding Beautifull yet Invisible, Exceeding Divine, yet not valued. Exceeding Great for it is a Living Sphere of fire wider then the world: yet very Little, for it is Shut up in Mans Body. Exceeding Rich, for it Illustrates all Things, includes and possesses them, yet very poor, perhaps Living in a cave with out house or lands. Exceeding High, for both in reach and Nature it is Higher then the Heavens, yet very Low for it walketh upon the Earth, and very Humble. it swayeth a Scepter over God and Man; yet is very weak for any Body may Destroy it, or at Loast the person in whom it Dwelleth. it is Exceeding Beautifull, for it Enflameth all Things, yet is invisible, for it Cannot be seen. It is an Endless Blessing Tho Not understood. All covet it, All admire it, all Delight in it. It is Rich and pleasant. every one Desireth it for it is Sweet to be Beloved. It is a Strange Dæmon for it is the Spring of all our affections, the Secret Mine of all our pleasures, the Rule of our Affayrs. The most Great and near and Tender Interest, of which all are Jealous; no man must Touch it.

65

As Lov is his wisdom, whose Essence is Lov: so it is ours. our Holiness Blessedness and Glory. for by it we become the End of all, of which God is the Author. are Glorified our Selves and Enrich others. Enjoy the Treasures which we Giv a way. Satisfie our Selves and Exalt others, knit all the Happienes of God Angels and Men in one. Enrich our Selves by Giving a way our Treasures, possess all in Such a manner as to be the Joy of all. be Like God by Lov a Lone.

66

Those that think our union with God so Incredible, are taught more in the Sacrament. He gives Himselfe to be our food. is united to us. Incorporated in us. for what doth he intimate by the Bread and wine, but as the Bread and wine are mingled with our flesh, and is nourishment Diffused through all our members, So he is Lov mingling with our Lov as flame with flame, Knowledge shining in our knowledge as Light with Light, An omnipresent Sphere within our Sphere.

67

There be many things wherein the modestie of Man is an Injurious Counterfeit. Not modestie, but Ignorance, Ingratitude and Thraldom, for such is that that is afrayd to acknowledge the Benefits of God; and unwilling to perceiv the Good it hath received. Had I said that the Son of man while we Sit Down will Gird Himselfe and come forth to Serv us; I should hav been accused by men to hav Spoken Blasphemie. But now he hath said it, it is Beleived: but Hastily, past over, and not understood. yea many read that never take Notice He spake any Such Thing. Blessed are those Servants whom the Lord when he commeth shall find watching: verylie I say unto [you] that He Shall Gird Himselfe and make them Sit down to meat, and will come forth and serve them. what kind of service will Jesus doe? Shall the king of Glory come and Gird Himselfe and come and Serve Such Abjects as we, who dare presume to think thus Arrogantly of Himselfe! O Man Consider, what Service wouldst thou have him to do! Were He like thy Servant at thine own Disposal what wouldst thou require? wouldst thou have him come and wash thy feet? He hath washed them with His Bloud! wouldst thou have Him reach thee New wine in the king-dome of Heaven, while thou Sittest at the table! He will do it! not in cups but in whole Hogsheads Seas and Oceans. Alas! couldst thou ever have Contrived Such a Service, either So profitable to Thee or So vile to Him, as His comming Down from Heaven to Dye for Thee! He doth Greater Things for Thee, then Thou darest presume to Ask. What Greater Condescention, then that the king of Glory should leave His fathers Throne, and be basely mangled Upon a Crosse for thy Sin! He is wont to do Greater Things then Man dare beleive. And now He is Ascended, Doth He Gird Himselfe as thy Servant (to whom Angels Minister) to Governe all Things and to prepare thy Joys in making them fit to be enjoyed. In the kingdom of Heaven Thou Shalt Sit at the Table; when Thou art awakened to Consider these Things,

71

That God should give us soe Divine a Power! To Transfigure all Things, and be Delighted!

72

Shadows in the water are Like their Substances. And So reall, that no Painter can againe Express them. even here beneath the sun is seen, and the face of Heaven. O give me more of that Spirit, wherby we strongly Lov and Delight each in other. whereby we Liv in each

other[s] soul, and feel our Joys and sorrows! The Father is crowned in
God the Son, The Eternal Son in God the father. And both obeyed in
obedience to the Holy Ghost. one will in three persons. But are they
not one in Essence too! one in Felicity, one in Lov! All Treasures are the
fathers in the Son, All Joys are the suns in the Holy Ghost, The Holy
Ghost is the Lov of the father and the Son Dwelling in us, or to speak
plainly seene by us. For as the sun when it shines on a Mirror, is seen
within it: So Love when it is seen, Ravisheth the Soul becaus it
toucheth it, and Dwelleth in the understanding by which it is seen,
and the sight of it Enflameth the soul with Lov againe. the Lov seen is
the Lov returned. or else Exchangeth, Dwelling there and Begetting its
Similitude. Three Persons united in Lov, are one in Essence: or what
ever Difficulty is in that word, one by the Best of all possible unions.

73

The Soul beneath is Like that abov, and the Image of God[s] Divine
workmanship. Theres not a streak nor a Feature, but HimSelfe that is
in it. we are Greater Treasures then the world to each other. We are
Flames and Lights and Thrones to each other. in either the sun serveth
us againe. In either Angels minister

75

Lov is as Great a Prophet as it is a King. Now Prophets see in their
Extasies, Those Things which no Eye of Sence can Discern. O what
Spectacles have we in the Heights and Raptures of Holy Lov! we are
often Blind to those Things that are about us: Becaus inwardly we see
Infinite Treasures Joys and wonders. Vulgar People can as well read
the Thoughts of Angels, or tell the Inward soul of all the sages, as see
or know what we enjoy. The Perfection of our Riches and the manner
of our Enjoyment make it Ineffable.

76

Love is as Great a Preist, as it is a Prophet. And finds every Place a
Temple or makes it So. It can Sacrifice as Acceptably, as Know
Profoundly. And doe it Beautifully, upon the best of Altars. Nothing is

so Effectual in sacrificing Thanksgivings, nothing So Substantial in offering Praises. The best of all Female Graces is not more Amiable. nor can she bring more Rich and Sweet Perfumes, Then this Masculine Perfection.

77

Love is the onely sacrifice. It is Like our Saviour its own Preist, and its own Alter, Perfume and Flame. A Prophet Preist and king. O my God it is like thy son, the Phænix of the world. Its comprehensiv sphere, a flaming Temple. The Antitipe of her who is the faigned Miracle of all the Birds and more then So. Its own Alter fire nest and Sacrifice. O Thou nest, and Bed of spices! In its Highest Agonies, ever Dying, Expiring and Reviving every moment.

78

Spir[i]tual Idleness is an Alienation of the mind from its Proper Objects, And worse then Death, because it is a Seperation of man from His True Happieness: whereas in Death He may enjoy it.

79

To see the Goodness of the Lord in the land of the Living is the Hope of men, and the felicity of Angels. A Good man even by seeing the Felicity of his chosen is made Blessed. for all people are his enlarged Selfe: and Delightfull it is to see the Happienes and Glory of His Kingdom. a Liberty and Exaltation to behold the Light and Joy of his People. Tho therefore thou Dwellest in Solitary places, if by an Active contemplation thou go out of thy selfe, in the midst of Darkness thou Shalt see his Glory and be comforted abundantly in the Light of Heaven. All the Blessednes of other people shall be thy Delight joy and satisfactio[n].

80

To Se God imparting Blessings, advancing his people, Bringing them out of Egypt into the land of Canaan: giving them Blessed and

Glorious Laws, promising them Rewards if they will keep his statutes, makeing them Higher then all the Nations, Blessing them in the City, and Blessing them in the feild, in the fruit of their womb, and in the fruit of the Ground, Blessing their Baskett and their store, and prospering all the works of their hands, Putting all their Enemies to flight, and giving them Rain in Due Season, Lading their Trees with Grapes and Apples, makeing their Harvest reach unto the vintage, and the vintage to Sowing, that thay might eat their Bread to the full, and Dwell in their own land without any fears, Giving peace in their Borders and sleep without Terrors, takeing a way evill Beasts and not suffering the sword to wast them, causing five to chase an hundred of their Enemies and an Hundred to put ten Thousand to flight: To see Their songs and praises and Thanksgivings, is to be entertained with sweet Delightfull objects, and to feed upon them is the Life of Heaven.

81

The sight of his Goodness unto Kings is Pleasant, and affecteth the soul with Joy and Glory. He that Defendeth the Poore and Needy shall possess the Double in his own Land, kingly feasts and the food of Angels. the Best of fruits both new and old, Eternal fruits, the sweetest Fruits and most Lovly, full of Marrow and satisfaction, Joy and Gladness, Happieness and Glory. O How Divine and Greatly Blessed is the Life of Holy Kings! which excelleth here in Temporal Things and forever resteth a-mong the Holy Angels, is nourished here with Earthly Delights, is clothed there with Eternal Glory, here is attended with crowds of People, thare is accompanied with Quires of Angels, here is Delighted with Multitudes of Men, there with the Blessed order of cherubims, here is observed by the obedience of Armies, there exulteth in Jesus followers, shineth here with a Princly Robe, is Adorned there with Immortal Glory. here weareth a Regal crown, there Danceth with Eternal Joy, [here] is stiled the Sun of an Earthly Kingdom, there a Son of the King of Heaven, hath here the Inheritance of an Earthly Realm, and is Beautified there with an Heavenly kingdom. To see a man in such a path of Lillies and Roses, and by such steps of Gold and pearl ascending to the Throne of Glory, is Enlargment and pleasure both in one. and maketh one Blessed when we Delight in God, rejoyce in his Bounty, and the Beauty of his will,

But Especialy when he seeth all these Blessings upon Good kings, imparted to them for thare Peoples sake, and those people Governed by kings, to be our Treasures.

82

Melencholy objects entertained in the Thoughts do like soure Onions Excite teares in the Eyes, Delightfull Sights and curious Gardens naturaly Recreat the mind of man. but never soe much as when our Interest is perceived. It is one mistery in the art of Felicity to keep ones Thoughts a mong pleasant objects for while we are affected with sour and Displeasing Theames we are walking in the valley of the Shaddow of Death. He walketh in the light of the living who seeth the Beauty of Gods Kingdom. Awaken therefore thy Thoughts, and Strongly apply them to see the Glory of Gods Kingdom, the Pleasing Excellencyes of his works and ways, for such meditations shall Transport thy soul and make it even to Dwell in Heaven. But how much are we bound to bless his Name, that in the world of Things there is an Amiable and Delightfull side, which the Happy man does always apprehend! as the same Pillar that Divided between the Israelites and Egyptians was a fire to the one and a cloud to the other.

83

To See Temples Erected by the care and providence of God, wherin Assemblies might Gloriously be received, villages Rejoycing and Cittyes Flourishing, while all the People see his Glory, to see his Apostles and successors teaching all the families, coming into his courts, and there resounding with joy his praises: all this is Exceeding sweet and pleasant to behold, because God Himselfe walketh a-mong them. But that all this Should be done for me, that they all might be Lovers in Eternal Glory, every man a God unto my soul, or Like a God, a Living Treasure, a freind, a Joy, an Immortal Lover, this maketh all His Thrones and Temples Mine: as it doth alsoe that they are spectators of my Glory. But How can I ever understand this, till I see the Benefitt of Lov. Lov a Lone maketh me the possessor of all their Joys, Lov aLone maketh me a Joy and a Delight to them. The Lov of Beautifull works, of Gods Glory, of Delightfull sights, of their persons,

the Joy of seeing them wholy pleased, and pleased wholy for our
sakes. we may walk over all Eternity and ever see all our own. But not
till the Benefitt of Naked Lov is thorowly Displayed. at Least apprehended, if not Displayed.

84

Naked Lov is the cause of all things, and Naked Lov is the End of
all Things. Naked Lov is Efflagitated by Laws and Nakedly Preferd
abov many Temples. Temples full of Gold are but Drosse in
Comparison. to Discharge this, Eternal obligations are Laid upon us,
and Joys Eternal prepared as Rewards. Naked Lov is Greater and
more Divine then the Tongue of Angels. till we Esteeme it Like God
and rest satisfied in its naked Excellency we shall never be rich,
Blessed and Glorious, never be satisfied, never value the meanes till
we apprehend the fullnesse of the end. For where the End is Disliked,
the meanes are ingratefull; where that is Despised, these are superfluous. Till therefore we see the Inward Blessedness of being Beloved
we can never Enjoy the Palaces and Temples of those that are to Lov
us: nor God who hath made them to Lov us, nor Kings nor Thrones
who Lead them to Happieness, nor Ministers nor sabboths that Direct
them to Glory. How much therefore doth it concerne us to know the
Nature of that without which nothing is Enjoyed.

86

All security and Power are in Lov: all riches, Delight and Glory. For
Angels and Men while they Lov as them selves, watch for our welfare,
Employ ther Powers to Advance and please us, Giv us all the Riches
they can command, Exalt and Honor us, Delight in our welfare and
promote our Happieness. yet all these rea[c]h not the Inward parts
and Depths of love. there is somthing beside for which these are
valued. Namely the sweetnes of Naked Love, an unexp[r]essible
sweetness, an Intrinsick Joy and pleasure which we feel in Naked Lov.
which God doth So strongly covett and Delight in, that for the sake of
it He created the world and all. therefore they are Dull and not
Spiritual, Ignorant and not knowing, Profane and not Holy, and must
needs be so in a 1000 Things that cannot feel it as God doth; whose

Happieness is Lov: the Delight of Loving and being Beloved. O that I could see the Hidden Sweetness of this Inward flame! this Queen in Glory, the Beauty of her soul, the End and crown and soul of the univers! O my God I pant after Thee as the Heart panteth after the water Brooks! could I see Lov in its Naked Essence I should see thy Glory. for God is Love, which is the sweetest Being.

87

God Himselfe cannot be Enjoyed till Lov is seen. Till we Delight most in being Beloved, we cannot Delight in God more then in his Gifts, nor Enjoy his Gifts, till we Lov to be Beloved. The Terestrial services of Heaven and Earth are Exceeding Great, as they serve our Bodies, but nothing in comparison of the service they do us in Exhibiting His Lov. which is Greater then the World, Brighter then the Sun, Sweeter then Hony, more precious then Gold, more pure then the Heavens, overflowing abov the seas, nearer then the Aire. It riseth in the East, moveth in the stars, is clad in sables by night, in Glory by day, Liveth in the soul, is visible in the Body, being as it were Embodied in our Lives, is Legible in his word, Promulged in his Laws, Glittereth in His ways, Flourisheth in the valleys, Springeth in the feilds, Shineth in the moon, refresheth us in the Gales, floweth in the winds that He bringeth out of his Treasures, cometh Down in the Rain, Reviveth in the Dew, Journeyeth in the clouds upon the wings of the wind and there overshadoweth. O my God how universal is thy Lov; it is wholy every where, all these are Effects and Types and Pledges of thy Eternal Lov, but without that Can never be enjoyed. The frame of Nature composed of these is Beautifull to the Eye, yet Infinitly Profitable underneath, as it Serves us by many Sweet and Secret Influences. As for example, the sun is as Bright as if it were made for Nothing but to be seen. Yet it doth Illuminate all other things, Melt waters, Raiseth springs, Disgesteth Gold, Impregnates the Earth with spirits, which transpiring thence, rais up the corn, ripens wheat, and fruits on Trees, Rayseth Odors from Perfumes and flowers, Quicken Men and Beasts and Fishes, animates the world, comforteth with warmth, Actuates all. Yet till we see the Lov of Him that made it All this is to no Purpose. were I alone in the world all these are necessary to me, and in Serving are my Delight, but till I See the End for which they are Employed, that is what Life I must Lead while these attend me, they all Distast me by reason of Defect. I cannot enjoy them in their original till I See the Lov from whence they came, I cannot enjoy them in their End till I see the Lov for which they came, and without these, it is Like a Man whose Head and feet are cut off[f] a Broken Circle. I cannot enjoy it with fullness of Delight till I like the Employment for which I Liv. To Lov and to be Beloved. Communion with God is the End of the creation. And He that sees it Surmounteth the world and Dwells in Heaven.

88

All these he giveth as freely as the beames of the Sun, which fils the Ayr with light and Glory, and are present without being noted. Since Lov from which they came is the sweetest Thing, He gave us Men that they might Lov us too, and the Holy Angels. That all these Things are soe freely Given, so Reall, common, near, being such infinit Treasures, Great in magnificence, Transcendantly Good, Beautifull beyond measure, of Inestimable Price, necessary yet common, Divine and Glorious, yet freely surrounding us: It makes his Kingdom reall and Illustrious. Did we walk a-mong Rivers of milk and Hony, Rocks of Adamant and Skies of Gold, Trees of pearl and Emrald Spires insteed of Grass, It could not be so sweet as to enjoy those Heavenly and Living Things. But that they are all given to such an End, it makes his Glory to shine so strongly, It is a Miracle He is not seen. A miracle to wit of mans Apostasie. Such an end Enricheth all for we are all now to live in freindship with God, Admiring at the Riches which He hath Given: but most at the Lov. whose Greatness seen in the vastnes of His works, Goodness also wisdom and power, in the fabrick of the world and uses of his creatures, are therefore contemplated that we may Know the Glory of Him that Loveth us, who is King of Heaven and Earth. And the Happines to which ourselves are Exalted, by a King so Great, and wise and potent.

89

In makeing men He hath infinitly Enriched the world unto us. For He hath made it to serve us in each of them, as it serveth us in Him.

whom it wholy serveth for our sakes, for it serveth them That They might Love us, and as Kingly freinds, yea God-like Emperors, Give them selves unto us. All the world upholdeth me, that I might minister to one of them, All the world upholdeth them that they might minister each to me. But oh the Depth and unsearchable Riches of his Eternal wisdom, Ages alsoe are prepared for me, and evry soul a sacrifice To me, an offering of God, a Gift of Lov, an Angelique minister, a Lov it selfe of infinit value: that can shine on all yet on me alone, can shine on all for my sake, be made more rich by shining upon all, and enrich all with Light and beauty on whom He shineth, while I enjoy both Him and them. He that loveth offereth Himselfe, openeth his soul, presenteth the Incense of his best affections, Exalteth us on High, seateth us in his Throne, Shineth upon us, Divideth his Empire, Giveth it all, rejoyceth to be enjoyed: Loveth to enjoy, Resigneth Himselfe, and taketh pleasure to be commanded: He lifteth up the Heads of the everlasting Gates, and rejoyceth to see us enter the Regions of His soul. But how Good is God, who giveth us the very soveraign End for which He made the world, maketh us to reign in his own Throne, and to be almost worshipped in evry Temple where Himselfe is Adored: By makeing us to be Beloved of evry Subject in all his Kingdom. He hath multiplied the person of evry soul, and made it to reign in Innumerable kingdoms. for every soul is an Infinit Realm or sphere of all Things, by giving us which He hath Given His Empire. for every soul includeth His Empire, and in every soul we are made to Reign.

90

To be Tumbled out of any Soul is to be Thrown from our Throne, infinitly more rich then a Throne of Gold, And to be Banisht that Empire, where we might talk with God and in the light of which see his Glory. The Effect of which is such Discontent, and Rage at our selves if by folly we loos it, that There needeth no other Hell to Torment, nor fire to consume us.

91

He that would be a wise, and well Adorned Lover, must remember Himselfe to be [a] sphere of all Things. That He is in the Temple of

Eternity, And that God hath put the Earth which is His footstool beneath His feet. That all the Engravings and ornaments of it, are the Riches of His footstoole, that his Head is a bove the Heavens, and his soul seated in the Throne of God, that the sun and stars minister unto Him, Angels and men attend upon Him, that He reignue also in the Bosom of God, shines upon Ages, and Governeth Kingdoms. In this Glory therefore He is to be unmoveable, and to love as the freind of God. All his affections are to flow out from this Centre. He is to Embrace his freind in this sphere, to offer up Himselfe with all his Glory at His freinds feet, and to rejoyce that His freind is Adorned here, in this Living Temple, that He reigneth here, is served and sacrificed to by the sweetest affections. such Living Perfumes are Paid to God, And such to His Image: becaus it is exposed as the Representitive of Himselfe to be Beloved.

92

There is in a man a Double selfe, according as He is in God, or the world. In the world He is confined, and walketh up and Down, in Little Roome: but in God He is evry where. Hence it is that his Thoughts can touch any part of Eternitie. And that his Soul is more then the Temple of it. An extensiv and Immateriall Being, which is Like an Indivisible Atom without Bulk, All eye and sight, is therefore every where, becaus its sight is so, which it selfe is. for the very substance of the soul is all sight, and Pure life as God is, when it is perfect as it ought to be, whose whole Eternity being Incomprehensible, and its presence evry where, immediatly toucheth the soul and affecteth it. which is therefore a Temple or Infinit sphere, because God is Infinitly present in this centre, every Intelligence being a sphere and centre at the same time, becaus God is so. whose nature is so perfect that he can wholy be enjoyed. that is, Tho He be altogeather infinit, yet being a-ble in power He can give Himselfe, which nevertheless He could never do, were it not for His Nature, so Exquisitly Glorious, which is wholy here.

93

Intricacies obstruct a little at present. Yet even these make for our

Happieness. for while we scarcely can tell how it Cometh to pass that the soul should be thus an Infinit Sphere; we see the Triumphs of Eternal Power over all its Difficulties: and Admire the Nature of God which is the Basis and foundation of all His power: See every obstacle which it overcometh made a Treasure, and read the Coincidence of his Lov and Essence, while both are present here. He doth all things at one conamen, and that is by being what He is, All Act. becaus He is Eternal, and eternaly here, infinit in Essence and Infinitly here, therefore can we walk over all the Regions of His Eternity and Infinity here, walk over all within our selves whose souls have neither Limits Walles nor Borders. Being therefore thus like Eternal spheres and so made by the nature of God, Temples whose Materials are Immaterial, Infinitly Richer then Materials are, not Lined with Gold, but Life and Lov, So Strangly Endued with sufficiency and power, that even in our own souls, we can offer sacrifice, Exalt into Thrones, Present with Riches, Exhibit worlds, Magnifie and Prais, Elevat a bove the skies, Caress and Embrace: all this we ought to do in our Inward Man, and Apply our minds to Enjoy it in others. for there All Things are most Delightfull, as they are being Seen in Gods counsels.

94

The Little Actions of our confined being, as we walk up and down a-mong the Sons of men, are like our Body compared to our soul, contemptible, feeble, worthless, shells and husks. all the Glory being of the Inward man. yet as the Body is inhabited by the Soul, it is a Glorious Jewel. And so those feeble and little Actions, which man doth in External affaires, as Animated and flowing from the Soul within, have an Imputed Greatness by the Inward Sphere, and a spiritual Depth or value like i[t], but all the works of joy and Glory are Radicaly there, And thence doth all the Beauty and valu flow which is on the Inside of evry operation.

94

Acts of charity, mercy, Almes Deeds, and Justice: are Such Diminutiv Things compared with the Grandures of this Eternal Sphere, that a Soul possessing it selfe seemes to behold them, from a-bove the Heavens, and to see the Limited person doing them, like an Ant beneath. external works bearing no more proportion to the Glory of Gods Image, then a sand to the world or a Drop to the Ocean.

95

This Inward Sphere or Temple of the Deitie ought to be Beautified with all operations: And is most Glorious as it is after Gods similitude, Enjoying in it selfe all Ages, kingdoms, Souls and Treasures, in a firme and unmoveable Manner, enjoying Eternity and the omnipresence of God in which it is seated. which while it is doing External Accidents are so far beneath it, So Inconsiderable weak and little, that How troublesome soever they seeme unto others, they cannot annoy it. The burning of a house, the Death, or Stealing of a horse, a wound in the Body, or Slaughter it Selfe, leav that untoucht because it is Immutable: And either in the Body or out of the Body Enjoyeth all Things. Yet are there Circumstances Considering our weakness and the place where we liv infinitly enriching Such Inferior Accidents.

96

For Two persons to love each other in all this Grandure, clothed with the Heavens, Surrounded with the Angels, Enriched by the Ages, Exalted by the wisdom and power of God, as seated in his Throne and reigning there, as it is to See either well, So it is to Liv towards each in Glory. And O that I could ever be Endued with this Sence! And be like him whose affections are all perfect and unmoveable! In Such a person they Draw toward rest and sacred peace, Inviolable Repose being the climat of His Soul. for he Seeth all Accidents clearly, in their consequences and causes; and How all calamities are to a Triumphant soul Sublime Advantages: And cannot therefore be afflicted at them; but rejoyceth in the Ingenuity meekness Humility Patience Prudence courage of the Author that Governeth in Turbulent Affayrs, and suffereth not her Soul to be ruffled or Discomposed. He that can do this is Invincible in all assaults, Shall be highly exalted by all Distresses, Reign with God over all calamities, Enrich Himselfe with all kind of vertues, and Beautifie Himselfe with daily victories.

97

Affections therefore I have to my freind calm and quiet, but Greater then the world, and wider then the Heavens. Deeper then the sea, Stronger then the sun. O that they may be sweeter then perfumes, and far more tender then a mothers Bowels! I confess I am Defectiv and Imperfect. But O that I might be compleate in all Things! I would yeeld unto my freind joy and consolations after the similitude of God: But then my freind must be clothed with his similitude and be Able to resent, as He resenteth. We are imperfect here upon Earth, but our Imperfections shall be blown a way: And therefore we breath after Eternal Life in another place, where all the purity of every Excellence shall Eternaly remain, the Quintissence and substance of every Treasure be made perfect; and all that is fals and Erroneous be Abolished.

98

Vigorous and violent, Tender and melting, compassionat affections, seem Inconsistant, with standing and unmoveable. but affections are capable of all perfections at the same time, being as Activ as profound, as forcible as unmoveable. O that God would Heal my soul and make it compleat, Especialy towards Him whom it is my Great Imployment to Lov and Honor, and while I would boyl on a Grediron or Dye for my freind, mak me able to Lov them Delightfully, Giving me Tender and Delicate Resentments. I would have all! a compleat Harmonie. a perfect Heaven.

99

To Him that is the Author of these delights, the fountain of these Beauties, the contriver and framer of these Glories, the giver of all riches, the Life and Guid of all affections: let my Soul in this world doe Eternal Homage. with Him let me walk as my Eternal freind, and daylie be engaged in those employments that will most delight Him. my freinds shall Relish me with a contiguous feeling: but all the Delights of His Eternal Kingdom must I enjoy. and those in them, and them, in Him. who is sufficient for these things? none but they in

whom the fullness of the GodHead ever Dwelleth! I shall appear more
Rich and Beautifull to all my freinds, when I enjoy all in the Similitude
of God; be a Temple of the Holy Ghost, a Shining Light, and more
their Treasure.

100

Keep my heart o lord always sencible of my created worthynes!
And when I enter into Houses, let me remember the Glory I saw in the
feilds and the Blessedness of thy Kingdom! it is imposible at once to
be present with Men and Thee my God, unless we oppose and Greive
at their Thoughts. For they are so far Like Runnagates run From Thee,
that it is impossible by consent to goe a long with them, but their
thoughts will lead us out of thy presence. The Heavens and the Earth
are Annihilated in their understandings, Thy laws forgotten, and thy
wayes unknown. They wander among weeds and gather vanities;
They goe out into the wildernes and Hide them selves a-mong Bryers
and Thornes; And know not How to return unto Thee. These Thinges,
the Glory of thy kingdom, They cannot understand. There is a Great
Gulph set between us, if they will not Come to me, O let not me goe
back againe to them, but weep in my secret Places; and Pray for them.
O my God make me faithfull, lively, constant; and Since Thou hast
Given me a Tongue; Tho I am an Eternal Sphere in Communion with
Thee, Teach me to use it moderately Prudently Seasonably to thy
Glory. Amen.

SELECT MEDITATIONS
THE THIRD CENTURY

1

The Greatest misery in Humane nature is forgetfulnes[s]. And yet is it a way to the Greatest Blessedness: if some have no[t] weighed amiss. for the poets faigned that all those who passed henc[e] into the Elizian feilds were Steeped in Lethe, haveing their senses Drenched in the lake of oblivion, that they might never more be Disturbed with the Remembrance of Earthly Troubles, but being removed in Spirit as well as Body from all sorrowfull and Greivious objects, be nakedly receptive of celestiall Joys. but I think the learning of the Poets here Defective, and that Solid Philosophie Descries a Treasure in evry calamity not to be forgotten. And Divinity teacheth that the Eyes rather are to be washt in some clear and celestial Stream that we might See the Beauties and the Jewels concealed under that rough and Shell. For Infinite Goodness wisdom and Power menaging every thing is every where to be Enjoyed. The Treasures of which are to Great to be lost by forgettfullness.

2

that wee are So Suddainly forgettfull of all our Glory is a solid trouble and Great Diseas. That we are Soe Apt to take the seal of impression from a nothers Thoughts, and suffer them to steal us a way from our Kingdom, And by a secret contagion, to Annihilate our Joys! To the Intent I may be more fixed therefore I will be more silent when they talk of vanitie. And since I cannot accompany their Imaginations and the thoughts of God; I will either overrule their Souls, or Depart the company. if I must needs tarry there I can goe away by Attending Heaven. yet will they be a burden to me and I to them. Tis a wonder how Souls should be such Ayds or Impediments to one another. O my God pitty my weaknes and remember that men were ordained pillers to Sustaine me, wings to carry me; lights to illuminat, and freinds to Aid me, who now are Enemies, Deceitfull lights, And floods goeing down to a final end that is Destructive, against which I must swim. That creature ill swims against the streame, whose Nature was made to be carried down it! O my God they are now Seducers who should be companions. Their Thoughts are so far Divided from Thee that one must Pass an Infinit Gulph to see them.

3

By how much the Greater the Difficultie is, by so much the more Glorious the soul is that overcomes it. And by How much the Greater Labor is in opposeing, so much the Greater care and fidelitie ought we to use in continuall Endeavours. And according to these shall our Acceptance bee. All Things are Treasures; And therefore are we to prais God for the Advantage of our Disadvantages. our Internal weaknes as we are now stript of our wings and Aids, which are the sons of Men, shall increas our Glory in the future Triumph: And if we pray Heartily be removed by the presence of the Holy Ghost. O that I might have his continuall Assistance and Always do the Best of Things. Tho I am restored, I shall not remember the love of God, without his Grace; by which alone I Liv in his kingdom.

4

To Liv in his kingdom is not by Body to be removed thither, but there to Abide in mind and Spirit. for there my Body Always is. where my Thoughts are, there am I. since therefore my Body is Always in Gods Kingdom, and cannot chuse while it [is] here upon Earth: it is by my thoughts alone that I can goe out of it, into I Know not what coasts of Emptiness and vanity. But if I will Contemplat and Lov his Divine Glory, and see the excellency of all his Treasures; The King Himselfe, His Territories and Laws, they are allways Near me; and so is one of his subjects, and that is I. Heaven and earth is full of the Majesty of his Glory. which to awake the understanding, is all within. his Laws are written in the Heart, His ways are Always before me, in his Territories, His works Surround me. It is easy to be a stranger to them, and Exceeding miserable; easy to be acquainted with them, and exceeding Glorious.

5

There is no Deceit in nature more Incident or hurtfull to a Brisk understanding, then a little weariness or contempt of Aprehending things already known. even by the change of a Thought is an Infinit Temple either Built or ruined. And as God by a perpetu[a]l Influx of Beauty and power upholdeth the world: in which respect every moments conservation is fittly stil'd a new creation: So will he have us by a perpetual Conflux and Activity of thought to maintain all Things and in our selves to uphold our Treasures: for they are no longer ours then they are within us. The world is in Him upheld by him, the world in us is upheld by us. If He should withdraw but the least moments sustentation all would be ruined. yet in a moment could he make it again. But he is Constant. And so ought we. for were we once seated in the kingdom of Heaven, the least withdrawing of the Beams of our Souls would be the Irrepairable Ruin of the world; that is to us. for it would never more be repaired in our soul.

6

Sweet Apprehensions strangly caus objects to vary. what is the reason why some account Gods Laws a Burden, others esteem them infinitly more precious then Gold and silver. To some the world is a kingdom, to others a Dungeon a wilderness a prison. Because some have pure and bright Apprehensions, others rude and vulgar and Deformed. when a Begger goes by a Noble Mans house what is the reason He sees all the splendor Beauty and magnificence with So Cold an Ey!

He Apprehends it not with any Pleasure,

His onely is the Joy whose is the Treasure.

But palaces and Treasure, which Noble men more sweetly Apprehend are truly theirs. so are the Heavens and all Things truly mine. True Apprehensions being always Best, becaus Nothing can truly be Appr[e]hended but it must needs be Aprehended as Treasure and Inter[e]st. Becaus every thing to God and his Image is soe. Truth and felicity are ever the same, becaus all the things in Heaven and Earth are Infinit Treasures: And are never Enjoyed but when truly Seen: nor ever indeed truly seen, but by a wise man they are truly enjoyd.

7

That every Thing indeed is an Infinit Treasure is an Infinit Paradox to Some understandings; but Infinitly Sweet, becaus truth is so Great, that in Divine Things there can be no Hyperbolie. every thing must be an Infinit Treasure becaus the Agent and the workman is Infinit: And becaus the Spectators are of Infinit Capacity, Depth and Reach: And there is by the one Laid in for the other an infinit Depth of Endless concernments, a fathomless mine of invisible Excellencies. Neither was it Possible to be otherwise. the Best things being always necessary, and upon the Admission of a God unavoydable.

8

In evry Thing God is enjoy'd, as it ariseth from His Goodnes and Endeth in his Glory: as it is Guided by Him to infinit Ends, as His Power and wisdom are seen in it, as it relateth to all Angels and men. every thing being made infinitly usefull by the Infinity of God creating them. For becaus every one of them can see All the Things in Heaven and Earth, therefore every thing in Heaven and Earth relateth to Each in every Age. And the Depth of God unsearchable in his ordinanc and way about it. For I being a Divine Lover of all Angels and men am concernd in their felicity as much as mine own. And evry thing that serveth them is mine in them, So that of all the Services which it doth to all I am the Heir. Tho evry one enjoyeth those Services for evry ones Sake. The Consequent of which is a fruition in Depth infinitly Infinite. Nor was it possible that any thing Should proceed from God any other way. evry thing must arise from His Goodness and End in his Glory. And in that respect be infinit alone. nay it was impossible but it must relate to Infinit persons and be of Infinit Depths and uses. for God could not doe any thing in vain, and therefore make nothing without makeing his Image (nor create any thing but to answer some Exigent and necessity conceived by Him), whom he would not make of limited comprehensions, becaus that would be a loss of infinit Happiness.

9

Because He would provide Innumerable pleasures for his Image to Enjoy, therefore did He creat infinit varieties and kinds of things, and multiply the Treasures of his Eternal Kingdom by wants and supplies. Had there been noe creatures made that could need the sun, the sun could never hav been made a Treasure: nor could God frame a sea, but first he must conceive a Person needing it: Air to them that need no breath, nor open liberty, nor Bodily Refreshment, would be superfluous and made in vain; Light, were there noe creature made to see, would be Always as it is to the Blind, And So were Sounds were there noe hearer, Beauty were there no Spectator, odors were there no smelling, Fowles Beasts and fishes were there no Dominion, no lord to whom they are given, no Thanksgiver, no Adorer. But he that is a Thanksgiver and Lord over them is meet for God and can return unto Him. Now Angels can Adore, Giv Thanks and lov. Yet without the Interposure and mediation of man cannot enjoy this Adspectable world, for haveing no Bodies, no smell, no feeling, sight, Eys or Eares, no need of Aire meat or Drink, all is Superfluous to them Selves, as it is to God. Till man be made. The Image of God in a Body being the Grand mistery of all Eternity: Gods Picture in a curious Case, besett with stars instead of Jewels, The Angels freind in whom alone and by whom they enjoy the world, the sphere of all Perfection and the centre in which all visible and Invisible thinges Sweetly Close, The Temple in whom the fulness of the GodHead dwelleth Bodily. For He is the Inclusive Head of all Spirituall and Material perfections. No wonder therefore that being Gods most [great] and Peculiar workmanship, He Should let Pass the Angels when they fell and giv his Son for the Redemption of man. But here is the wonder, that man being so Great and peculiar Should So little understand it: and accustom Himselfe to the feeling of vanities, Being a Dead Apostate to all his Glories.

10

Those things I call vanities which He is Apt to feel, taxes Injuries clothes and Monies, Musick feàsts chambering wantonness, Sports and Losses. All these, yea crowns and Scepters, in comparison of the Naked Grandure of his High Estate, (for his True estate is exceeding high) are most visible and plainly worthless Trifles. Lord what is a Thousand Kingdoms, compared to mans Dominion over the world. Can hats and knees, and Thrones and scepters and Silver and Gold and Splendid Palaces, appear any other then Shells and Patches, and Tinsell vanities, when they are put in Competition with all the Glory of Heaven and Earth! Man for whom all the things in Heaven and earth were made, is exalted likewise over all his Brethren, and by Sacred laws made to reign in all their affections. his Dominion extendeth thro all Ages and reacheth unto Angels. For wherever God [is], He reigneth. His eternall Freind that made all things for Him, so Loveth Him that He shall Triumph even in the Souls of cherubims. And if kings did understand this, and see the Grandure of their Subjects, so as to know over whom they reigned, Did they reign in all their Hearts, and Triumph in the affections of such Glorious Creatures, were they exalted in the Throne of their Immortall soul, and did they liv like God sincerly Honoured and Admired in their Temple; as by His laws and Statutes every son and freind of his ought to doe; this were somwhat. But else all the other tinsell vanities are shews without substance and Beggerly Elements without Significations, onely as they restrain the Inordinat vulgar, and Breed a Reverance in Dull Spectators. For the person of a King and the Benefit of His office ought to prevail, whoe is most Beautifull in His Naked Authority: But a Blinded people that see noe Truth would tread upon Authority without some Ensigns Exhibiting it to them, in such Ideas as they can see: And this intimateth the original of kings, their use and Glory.

11

The Estate of Innocence needed no such supereminence. Being all Lov every man was supreme and subject to other. A King to Aid, Protect and Defend, but that there was no occation. For Lov naturaly makes all a king, a freind, a sovereign. Becaus it naturaly makes Him Tender of a nothers Glory. There Sweetness, Innocence, Justice kindness mercy liberality flowed, where these flowers Grew there needed noe Judicature, nor higher Power. Sin onely Bred Inequality among us. But when man fell into Sin, became Blind, Had lost the Sence of His Happines and Glory, And did not see the Beauty of obedience and the sweetnes of his Duty: that Lov which before was his Delight, became a Burden, those works of mercy and Justice that were before the natural Acts of freindship, the Pleasant Emanations and Delights of Lov, the free and voluntary choys of his heart, the ornaments of Life and Exercises of felicity, were Discoulered now with the sence of obedience being not freely but ingratfully don, Irksom and painfull, to Blinded Souls; Injustice violence and wrong, malice Envy Covetousness and oppression succeeding in their Room. Then did Citties need a Governor, societies a Gardiner, Kingdoms a Phisitian to Pluck up those noysom weeds, to Heal those Diseased, to Terrifie with punishments, to Alure with Rewards, to here the cry of orphans, to plead the caus of the needy, to Strengthen the hands of the weak, and to be an impartial judge of Right and wrong, Banishing and suppressing those Dreadfull poysons that sin introduced. so that the officce of kings is exceeding Glorious wheather they be Beloved or no: Provided they understand and Discharge their Duty. for they are Healers and correctors of Natures Malice, Restorers of the world to Its first Beauty, Rules of Justice Equity and Right, Rulers a mong the Gods, Shepherds over the flock of the Almighty, Conduits of Living and Refreshing waters, Defenders of the poor, and Like God fathers to the fatherless and Husbands to the widdow. But that which yet is extremely marvellous, is, that if with a clear Wisdom courage and Benignity, They manage their Reign and Scepter well, they Shall be Beloved, and had in Reverance, and in Exceeding High Honor of all. For the welfare of His People is intrusted with Him, And tho Men are Apostates yet they Lov their Ease, and Delight in Him that maketh them to flourish.   .

12

Men by Divising other Riches, and Encreasing their moveables, have made them selves capable of being injured, more then they were, or could be in Eden. For their Treasures there were Permanent and Steddy. The Skies and the Rivers, the sun and the stars, the Beauty of the world, their Dominion over Beasts and Fowls and Fishes, the Dignity of their Nature and the Image of God which none could Deface, but each man Himselfe; these were permanent and stable Treasures: and worthy to be so becaus they were Great and excellent. movable Treasures They had none other, but their Hands and Eyes and Lives and Sences: And these Gods most Sacred Laws, and the Light of mens souls did always secure. So that they Lived in the light [of] Heaven, And were to celebrate the praises of Almighty God for all His Goodnes, having Herbs and corn in evry feild, and precious Liquors in evry brook. Their joy was that they were Belored of the King of Kings, magnified by Gods Laws, and so exalted in evry Bosom. The costly Delicate[s] we have invented have made us miserable. we must needs be as Gods, and by creating Riches of our own devising made work for Robbors.

13

To See So plainly the Distinction between True and fained Riches Should make a man Happy. And Teach Him to leav Deceits and vanityes: For the Lov of money is the Root of all evill, which while some covetted after, they Erred from the faith and peirced themselves thorow with many Sorrows. To return to the Living waters, and leave sophisticat puddles, is to Returne to the simple Treasures of Eden, an ounce of which is more worth then all the Mass of compounded vanities. Sophisticat Joys delude us always: Sincere ones Delight us. The Treasures of Eden are Simple and Divine: Simple, but Illust[r]ious; Necessary; magnificent, Great; and Glorious. O my Soul walk a-mong these Trees, Reckon these stars, Admire these Heavens, they are the Pavement of thy feet. And the sun it selfe is made to serve thee, lye down by these Gentle Streams and feed in these pleasant Pastures. Revive them frequently, God spreadeth Thee a Table, feast upon His Joys: And Remember Diogenes his wise Description of the Happy man, whoe beleived, That the World was a Temple Worthy of GOD, in which an Excellent Man, living Sweetly piously and joyfully, feasteth always in the Sight of the Deitie.

14

Lov knows no Distance, but is imediately near to all his objects. It shineth upon Things without sending forth Beames or if it doth, those Beames are Spiritual and Invisible, they can permeat walls, and extend to the very Heavens. Yet no man can see them on the outside. Surely Lov is an infinit Sphere, and Shineth on all objects within itselfe. It must needs be, the Possessor of all it Includeth. And if it be so it is a Sphere in a centre. All Things being without it, yet all Things within it. It is strangly Eminent! It is an infinit Mistery, Behold it from without and it is no wheare, Look into it, it is infinit lik God, it is not in the world yet fils it, and Surrounds it. The Bodily Ey sees all Things abroad, the Soul within. That I can thus in my chamber Travel spiritualy and visit kings, that the Beames of my Soul can penetrate the walls and extend to Emperors is a pleasing power, and more pleasing Exercise. There is somthing in me more noble then my Body. And so much Better then the Heavens and the Earth as it seemeth lesse, so much Better as it appeareth Greater.

15

If I live truely in the Divine Image I shall appear among kings a Greater king. For to be a King like God is a thing more Divine then to Reign like a Man, unless that Man Reign Like a God. To be a King like God is all mens hopes, some men[s] fruition. If it be mine, O let me Liv with kingly manners. God that made and ordained Thee for his Throne, made thee for himselfe. He made Thee for Himselfe in makeing Thee Like Himselfe. Despaire not, Forgett not, Be not careless, but Liv alwayes at this Height. He made Thee for Himselfe, by makeing Thee Like God. when He made Thee His Image He Intended that thou shouldst Live Like a God, and therein Delight Him. Heed not the Trifles of thy Body, nor the Impertinoncies of mens Ignorances. pursue not the flies, Liv not a mong the frogs of their Empty Thoughts. for such swarm in their fairest chambers. But keep at home and retain thy Majesty within Doors. Remember thy Treasures; be sencible of thy kingdom. Move always with a Due Estate, and Reverend Behavior. A venerable Deportment becomes a God. Be more Silent. Less apt to mingle with other mens words; unmoved in thy passions. The Eternal Deity is seldom Angry. Be Great and Active, And becaus thou art a Man be ever Watchfull.

16

Plato in his Dialogues moveth such a Question as this, How many things are necessary to vision! wherein the Respondent Answereth two. An Ey rightly Disposed, and an object Seated at Convenient Distance. He asketh the Question wheather nothing else, The Answerer cannot find what else should be Requisit to Sight, but the object and the Ey. Plato finds a Third Thing, and that is Light. for Tho the object be never so rightly Seated, and the organ never so well disposed, if there be no light there can be no vision. this being Granted He then asketh, How many Things are Requisit to Perfect understanding. The vulger Intelligence answers two. A faculty of Knowledg in the Soul of man, and an Intelligable object. He asketh if nothing else; It is answered, nothing. He replieth Three. for there must be an Intelligable light, In which the understanding may see its object. And when the citizen asketh what that is? He answereth thus. as Light it selfe is a Thing that may be seen, and the meanes by which wee see other Things: so is this Intelligable Light whereby we understand, An object that may be known and the meanes by which wee may know all things. and that is God. For as without light we can see nothing but are apt to mistake a cart for a coach, or a Tree for a man; So without the knowledge of god we can see nothing: as in the Twylight we are apt to mistake, vice for felicity, and vertue for misery. All Things haveing Lost their figure and couler. To this Purpose the Heathen Speaketh. Profoundly intimateing that all Eternity was the true Light in which we ought to see and Discerne any thing. For till the originals and Rewards of vertue appear: till we see a God, to whom we must conform, whose Eys are ever upon all our wayes, whose Judgments we must Revere: we can never distinguish nor Se a right, what Things are felicitie, what is miserie. For his everlasting counsels and the Ends where they cease are Appurtenances to virtue and shine upon it, and Beautifie its face with Infinite Lustre. Nor can any see what is riches nor what is Poverty: till in the Light of Eternity they have seen the Treasures of Allmighty God, and how all Things are enjoyd by his Eternal majesty. How much therefore must the soul of man be mingled with Eternity; that Deriveth Light from all its parts: And what need he hath to be conversant with the Deity, since God is the Light of his understanding, in whose Bosom, and manner of enjoyment, He Seeth all things? Infinitly a bove a Beast, and like a God must He be, to whom all these are for ever Open.

17

He hath Shewed his word unto Jacob, his Statutes and his judgments unto Israel: he hath not dealt so with any nation, and for his judgments they have not known them. This was the Joy and Glory of Israel, that She alone of all the nations in the whole world was acquainted with the wayes and judgments of the Lord. But it is His Glory and Joy, that notwithstanding our Apostasie [from] his covenant in former Ages, (When it was offered to us in Adams house, and in Noahs Family) After a long night of Ignorance Fantasies and Apparitions wherewith we weare troubled, by the Labor and mighty power, and miracles, and sweat and bloud of his Apostles, He broke open the doores of the Nations, and came in upon us. We had Shut them by our Rebellions against Him, and barrd them fast on the inside, While we kept wreaks within doors, in wantoness and Lusts and Banquetting and Revelling in our private chambers, in Idle Superst[it]ions, Bloody Sacrifices, monstrous Idols, with cheating Preists in our Higher Places, Yea Drunkenness and Revelling, in our Lower Roomes. All the House was out of order, Till He came in upon us, who might in Fury Like an Armed man, have overwhelmed and Devoured us. But He came in Mercy to restore the Family and Set us all in order.

18

Oh the Inestimable Refreshing Light! The Rosie morning breaking Forth upon the mountains! The Rising Face of that Glorious Bridegroom. Light is not more Beautifull, and Healing in the sun, then the Beams of his Gospel Shining in our chambers. we were before Like Dragons inhabiting the Parched Places of the Desart wildernes: now Streams and Rivers flow upon the Top of evry Hill. we did eat the Dust for very need of meat: but now we have Manna and bread to the full. We were Like owles and Satyrs in the night, we are now Like Angels and cherubims in Day. We were the Reproach and abuse of Devils, who are their Conquerors. ...
In thy Name [shall they] rejoyce all the Day and in thy Righteousness shall they be Exalted. For thou art the Glory of their Strength, and in thy Favor our horn shall be Exalted. For the Lord is our Defence, and

the Holy one of Israel is our King.

19

Shall Abundance make me Poor! The Earth is the Lords and the fullness thereof. Were there but one meadow, one Garden, one feild, one River, one orchard in all the world, And were all the rest Gold and Pearl: oh how Divine and Sweet and Living, how Glorious Rich and Heavenly would those few appear. All the Rest would be ungratefull Drie and Parched Places, And those the onely Jewels to refresh and feed Immortal Souls! that therefore they are spread over all the Earth, and in every Age and kingdom feed fowles and Beasts and fishes, That these might Sustain a Race of kings, and make all the world an Heaven unto me is more Delightfull. But far more abundantly am I to Praise God, for the copious Riches of the meanes of Grace, Religion received into a kingdom by kings, and Established by Laws. Temples Erected to the Glory of Him who Died for our Sins, His Sages magnified and crowned in the Assemblies.

20

The Angel flieth haveing the Eternal Gospel in his Hand throughout all christendom. the Lion and the calfe feed togeather and a Little child doth lead them. Preists are Stars in our Saviours right hand, and Holy Bishops Angels of the churches, our Saviour walketh a-mong his Golden candlesticks, Even here on Earth. And God is with us as He is above the Heavens. O for clear Eyes to See his wonders! He numbreth the Stars and bringeth them all forth by their Armies. He maketh vapors to Ascend from the ends of the earth, and bringeth the winds out of his Treasures. He maketh the clouds his charets, and watereth the earth from his chambers, and Blesseth the Springing thereof. He causeth Grass to Grow upon the mountaines, and heareth the Ravens that crie. He boundeth the seas with a Girdle of Sand, and clotheth the vallies and the feilds with corne. He Standeth in the Gates and judgeth a-mong the Gods in the seat of Judgment. His voyce is heard in many Thousand Temples sounding from the Pulpits a-mong all the People. He pleadeth the cause of the poor and needy, Defendeth the fatherless and is the Husband of the Widdow. He

Healeth the Broken in heart and bindeth up their wounds. He Governeth the Nations, is Adored by Kings, praised by Senators, and Reverenced Greatly in the Assemblie of the Saints: His eys run to and fro in the whole world to behold the evill and the Good, and to shew Himselfe Great in behalf of the Righteous. He observeth our Thoughts, He compasseth our paths and our Lying Down, and there is not a word in our Tongue, but He knoweth it alltogeather. He numbreth our Hairs and Suffereth not a Sparrow to fall without his Pleasure. He maketh the springs to flow and the Righteous to flourish. Behold I have created the smith that Bloweth the Coal in the fire, and that bringeth forth an Instrument for his work, in the very marchants shop all the weights of the Ballance are his work. He teacheth the Plowman to Threash and Sow. It is God doth instruct Him and teach Him Discretion. Oh what a Glorious place must this be: where God is soe Daylie Present. He is not more frequent a-mong all the Angels then he is with us. I do not See a Carter on the Road, nor a carpenter Building a Little Cottage, but in the Light of Heaven they are before mine eyes. Deep Misteries are beneath the Surface of common works; This also cometh from the Lord of Hosts who is Wonderfull in counsel and Excellent in working.

21

That which refresheth and reviveth me is, that I have Light now, wherein I may see the odiousness of Sin. And feel, and fear. My Soul was Parched till I knew my God. Confounded and Desolate till I could apprehend his GLORY and Reverance Him. He is a Mighty and a Terrible one unto me. And it is my Joy that it is so. The Giver of all Treasures, and the Just exacter of all obedience. My Soul was never a fountaine of Living waters; till it was fild with fear, and The tears of Repentance. It was a Drie and Broken Cistern: a Parched well: till He was Known: till Greife it selfe and mourning did revive it. when it toucheth the Centre of Hell with Despair, it reacheth unto the Throne of God, with the Eye of Hope, and is made what it ought, wide and profound. I had rather fear by reason of the Disquietness of my Guilty Heart, while I have God in my presence; then rejoyce with Kings, where Sincer[i]ty and truth and God is absent. It is a Comfort to See Him Even clad in Thunder. Oh my God! what shall I render unto

Thee, for all the care and Lov which Thou hast shewed in Building Temples, Adorning Quires, preparing Bibles, conserving Universities, Sending ministers, Affording Sabaths, Administring Sacraments that I might be comforted in my Tears of Penitence! I had rather have Thee Living in my conscience, and judging there, then be the judge of Heaven and Earth. O Thou who art Amiable in thy Reproofes, Reveal thy Selfe unto me, and teach me a venerable Life, with Holy Reverance.

23

Two things there are, that make the kingdom of Heaven Desolate upon Earth. The one is the Blindness of those Profane ones that cannot See celestial Joys, the other is the Ingratitude of those Holy ones that kick at Heavenly Treasures. Drunkards and whoremongers and Revilers with all covetous men and Lyars, See not those Joyes for the Sake of which Temples are erected: Ingratefull Pharisies, and Lofty Hypocrites, Disobedient Hereticks, and selfe conceited Holy ones, that make Devisions, and are Despisers of union, Peace, and External Flourishing, see so much of celestial Joys, that they Forget inferior Heavenly Treasures. A Flourishing church, converted Citties, Religion Established by Laws, kings and Magistrates turned From Paganisme, the Freedom of the Gospel, and the shining Light which a Golden candlestick giveth in a National church, The Joyfull Sound, and the Light of Gods countenance in which we walk under the wings of Magistrates and the Protection of Laws, Solemn Assemblies meeting in Peace, Stately Temples Erected for their Entertainment, Quiet and Ease and Repose and Safety, and Such times as those were, whereof it is Sayd, Then had the churches rest, throughout all Judea, and Galilee and Samaria, and were edefied: And walking in the fear of the Lord, and in the comfort of the Holy Ghost were multiplied. Such Times and Things as these are the Diseas and Scorn of Such mens Souls. churches flourishing under careless Magistrates are far different from those that flourish by the care of Magistrates. in the Apostles Dayes they had a Little rest becaus kings and their Infferior officers Let them alone. In these because they are Maintained by the care of kings, who Themselves with their magistrates have offer'd up their Scepters at the feet of christ. That they are not Sincere in their Interior man is their

Eternal Shame. But Shall we therefore Despise all the External Blessings, which God hath with Great Labor and cost and care been thorow Ages in providing? These Disturbers of my Joys! when will they be reformed! Little doe they Imagine the Tears and Groanes and the Bloud of martirs, the conflicts and Persecutions and Bonds and Imprisonments, the Sore Struglings and compassions and perswasions, that were felt and Endured before it came unto this Pass: And therefore not seeing the Treasures with which our fruition is Lined, they Sel that in the time of Abundance which in the Day of Distress Martyrs would have bought with their Deerest Blood.

24

It is the Art of Satan by all ways possible to Attempt the Ruin of the world. By spreading forth the snares of Pleasure and Gain He entrappeth some: and others He Eggeth on to Destruction by Malice and Revenge: But in all these, he playeth at a particular and single Game. The Goverment of a church Established by Laws is a Great fortress in which the welfare of Millions is concerned. A Bulwark hindering his Ancient Revels, wher He was Sole Lord over Pagan Kingdoms. Against this therefore he Laieth all His Batteries. Assaulteth it with manifold and Subtile Engines. of which the Ingratitude of Pious persons, that would tear out the Bowels of that church which gav them a Begining, is one of the Greatest. No mean Engine will serve here. unless He may Transform Himselfe into an Angel of Light, He cannot prevail. Therefore must He crie against the Prophaness of the church, and call it Sodom and Babylon and Gomorrha: and by that means He shall perhaps be able againe to Reign. Secretly unhook her from all her Laws, break down her Hedge of care and Goverment, Disarme her magistrates, Revile her ministers, Pill of[f] the Rind from all her Branches, take a way her leaves, break of[f] the Boughs from the Body of the Tree, Trample under foot the Husks, and Expose the fruits to the open Air: Then may the Boar of the forrest come in and wast it at Pleasure. Blindness, Atheisme, Libertinism, Exposure to all kind of Storms and Enemies being the Joy of Satan becaus by these He hopeth to attain His Ancient Seats and Sweet possessions. It was a kind of felicity Such as Devils were capable of to see them selves Adored by them who were Redeemed with the Blood of christ. And perhaps He may again have Idol Temples: could these be thrown Down, wherin God is worshipped! The wickedness of the wicked, and the foolishness of sectaries jumping togeather, as His Engines to do it. But Holyness Shall Tryumph notwithstanding His Devices.

25

was it a joy to mount Zion that She was the vineyard of God, and shall it not be so to the church of England! might every man do what is right in his own Eys we Should all run into confusion. They do not understand in whose Light they see, whose milke they sucked, on whose Knees they were Dandled, or what womb gave them their begining. They owe somthing to the Nation for their Being, more to the church for her Education, yet understand they neither the one nor the other. No Beauty do they see in the Nations union, much lesse any Benefit in the union of the church. Narrow Souls! and acquainted onely with Little Things! was it so Great a happieness to the church of Israel, that they walked in the Light of Gods Countenance, that they had the Joyfull Sound, that all their Tribes were united into one, that She was a vine planted by God Almighty, that She was fenced with hedges, that non might pluck her, that Shee was rooted by Laws, and that Kings and Queens were her nursing parents: and Shall it be non to us! And for every Trifle and for evry Scruple must ye all Abandon her and Lay her wast! O prodigious and unreasonable men! And do you think that it is unlawfull that she should be united! must we all be Independent, And cannot we Live, unless we pluck up her roots, and pull down her Hedges? do you verily beleiv it unlawfull for kings and parliaments and Elders in a National manner to covenant with God that they will be his People, and Employ their Power and Authority for his Glory. Is it unLawfull for Kings and Lords and Senetors to Establish christian Religion in their Dominion; to Advance His ministers and Erect Temples wherein they may Sing his Praises? verily Such men have I seen in the world, and their thoughts are so absurd, that [it] is even a part of felicity to detect and hate them.

26

The Enemies of my Soul and the Little foxes that would Spoyl our

vineyard, doe me this Good; they Quicken my Sences, and by irri-
tating my affections make me more vigoriously to Apprehend the
worth and sweetness of my Treasures. And while I see throw them, to
Admire more the Goodness of God, which in the midst of all Enemies
preserveth our Possessions. Tho they are very proud Incorrigible and
selfe Conceited; yet are they to be born, instructed and Desired. And
if they will not Learn, yet are we to see thorow the snares and shining
clouds of their Sanctity, yea thorow the snares of Riches and the veil of
kingdoms till we behold the Simple Innocence of Eden, And the true
Treasures Lying at the Bottom. Then shall we return and see how God
ordereth these and maketh them Riches and pleasures too. For there is
nothing in being but one way or other it becomes a Treasure. Becaus
he would not p[e]rmitt it, if he could not surmount it: And by
surmounting it, makes it 1000 times more Delightfull, his kingdom
more Rich, and Himselfe more Glorious then if the evill had never
Happened. What soever happeneth it is happy for us. Little did I
think when I was confined within the citty wals I was born, that the
king and Senators of this kin[g]dom were mine: yet was there a time
when I was unconfined: and saw evry Kingdom mine which mine ear
heard of. in a clear light it appeared to me as mine own possession tho
beyond the Seas.

27

Till custom and Education had bred the Difference: it was as
obvious to me to see all within us, as It was without. As easy and as
natural to be Infinitly wide on the Inside, and to see all Kingdoms
Times and persons within my Soul, as it is now to see them in the open
world. Nay verily it was more natural, for there was a comprehensiv
Spirit, before ther was an Eye. And my Soul being Like him, did first
expect to find all things in it Selfe, before it learned to See them
without it. It would be a Great wonder if God Should See any thing
out of himSelfe. And but that he hath made the world would be still
wonderfull. Were nothing made but a Naked Soul, it would see
nothing out of it Selfe. For Infinit space would be seen within it. And
being all sight it would feel it selfe as it were running Parrallel with it.
And that truly in an Endless manner, becaus it could not be conscious
of any Limits: nor feel it Selfe Present in one Centre more then

another. This is an Infinit Sweet Mystery: to them that have Tasted it. For before I had Bodily Journeys I was immediately Present in any kingdome, and Saw the people in it, Trees Ground and Skies in as strong a Light, as ever I saw the Kingdom where I am. I scarsly Dream'd of any outward way that Led unto it. And did as vigorously feel them to be my Treasures Delights Enlargments as ever I did feel any Money mine or Tree or Gardens or meadows since.

No Tongue can tell what Treasure are in Store
What Joyes shall Dwell in those that him Adore.
Mens souls unless they better measure keep,
Are most a wake when most they seem to sleep.
When most they seem to wake are most a sleep.

For when they are awake, they see Things with their Bodily Eys: but their souls sleep, becaus they see not with their understandings. If their souls are Drownd and hav Lost their Liberty, they Dream and are asleep wakeing. being therefore asleep, they think those who Liv by their soul to be onely Dreaming. How is it possible that all the Things in the whole Hemisphere should be represented in a Looking-glass, and that all the Things in Heaven and Earth should not in a Soul, which is a more Glorious Mirror. Seest thou not How vigorously and realy thy face is seen in a Glass, bring it out to the open Heavens, and the Heavens shall be as truly represented in it. The sun shall shine as strongly in it as it doth in the skies, O the Reality! O the Room! O the lenght and Breadth and Depth that is in the molten steel! And shall not all Things more realy Individualy and truly be seen Abiding in the Hous and Temple of Almighty God! O man, thy Soul is capable of an Eternal Day, far more then a Mirror is of the Earth and skies!

28

Being capable O my soul of an Eternal Day: And Since all things Shine in the Light of the understanding, far more Gloriously then in the Light of the Sun: what things art thou cheifely to See in this Eternal Day? And on what things are those Beames to Shine, which are so Divine and Excellent a bove the Sun? what objects art thou to Beautifie? what Treasure to Lay up in So Divine a Treasury? For certainly Thou oughtest to be very carefull. Thy Bosom being Like that of God, more rich then Gold, more Amiable then the Air, more abundant then the seas, more Heavenly then the skies. And thy Beams so Divine; that the Fruits must be more Excellent which they rais and cherish, then those which the sun thrusteth forth of the earth by shining on Things here beneath! O my Soul, Gods kingdom and the Things in it, must appear in the light of thine Eternal Day: on his Territories and on all the objects there must thy understanding Shine. In Gods Bosome Things abide after a Diviner manner, then in the open Air. Thy Bosom is the Similitude of his. Let thine understanding therefore shine on the Sun it selfe and on all the flowers which the sun raiseth. on God the King, on all his Subjects, on all His Laws. It is a strange thing how they will be advanced in Thee. They are all Treasures, committed to thy care: as the feilds are: to be improved. And the Fruits which Thou dost rais from all these by shining on them will be as much more Excellent then fruits and flowers; as Thine understanding is more excellent then the Shining Sun. Yea as the objects are on which Thou Shinest, above the common Earth we see in feilds. O what a harvest will this be if thou Continue diligent! O what Zeal! O what care! what care is that which Thou oughtest to use; Since by How much the more precious Divine and Glorious the fruits are, so much the more Drie Greivous and desperat Barreness will appear, in the Day of Sorrow.

29

Gods kingdom, His subjects and Laws are Divine Things, when I Look upon them in the Light of the Citty wherein I Lived. I remember the time when its Gates were Amiable, its streets Beautifull, its Inhabitants immortall, its Temple Glorious, its Inward Roomes and chambers Innocent and all Misterious, Soe they appeared to the little Stranger, when I first came into the world. As sweet every thing as paradice could make it. For I saw them all in the light of Heaven. And they were all mine, Temple streets skies Houses Gates and people. I had not learned to appropriat any thing other way. The people were my Living joyes and moveing Jewells, sweet Amazments, walking Miracles: And all the place a Grand Hive, and Repositary of Delights. But little did I imagine there was a-nother Kingdom (then) to be enjoyd. I was as far from conceiving that, as I was from apprehending any other way of appropriating Riches then sight and Love. That was the way of Angels, and that was mine. All I saw was Still mine own. They in Heaven have no clossets Tills nor Cabinets to hide Treasures: and more precious then to be called Jewels. They most enjoy them while they see them all the Delight and joy of other persons. Those Gates and those wals did then confine, seeming the Limits Surely of the world, if not of my desires. And when I place my Selfe now in that Citty, and see Ages all mine! and Divine Laws, and Gods wayes in many kingdoms, And my Soul a Temple of that Day! exalted to be the Image of allmighty God among them all, A companion of kings and of the Holy Angels: me thinks those are very Glorious things. New and wonderfull, yet more High Divine and Great then New and wonderfull. that city being in the midst of all my Divine Treasuries so surmounted. Which once seemd it self Divine and Glorious, and yet in that city all enjoyd.

30

When I come from the Scholes, haveing there heard them dispute De Ente, De forma materiali, D[e] Quid-ditate, and Such like Drie and Empty Theames: when I came from the Heathen Poets, Having seen their vanities Dreames and fables: or else from the market haveing there seen a great deal of chaffering about cloth and Money, and things more Drie then Hæcceities and fables. Yea when I come from Taverns haveing there seen Roaring Boys, that can swear and swagger and wallow in their vomitt: O what a Glorious thing is that Kingdom which in the Temple I behold! How doth it overflow with Living waters to Refresh a Droughty Soul. whence ever I come I find it. Amiable and Sweet. my only and resting Place. seas of Amber, or far more Rich, Mountains of Gold, or far Better, Territories more Kingly, then Angels else can tell How to frame. Laws sweeter then the Hony comb, souls and mansions more wide then the Heavens, such Heavens as Adam Saw, affections Better then Sun Beams, yet Sun Beams Better then Rivers of melted Pearl, Golden Thrones and crowns of Love, and all these endlessly multiplied in all Ages. O the joy, the food, the Satisfaction! where ever else I am, being a Stranger unto these I am a Husk with Swine. not a Prodigal but a very Husk a-mong them. A Husk in respect of Emptines. A Prodigal in respect of want, nor ever am I Happy till I return Home.

31

O my God teach me Things concerning Happieness Soe Divine, and So Illustrious in their Native Light: that it may be very certaine assoon as they arc Named, that neither Angels nor cherubims can bring any tidings even from Heaven it selfe more Glorious. Nor any of the Blessed and celestial Hosts inform us with more Profitable or Divin Misteries.

Instructions Teaching us how to Liv
the Life of Happieness

1

Remember that it was possible that thou alone mightest have been in the world: and that then there had been no cities no Temples no palaces no kingdoms, but an open wilderness of Briers and thorncs, and Dolefull creatures Endangering thy Life. Yet that the Sun would rise and Set, the Day be Beautifull, the Starrs Shine by night and minister to Thee. And all these be wholy thine, as they were once Adams. that waters would be thine to Quench thy thirst, And corn where thou couldst find it. and that all these were in the wilderness nevertheless to be enjoyd, and that they ought to have been prized according to their value.

2

Remember that the world is the begining of Gifts. And that the Sons of men in destroying the wild Beasts and Dressing the feilds, take a way the Briers and Thorns and Restore the world to the Beauty of Paradice. In Adorning the meadows and building villages they Sweat for Thee. And make the wilderness an Habitable Kingdom full of Cities Trades Temples and Beautifull varieties, which were it not for these would be an horrid and an Empty Desert. that all these are Superadded Treasures, Yea that all their Trades and occupations are thine. For without them Thou must go Naked and Lie in a cave, who now hast comfortable clothes and Houses.

3

That Gods Laws Command them all to Lov Thee as themselves. by which He hath given Thee all their Riches Authority and Power. and that How ever Disobedient men are, Things are to be Accepted According as they are intended. And thou infinitly Enriched by this Promulgation in the Bosom of God.

4

That Thou art made to Live in the Image of God. To Lov them. To be a Joy a Blessing and Treasure to them. And that it is a Greater Happiness to be a Joy and a Blessing unto others, then to have Millions of Silent worlds in Quiet Possession.

5

That haveing all these by the Gift of God Thou art to Admire His wisdom Goodness and Power, for makeing thy Soul the End of all Things. And as the freind of God to Live in the Contemplation of his Eternall Love, and in the conti[n]ual exercise of Singing Praises and Loveing God.

6

That Swerving from this Glorious and Happy Life Thou art faln into sin. And needest a saviour to make an Atonement and Reedeem thee from Hell. which by reason of the Infinitenes of the Guilt, and sin, no man could do but the son of God. who therefore was incarnat and became man. whose Incarnation, since it is soe Difficult yet necessary to beleive; All the wayes of God in promises prophesies miracles Tipes and figures, Ceremonies of the Law, and Revelations from Heaven in the Ages before he came were Busied to confirme. And all his ways since in the Evangelists and Apostles, preist[s] and Martirs, Bishops and fathers, in converting kingdoms, Erecting Temples, Translating the scriptures &c are busied to reveal.

7

That all these being requisite and ordained to confirm thy Faith in that Glorious person are thy Treasures, and Sacred Blessing in thine Inheritance.

8

That Jesus christ redeemed all mankind to be thy Treasures as well as his. And that He Himselfe is thy Soveraign and Supremest Treasure, who purchased all these.

9

That now thou art to Liv as the freind of God, in a more Glorious union and Communion with him then before. All things being thy Treasures of a double value, if not by a double Right. And that the Lov is double to what it was in the First creation. That therefore all Ages are Thine Inheritance and Thou Like Abraham Heir of the world and now to Liv in communion with him, as an High Preist to prais and offer Sacrifice.

10

That the works of Lov which Thou returnest are pleasing to his Eternal majesty, and to all his Hosts that see thee with him. And so much the more by how much the more precious, costly and desired.

11

That the works of Lov which Thou returnest to God, being sought by all these meanes, are more precious then Thousands of millions of worlds. And that thou art to enjoy thy selfe as the joy of all after this Manner.

12

That in this Life Thou art to Liv Eternaly, as the Holy one of God: Angels and men being better then ministers officers and Attendants, Freinds unto Thee. That all the Things in Heaven and Earth are thy Delight, for Pleasing them. And finaly that a time cometh when all Things Shall be Naked and open to thine eyes, all thy Sences and affections perfect, All Angels and men before Thee, as realy and more effectualy then now thy freinds and companions are. Every one of them being as Great a Delight to thee as Thou art to God, and thou a delight to evry one of them in His Image.

The seeds of all wisdom Happines and Glory are here Included. And these Instructions So Great, that I would have given in my childhood Millions of worlds to have met with one teaching them, so earnestly did I Long after them. How much therfore am I bound to Bless God for haveing Satiated my soul and Replenished me with Good Things. It makes us see the face of Religion as Bright as the Sun, as Fair as the Heavens, as Real as the world.

It Discovereth an Infinit weight and Depth of concernment in evry work in evry Person. And Lifts a Holy Man above Thrones and Kingdoms, as much as Stars are above Sands or Angels above Pismires.

It maketh a man at home in his own kingdom. And even as a Pilgrim here to Liv in Heaven.

It Sheweth the Infinit Dreadfullness of any crime: and with what profound affections we ought on all occations to walk with God.

It Shews the infiniteness of the Love of God in the contemplation of which we ought to Liv for ever.

32

O my God with infinite affections I desire to Adore thy Glory! O that I could See and Answer thy Lov forever more. it is as Easy for a Mirror to be Put against the Sun, and yet no Sun Shine upon it: as it is for a clarified Soul, to see

36

that He is infinitly Good to Innumerable Thousands. that He multiplieth his joyes by Communicating His Treasures. That by Advancing others He exalteth Thee. That He maketh the Heavens and the Earth his Riches. That His Kingdom is over all and His Dominion Endureth from Generation to Generation. That His wisdom Goodness and Power are Infinitly Employed for thy Advancment. Had He made Thee alone These had been absent, and He Defectiv: that is, not the Same God that He is. He Advanced Thee, by Admitting Thee into an Eternity of Delights. But why do I not See them all at once? at once Thou mayst see them in a more clear manner, if thou wouldst be more Solicitous and more Diligent. But had He made Thee to see them all at once, thy Joys had been Alterd. which would have been infinitly Inconvenient Since they are the Best that can be. Neither Thou nor He had enjoyd the fullness of All Delights. God Loveth for speciall Reasons to proceed by Degrees. Why doth He not make all fruites perfect in the beginning? Becaus then he had onely had ripe fruites, now He hath Buds and Blossoms and Green ones, as well as Ripe ones. Now he Hath all: the very time that was Empty, before they Grew, is in its place a Treasure. Had He Seated all in the kingdom of Glory, the kingdom of Glory Had been Infinitly Less, then now it is. He had had onely that. But now he hath the kingdom of Legal Righteousness before the fall, the kingdom of Grace here on Earth, And these enrich the kingdom of Glory which He hath besides.

37

Had there been no kingdom of Legal Righteousness there had been no king of Such a Kingdom, No place for Rewards or Punishments, no Goverment nor use of Laws, no Trial of Ingenuity and excellency. No Godlike and Divine Delights, wherein God might Rejoyce in Such a kingdom and the Eternal Righteousness of his nature bee Seen. So had we been bereaved of all these Delights in communion with Him. never such a man as Adam had been known, never such a place as Paradice been, nor the Innocency and Beauty of such an Estate found in the world. Had there been no kingdom of Evangelical Grace, The Incarnation of God, the Redemption of man, mercy towards sinners, Long suffering and Patience, the truth of prophesies, the sight of wisdom in the ceremonial Law, the ministery of the prophets patri-archs and Apostles, the shedding abroad of the Holy Ghost, The Triumph of Saints, The Praises of God in his Holy Temples, the manner of our union and communion Here, our Labours and Travels and sweat in his service, All which will be Sweet Delights and Eternal Prospects in Heavenly Glory, and are now the Amazement and joy of Angels, had never been. And so these parts of Eternity Empty of Delights, at Least Such as Compleat our Glory. wheras now we can Stand in any part of all Eternity and See them all; All the variety of Service in his Kingdom, the varieties of Life wherein we appear, He and we being infinitly Richer by this means. for without these what Should we enjoy; where would his Justice, where would His wisdom, where his Equity, where his truth, where his mercy appear? where could there be any place of Patience which we So Admire. For patience without objects towards which we may be Patient, there can be none. nor mercy nor compassion without Exercise and occations. In these the Diety is Delighted and Delightfull. So that all Things must be as they already are, else Heaven it selfe would be Defectiv.

38

But why doth he desire Good works? And why leave them to us to perform, Tho He doth infinitly desire them? The Answer is, Becaus He desires they should be ours. for unless we do them, they are none of ours, and unless they are ours, we cannot be Excellent. for nothing is Excellent that cannot do good Works. Since without doing what is Excellent, no Substance can be of any valu, no Power hav any Glory. Had the Sun no Power to Shine it would be useless; had it Power, and did it forbear, it would be more Abominable. But the Act of Shining is not the suns since it cannot forbear.

40

He hath infinitly Loved us in Giving us His works: infinitly Loved us in giving us his Laws: in giving us himselfe, in Giving us his Son, in Giving us our Selves: But in nothing more hath he infinitly Loved us; Then in Desiring Good works and Infinitly desiring that we Should perform them.

41

In all other Things we are passiv and Receptiv but by Doing Good works are our selves Activ and Reign in Glory.

42

The Reasons why God desireth Good works, and why He desireth us to perform them: may be Derived from the Nature of God, from the Nature of Happienes, from the Nature of Good works, and from the Nature of the soul. But Jesurun waxed fat and kicked. men are so apt to Despise the Best and choysest Treasures when they com easily, that it is their very Interest they Should be Difficult. It is one Emolument that we have gained by sin: that wisdom is now become profound, Happieness concealed, Felicity Buried: we must Sweat for her as for Hidden Treasures. Nevertheless we shall Discover infinit causes. For till we know the Reason why God desireth Good works, and us to do them, we Shall never understand the Riches of his Lov, the Greatness of His counsels, the Glory of His Kingdom, nor See His Sincerity, nor the Reason of His ways, nor the Beauty of His Doings. It is a Question of infinit Importance, the Solution of which is in the next mine, but thou Shalt Dig for her.

43

God is Goodness infinitly Communicativ. God is Lov - infinitly Delighted to see us Happy. God is Wisdom and Delighteth to giv us all His Treasures, in the wisest manner. God is Almighty, and loveth to Satisfie his Infinit Goodness, and Delight His Lov, and shew wisdom, in makeing our Happieness compleat and Exquisite. Being all these he Delighteth in the utmost Exaltation and Glory. Doing theref[or] for us the Best of all possible Things, to satisfie his Nature He would make His Image, concerning which Image the Divines and scholmen hav apprehended too short, and spoken superficialy. They tread over a living River to the other side, and Leav all that which should reviv the Grass and cherish the Trees and make the Shore to flourish behind them. Bounty follows the Nature of God, as Light doth the sun, or a shadow its Body. Being therefore infinitly Bountifull He is infinitly willing to Give all Things. And that He may so do in the most perfect manner, creates His IMAGE to giv it unto. which Image they tell us consisteth in Righteousness and true Holyness, but for want of Drinking that River I Spoke of, Diminish the Beauty and Glory of the Shore by arriving at it to suddainly. They are silent in this, that man is made after Gods Image in respect of Ability capacity and power. And because I never had the Happieness of seeing this, I knew not the Glory of the Divine Image. Nor the Beauty of Holiness, nor the Excellent nature of that Righteousness unto which it was made. nor did I see the reason of Gods wayes, nor the Greatness of his Lov. Being Infinit in Bounty, and willing to make His Image, He made a creature Like Him to behold all Ages, And to Love the Goodness of evry Being in all Eternity, and of every Excellence in evry Being. That by Seeing, it might receive, and enjoy by Loving, all the Things in Heaven and Earth. And be as God Himselfe who enjoyeth all by Seeing and by Loveing them. His works being made thus the Image of God in Similitude of power, and Infinitly Beloved, God desireth His freind or Son Should use these Powers. Apply his mind to the Beauty of all His wayes, and render all Things a Due Esteem, Loveing the Goodness which therein is Seated. By Doing this I become Righteous and Holy, the Image of God in Exercises most Blessed and Glorious, His Admired Idea, among men and Angels. The Sole Possessor of all His Treasures, most pleasing unto Him In all the works of Happiness and Beauty. For the perfect complacency they take in me Reigning in the Bosom of all spectators. For then are we Righteous when we render to all a Due esteem. And then Holy when we do thus with such Infinit Zeal, That we would not for worlds miscarry in a Tittle. Being more Glorious as we are our Selves workers, then as we are our Selves Receivers of all things. God desiring to accomplish His work, not onely in Giving, but in makeing us to receive in the most perfect Manner. which is so to receiv that we may be Glorious in Receiving as He in Giving. more Glorious in Returning then we are in Receiving, more Happy as Suns, then Temples, more Happy as Sons, then Suns, but most Happy in being Brides and Freinds.

44

It is not Imaginable how many Thousand places of Scripture this passage doth interpret and Enrich, nor into How many it Diffuseth it selfe, nor what a Grandure it Inspireth into all our Lives, nor How clear it maketh the face of Happieness, nor How Nakedly it discovereth the Truth of Religion. nor How Potently it enflameth the Soul with Love. nor How marvellously it enricheth the works of God, nor How Apparently it manifeste[t]h his Eternal GodH[ead], nor how Deep and Amiable it maketh the Glory of His Holy Kingdom. For it Lyeth at the Bosom and Diffuseth it selfe being close at the Root unto all the Branches. Happy is He that sees to the Bottom.

45

With what State and magnificence would the Souls of Men Lov one another, Did they thus convers as the Divine Image. I Should see evry soul as the sphere of all Things. A Living Sphere whom I could not chuse but Lov and treat with Grandure, because he is the Soveraign End of all Things. The infinite Beloved of God, for whose sake God is, and All Things are Done, for whose Sake Angels and cherubims and men are exalted. yet most Blessed in being not onely the Temple, but the sun of all Things shining upon them with infinite affections, or rather more in being the Son of God, a voluntary work-man.

46

The Divine Image consisteth more in Doing then Enjoying, in Shining then Receiving; in being then in haveing all Treasure. By this we are, what by the other we are Intended, And Imitate God in Blessing and Giving. we receive all Treasures for this End, that we may be a Treasure. A Treasure unto God, a Treasure unto Angels, a Treasure unto men: an Infinite Treasure Deep and Exquisite, in the full enjoyment of Infinit Treasures. And Highly Beautifull in all their Eys by Imitating God of our own Accord. How wonderfully am I bound to magnifie his Name, that I am a Treasure to Such Infinit Treasures. How Rich is the world, wherin I have Such possessions. How Glorious is God who is a father in a family of such children. How Beautifull are those works which He Infinitly Desireth. How Joyfull am I and how Blessed a-mong all my Treasures. How odious is a Sin after such obligations. How Beautifull and Glorious is Gods kingdom. How Dreadfull and miserable is mans Blindness. How much are Souls to be thirsted, How Strait is the way of returning Home!

47

God is most pleasing to Himselfe, and made all most exquisitely to please Him, full of Infinit Beauty, variety and use for Infinit Ends. His works and Himselfe are most pleasing to all others, And becaus in this He is Most Blessed, He would make us in this Infinitly Like Him. for Doing which He is alsoe most pleasing. The Nature of our Happieness and our Souls requires that we should be pleasing to our selves, and that all our works should be full of Beauty variety and use, pleasing unto others. And that we should be Amiable in the midst of our Enjoyments. for if in the midst of all these Treasures and Possessions we should be stocks and Stones, or Abominable Dirt, or Ingratefull Rebels, which is worse then all, we become vile as Divels. That there-fore on the Contrary we might be Beautifull and Glorious, He would Have us wise and make us Holy, and giv us Ability to do Works, wherein we might Delight Him as the Brides of God. And because our works if they excell in Beauty will make our Happieness excell in Excellency, He would have those works infinitly Beautifull as well as Beautifull, that we might be infinitly Blessed, as well as Blessed. of which Beautyes you may take this prospect

48

1. He made them in Nature and Essence to be compleatly the Similitude of all His own. In respect of Life wisdom Goodness Beauty Liberty, Spirituallnes, Glory. So that all being done, all the Similitudes of those causes are found in them that make Him to Delight in His own. whatsoever there is that can move Him to Delight in His own Holiness Wisdom Goodness mercy will make Him to Delight in ours.

2. they are infinitly necessary to our Happieness, and being all founded upon Sight and Lov, or following from them, tend to make us either the Individual Possessors of all the Treasures, or the Publick Good of all Spectators: therefore He, infinitly Desiring our Blessedness and Glory, Infinitly Desireth and prizeth our works. His Nature which is Lov, Lov to Himselfe as well as to us, makeing our works an Infinit treasure to God Almighty. And (which is sweetly observable) His Goodness enriching all His Doeings even His and ours.

3. He findeth it the Delight of all his Angels Saints and cherubims, even evry Good work, as it is His. And that for His sake and ours and evry one of theirs.

4. Good works don by us, Thanksgiving, fruition, Benefitting others &c., are the very end for which He made the Heavens and the Earth. And therefore as much Better as the End is above the meanes, As much more desired by Him, as they are more intended, and as much more prized as they are desired. So that they are the Answer and full-filling of all His Design.

5. if we do Good works, apply our minds to see and enjoy, we put the crown upon all His Endeavors, we crown His works, and Accomplish

all. That being reserved for us to do for our Higher Glory. But if we delay we Spoyl all His endeavors; and Leav them Naked.

6. Good works wrought and done by our selves, Take a way the Danger of our Eternal Ruine, and make us Delightfull to God Almighty in an infinit manner. becaus a Treasure whom He tendreth as the Apple of His eye is preserved from Calamitye, and there is a gate opened for the Delightfull exercise of Eternal Freindship, between God and man. which would be all Abolished and Layd wast by our fall.

7. Good works don by our Selves are of Greater necessity and concernment to our Happieness, then all the Good works of God unto us, Nay then God Himselfe, Angels and men, our Souls and Bodyes and the Heaven of Heavens. O the Prodigious Excellency of all His Duings! That His Creatures Should be Advanced to these Heights of Power, that they should be able to do more Good to them selves, then God Almighty Can without them Do! How Incredible is this at first yet how easily attained when we Look into it! yea How unavoydable, how certain, how infinitly necessary! What would the Heavens of Heaven be were we Dirt in the Middle! We must be the joy and Blessedness our selves; we the Delights and we the Treasures, if we meane to be Happy. yea we must crown even God Himselfe, for His Nature so Necessitates Him to thirst our Lov, that He infinitly Desireth to be Beloved.

What Shall I Say more? He hath shut up all these in one work, in Lov alone. In which all Holines wisdom Blessednes and Glory concentre and abound and Dwell togeather. This He Efflagitates by all his endeavors, this he commands by all His Laws, this enjoyneth by all obligations, This allureth with Infinit Rewards. His Satisfaction and our felicity being Shut up in one, without doing this we Leave the Faculty of our soul Idle, and His Kingdom Empty. frustrat His Designes, Lay wast His Temple, and Deforme His Image. Rob Him of His Treasures, Break His Laws, Ruin our Selves, Greiv his Lov, Bring an ugly Act into His eternal Kingdom. being fled from his Works we Leav them Desolate, and the powers of our Soul Like Arches Threatning Heaven and earth, halfe finished, made in vain.

49

Leaving his works imperfect, that we Should crown them: if we forbear to do it we Greiv him infinitly, if we doe it we please Him, and Shall be infinitly rewarded; if we du it nut we give Him Dragins Blood to Drink and the Gall of Asps: if we do it our Lov is better then wine. we compleat His Image, we over flow with Living waters, and are made a fountain of Gardens, Refresh all his works and make them to flourish Like Grounds Tilled by Laureat Conquerers, they bear fruits unto Him, and his soul is Pleased forevermore. if we do it not, He made all Things to be enjoyd, without which they are Good for nothing. And us to enjoy them. All His counsels Thoughts and endeavors tend to this: eating, Drinking, Procreation of children, the Labors of the Sun, and the Subjection of Beasts flowers Rivers fruits and stars minister for this and without this are all in vain. This is our Supreme End, and every other work but as it Leadeth unto this Impertinent. we are fittly compared to a vine. for as that was mad aLone to bear and if it beareth not is Good for Nothing, so are we made onely to enjoy and to Delight in God and Glorify him and if we do not this we are Good for Nothing: scarce for the fire.

50

By doing this God hath given us a Greater Power then that of creating worlds. That External Power being as we Plainly See Superfluous and unprofitable without this, of pleasing Him, by our Internal affections. It is Infinitly more Delightfull to crown all His works then to create them; He haveing Advanced us to the utmost Heights of all Blessed and Invisible powers. Having given us a power infinitly to Greiv Him, or infinitly to Pleas Him, by not perfecting what He begun, but desisting for our Glory. neither indeed was it Possible that God should perfect it. As when we Look narrowly into the Depth of Things, Nothing is Possible but the most Excellent. For Gods Desire is that we should be Blessed and Reign with him. Now we cannot Reign without Liberty nor be Blessed without Glory. Gods Desire is to Se a creature Advanced to the utmost Heights of all possible power. of which he would bereav us by necessatating our Souls. we are conversant with Him in the Heights of power by being

Able to pleas or Greiv him infinitly. We Reign in Glory when we choose to please Him. Gods Desire is to have sons and Brides that can be Activ and vigorous, Living and Delightfull, Amiable and Beautifull, Loving and Thankfull, wise and Holy. non of all which could be without Life and Liberty, to see what was Best and doe what we pleased. Gods desire is that the works should be our own, becaus else we should be naked unprofitable Cyphers. else it is impossible that the Glory should be ours, impossible that his works should yeild him any fruits. Impossible for Men or Angels to be, Impossible that there should be any use of Laws or Rewards, impossible that we should be joys and Delights unto him. Good works are of infinit value, yet Desiring Tho he infinitly Desireth them, He may be Bereaved. The Reason is Plain. For tho He be Almighty Power, yet He can never make us freely do, what He doth in us. His Desire is that we should freely Do them, that they might be our own. Now they cannot be our works which He performeth. And our Works must Crown his. for our Holines and Joy are the End of all.

51

We become His Treasures by behaveing ourselves rightly in Such vast Exigences, Dangers and Concernments. If we do miss, It is infinit Loss. For Torment is not Pleasing to his Nature. Yet He returneth, and maketh up his Treasures by a Surmounting wisdom in useing the Advantage He hath gotten by our Sin, Punishing and Sparing according as He pleaseth; and as shall best suit with the Perfection of His [   ] Beauty and variety in His Eternal kingdom. Satisfaction is attained by an infinit fullness.

52

Among the Learned in the metaphysicks there is a Great Question De futuritione Mali. For as Gods Power is the foundation of all Possibilitie so they say his will is of all existence. How therfore Evill should arise which He willeth not is a Great Question and indeed an Inextricable controversie, so it hath been Thought, but felicity is a key that opens all things, whose motto is, facillima suprema. Nothing is a

Riddle, nor Inexplicable to it. But all Things are Easy, and the Highest Most. Deus faciendo creaturas Liberas, fecit Po[s]sibilitatem Mali, Ipse nec faciens nec volens Malum. God for the Advancment of his creatures made them free; And in so doing made a Possibility of Evill, Himselfe neither Doing nor Willing Evill. for He had don Evil had He not made them free: Against Himselfe, and against them: against all Things! all had been in vain, All uncrowned. But when he made them free He utterly Hated the Abuse of freedom. The Abuse of freedom Being the Highest crime. nor was it convenient that sin should be committed nor was it possible to be committed with Gods Desire. Had He desired sin Himself had sinned. or els there could have been none. For there can be no sin but against Gods Desire. That sin should be committed with His Desire was infinitly Inconvenient. And it was Repugnant to His nature not to hate it. But when sin was brought into the world against His Desire: that then He should improve it and make it a Treasure, was infinitly convenient. And it more tended to the Perfection of His kingdom, then if it never had been Committed. Yea Hath made all Things Richer, Infinitly Richer by its Wise Admission. without it there had been no Punishments: no Patience no Longsuffering no meekness no contrition no Penitent sinners, no Incarnation of Jesus christ, no Redemption, no new obligations, no Heights and Depths and Enlargments of soul in the Abisses of misery and the Heights of Blessedness seen at the same time. No victory and Triumph infinitly Sweeter then Quiet Possession, no miracles, no Revelations from Heaven, no use of patriarchs Prophets and Apostles. no Exercise of ten Thousand Resentments that are now in Being. yet we should have seen all these in their Possibility and have been Enlarged. And yet since they are, it is better that they should be. And that we Should see onely the future Emergencies of the Ages in Eden, (which would have followed mans Abiding Innocence) in their Possibilitie. For which cause, we may think all to have been in God from all Eternitie. Yet with all their varieties of occations, Beautyes, circumstances, Liberty, necessitie. That Liberty should be in things that from Everlasting were in God, and free; is infinitly necessary. And yet the necessity of that Liberty, yea of necessity it selfe, infinitly free, Since from all Eternitie, Beings even the most necessary Depended soly on the chois of God. Liberty and necessity with infinit Beauty meeting evry Where. His Image, being stamped on Things, Who is

Himselfe the most necessary yet voluntary Being.

53

By studying Felicity we are brought to the Delineation of Gods kingdom, to the Discovery of His nature, to a sight of Eternity, to the original of Sin, to the Excellency of Good works; to the nature of the soul, to the Reasons of Liberty, to all the things in Heaven and Earth. Little did I think when I first began whether I should be Brought. But I was brought it seems to the House of wisdom where all Things appear with a new face. nay verily we are made to conDescend to the meanest objects, in studiing to reconcile the Distractions of a Family or the affaires of a Trade to the Tranquility of Religion. And How we shall go Thorow the Stormes of this world into Eternal Glory. yea rather How we Shall ride upon the Storms of this world in Greater Triumph, Rais Beauty out of the midst of Disorders, turn poisons into cordials and Rubbish into Jewels. In the study of felicity also we have been brought to vertues, to see their original, Nature, offices, Effects and consequences. Some of which we find Belonging to the state of Innocency, and some to the Estate of misery and Grace. Goodness and wisdom and Temperance and justice have immediatly their original in the Divine Essence. And fortitude also to Adventure upon Great Things not withstanding infinit hazard. which is fed by Lov, Encouraged by Goodness, Sustained by Power, Aided by wisdom, and Deriveth strength from the magazines of Hope, and certain Prospect of what will follow. For thus God by Doing all Things by measure, did attain the utmost: Make man free. being encouraged therto by the Greatness of His Love, and allured with the Hope of what would follow notwithstanding the Danger. The similitud of which were in this Kingdom of Legal Righteousness by us to be used. an Exact Retribution of Justice to all creatures, with wisdom in seeing, Joy in Esteeming, thanksgiving in Enjoying all creatures. And these continue throughout all Ages. upon mans sin and Redemption by the Bloud of Jesus there rose up a new mine and offspring of vertues, which are Properly conversant in that estate: forgivness Penitence and Patience Faith meeknes &c. of all which Penitence and patience seem hardest. But if they be hard, Remember that we first made God Endure them. It repented God that He had mad man, and till we sinned there could be no Patience. But how Infinit is His Glory who could rais such children out of [the] Horrid womb of such a monster.

54

if Good works be so Rich and lovly O what Fruitfull Trees are they that bear them, O what living fountaines! O what Treasure is Laid up in the Ages for God and us to be Delighted in. They are Invisible but more Precious then many worlds. A world full of souls and Good works clearly seen in an Infinit Treasure. And the skill of God infinit in makeing it infinitly to be enjoyed, for in evry enjoyer we are the enjoyers of it. O Distinctiv and Eternal wisdom! How do I Adore and Delight in thy Glory. By Assuming us unto thy Selfe, and making us fellow workmen Thou hast Raised us to thy Throne who had we been onely Passiv, we had been Good for nothing. I no more wonder that Thou usest Angels or the ministery of man in the Saving of the world. Since shouldst Thou do all Things Immediatly thy selfe thy creatures would be Idle. And being useless would be Good for nothing. We all are Glorified by ministring to each other. And by Loving each other as we lov our Selves are infinitly Magnified. Having infinit cause to Delight in Thee more then in all. Thou enrichest thy selfe by enriching us, and magnifiest thy Selfe by exalting us, and by Leaving Things Imperfect hast made us perfect. O the Realty and Sweetness of thy kingdom! We are most Glorious Creatures in respect of our Comprehension. For what can be more Glorious then a sphere of Life including all Things! but far more Glorious in respect of Liberty. for How infinitly are we Exalted as Lords and Kings, in being created free, And how infinitly shall we Reign with thee, if we use our freedom as we ought to do! O giv me Grace to remember this, and to feel it always!

55

Most sweetly do the comprehension and freedom of the soul Beautifie, Enammel Each other. Oh what curious Relishes and Graces are there in the Divine Image! who would not famish to Gaze upon it! yea who can famish while He is Gazing there! Comprehension Enlargeth and Beautifieth freedom, freedom ennobleth and

Beautifieth the comprehension, both make the Soul of Him in whom they meet Divine and Admirable. Divine! what is that? Glorious before all, while he possesseth Treasure. For So to enjoy as to be a Treasure is to be a God, or else His Similitud, And it is Impossible to enjoy but onely that way, by which we become a Treasure. How Sweet and Highly invaluable are His works, who is a king of kings and Lord of Lords. who seeth all Things and is omnipresent in the Diety. wherever He seeth God, is. God is wherever He Loveth. Is not the soul so? yes by Lov, which includeth sight: in the Best of manners. What is it that we Shall most esteem in evry man? his Gold; his clothes, his face, His Houses! O His Soul! And the face of God in a mirror there! His unlimmited comprehension! His clear understanding, His endless affections, His Life and Love, His Exaltation and Liberty. But if a man be to be esteemed becaus He is the Image of God in Abilitie, How much more is He to be Esteemed that is the Image of God in Act Exercise[d]. The one may be a Dry Barren soul infinitly Desired. But oh the flames of Living waters that flow in the other Revive and flourish in the soul for ever.

56

That which infinitly magnifieth and crowneth all, is this final consideration. That with the whole Lov wherewith God Loveth all, He Loveth every one. nay such Inexhaustible Abisses are in His Eternal nature that the more He Loveth all the more He Loveth every one. For He exalteth one Abundantly the Higher by exalting all to the utmost Height. And He enricheth all by enriching one. By giving Heaven and Earth to Him, He exposeth Him the more enriched and Glorified to their veiw: And Him more Richly their Eternal Freind. It is Imposible but Himselfe must be the end of all Things, It is impossible but His Image must needs be so. For Let what will be don to God or man, such is the perfection of sight and Lov that it is don for it, and so much the more, by How much the more for others. All Angels and men are created for one. And God in communicating His Goodness to all is the God of one. In Blessing all He Exalteth one. Intendeth one as much as if He intended none Beside. Yea more then if He intended none beside. for He intendeth others for His sake. And in intending all intendeth Him aLone. And intendeth Him more by intending Him for all. O my God when ever will perfections cease? or How ever shall my Lov be small, How small, but with infinit Guilt, to Him whom God so infinitly Loveth? can I cease to Lov a man whom all Angels Lov as they Lov God! whom God Loveth as He Loveth Himselfe. whom Jesus christ Loveth more then I Himselfe! Shall I not sell my selfe to do Him Good! My very Love to God will make me Lov Him more then my selfe! were not all the creatures redeemed for Him by the Blood of christ! Shall I suffer an Heir of Heaven and Earth to Perish! Oh How Greedily ought I to Snatch any opportunity to do Him Good. And to a creature so much Beloved of God and christ, with what Zeal to Annihilate my selfe for His sake! with how much ease can I Liv and confide in God, Tho being ready to Perish, I releive Him! neither is that noble Inclination against nature, wherby I can more Delight to do Him Good, Then me. What, not Lov the End of all Things? I do not Lov Him, unless I prefer Him: what tho I am the Image of God and an Heir too! Lov forgetteth and Despiseth it selfe. I shall be the more Like unto the Son of God in Dying for Him. But I would do it, onely to save His soul. O my soul, Jesus when He was upon the Earth washed feet. Little Things are made infinitly rich by Love aLone. snatch the occation: become Divine: do Him Good and Liv sweetly in thy Grave. But ever Remember that the best charity is in Giving Counsels.

57

O my Soul! Learn Thou, in the Greatest Things to Impart all, even the Love of God, and Jesus christ with joy unto thy Brother. This work, Shall make the very Earth Heaven! By How much the more Precious Her Lov is, by so much the more Prodigal it [is] abroad. By How much the more He is a Treasure unto Her, by so much the more Let Him be thy Delight.

58

1
And now my Soul Enjoy thy Rest.
O Sit at Home
For He that seeth what is Best
Begins to Reign within a Throne.

In Silence See the Deity
The God of Love
And ever be
Within thy selfe with Him a bove
He onely Reigneth in the Highest Throne
Who sees Himselfe Advanced there a Lone.

2

At Home at home! there all the Joy
And Bliss doth flow
[   ]
But in the Inward Garden Grow
In silence see the Deity
And Liv a bove
for ever be
most Like thy God, the God of Love.
He onely Reigneth in the Highest Throne
Who Reigneth there more then if there aLone.

3

Attend, Attend; let no Disstress
Thy Heart annoy
no outward force thy Soul oppress
nor Accident Eclips thy joy
In Silence See the Deity
The God of Lov
And ever be
Within thy selfe Like Him a bove
In union Liv with thy most Glorious Freind
Thou hast Leasure outward Things to tend

4

Yet see them all, but see within.
For in the sight
of wisdom cleansd from pride and sin
Things shine more rich and fair and Bright
The world thy Freinds, the Glorious Ends
of Heaven and Earth

Thy Soul Attends
with Inward Joy with Greater mirth.
Souls in them selves are when they seem aLone
Most Blessed Great and Rich and most at Home.

5

O Blessed Soul Let wisdom Shine
The onely Light
The Light of Heaven, of God, is Thine
Where in thy Soul and Bliss are Bright.
Mens Bosoms Seem in mens eSteeme
But Dark Like Hell:
yet Inward seen
when Heavenly wisdom there doth Dwell.
The souls a world wherin we all things see:
An Endles Day within a Deitye.

58

What is the conclusion of all these Things? And what are the
Things included in Religion. The 10 Commandments, the Lords
Prayer, the two Sacraments, and the Articles of o[u]r faith. And who
are they that most enjoy them! The Sons of God and the Freinds of
God, the Divine Image, The Redeemed of christ, called and made to
Inherit all Things. Heirs of the world equal to the Angels, and Temples
of the Holy Ghost. How Long must we enjoy them? forevermore.
where? on Earth here, in Heaven here after. In what company? in
communion with God Saints and Angels. after what manner? In His
Similitude. The manner crowneth and perfecteth the Enjoyment. The
company Enricheth and Exalteth the manner. The objects Please and
Delight the Company. Duration and Immortality Beautifie the
Objects, And we who are the Persons Enjoying Enrich Eternity. The
two Sacraments are the Exhibitions of God, and the Seals of His
Covenant. The Ten Commandments are the Laws of His Kingdom.
The Lord[s] prayer is the Liturgie of His church and pattern of
Devotion. The Articles of our faith are the objects of Enjoyment
proposed to Speculation. which we ought to know as clearly as our
faces, as familiarly as our Goods, as fully as our Houses. What Shall

not God the father creating the world, God the Son Redeeming Mankind, God the Holy Ghost Sanctifiing the Elect, be [more] known then Stools and chairs! they are more Divine, more worthy, and of Greater concernment. we should feel them more then our toes and fingers. The Passion of Christ, His Resurrection from the Dead, His Ascension into Heaven, the Day of Judgment, the forgivness of Sins, the Holy Catholique church, communion of Saints, The Resurrection of our Body and Life Eternal, being objects of joy far Greater then all our Treasures Jewels Lands and palaces. The world is our Land, God our Hous and these our Jewels. It is the Duty of man as a son of God to be Great among them.

59

That one Single person is to enjoy all these is exceeding miraculous: yet very certaine, and Exceeding Amiable. It Strangly enricheth the Communion of Saints and Life Eternal, Sheweth How every [one] may be a King in that Kingdom. The marvellous use and Excellency of His Comprehension. The Possession of Heaven in this Life, and the Greatnes of Glory in the Life to come.

60

Eternal Life is an object of our enjoyment here beneath. God the father Creating the world, Hereafter. There being a Thin vail in this Endless Tabernacle, between the Holy, and the Holy of Holies. which vail was rent at the passion of Jesus christ. by Tran[s]formation to the Divine Image is Tran[s]portation caused. The objects of our Glory are ever present: but our Thoughts are Absent. If our Souls were present we should be present with them. For our Treasures Glitter round a bout us evermore.

61

O my Soul, Thy Happieness is not above the Heavens nor beyond the Sea, that Thou shouldst say who Shall fetch it who [   ] and Bring it unto us. but it is very nigh thee even in thy mouth and in thy Heart that Thou mayst Hear it and do it. what a Shame is it O Immortal Soul to be Ignorant of thy Glory! What a curse is it to be Brass and Iron in the midst of Treasures. what a Sin to be a [   ] Dul and Stupid among all obligations. a Lump of Lead to Divine Allurements, Dross and Dirt in the midst of Jewels! The Sun Shining upon a Marble wall reflects a Lustre: but not from a Mud wall. Light returning from a Palace is Beautifull, but not from a cottage. It raiseth Sweet Exlialutiuiu from a Garden. Stinking ones from a DungHill. A DungHill Soul is that Soul, a Thatcht Hous of mud walls, that is a Mole a mong Angels: Ignorant and Little in the midst of Treasures.

62

O my God revive my Soul, and refresh it with the Stream of Liveing waters! Life, sence, affections, Zeal: these, O these are the Living waters flowing from thy Throne. Replenish me with these, and I shall no more be a stony well of Dust, but a spring and fountaine of Living waters, Enriching and Reviving all thy works; Satisfying the thirst of God Himselfe; to whom also the Angels may come with Golden Buckets. The Ages Drink and Let in their cisterns.

63

God being willing to giv all Things creates His Image to Giv unto. We cannot Deface that Image but of necessity we become the most Horrid Divils.

64

Oh that I could Liv a-mong all my Treasures as God Liveth! A Divine spotless and Perfect Life! O that I could render Him that profound veneration, Perpatual Thanksgivings, Holy Reverenc, and constant obedience as I ought to doe. O that [I] could Liv without Transgression. How miserable and Little hath sin made us! How vile who were most Precious! How weak, who were Strong! How forget-full, who were Glorious! can an Infinit Sphere of Life and Love be Less, An Heir of the world Stoop at a Trifle, a Son of God Leav all His Glory to catch at a Shadow! And the Divine Image be wholy taken up with a Straw, or Devoured with a censure. The Lightest occurance breaketh our frame. we have need to be carefull, for our most Glorious frame is more Brittle then Glass. Infinit Care. O Infinit Care!

65

Profound Inspection, Reservation and Silence; are my Desires. O that I could attain them: Too much openness and proneness to Speak are my Diseas. Too easy and complying a Nature. Speaking too much and too Long in the Best Things. Mans nature is Nauseating and weary. Redundanc is Apprehended even in those Things of which there can be never Enough. by Exposing Himselfe a man Looseth Him Selfe, and becometh cheap and common. The vices of men have made those Things vices, that are the Perfections of Heaven. There Shall we Sing His Praises all the Day Long. With David my Soul Shall make her Boast in the Lord. Here it [is] Tediousness and vain Glory. There it is the Joy of all to be Communicativ and He most Happy that is Infinitly So. Here He is unwelcom. The Ignorance of man maketh those Things obscure that are Infinitly Easy, those things ugly that are in them selves Beautifull, those Things inconvenient that are in them selves Blessed. Here I am censured for Speaking in the Singular number, and Saying I. All these Things are done for me. Felicity is a Bird of Paradice So Strang, that it is Impossible to flie a mong men without Loseing some feathers were She not Immortal. There it shall be our Glory and the Joy of all to Acknowledge, I. I am the Lords, and He is mine. Every one shall Speak in the first Person, and it shall be Gods Glory that He is the Joy of all. Can the freind of GOD, and the Heir of all Things in Heaven and Earth forbear to say, I. we must attend the Reverence Due unto our Persons. And so far yeeld to the corruptions of men, as to strengthen our Influence in Bringing them to Glory. Their Incapacity hath made that saying Eminent and necessary. Silere Tibi, Laus est. There we Shall have one open and Eternal Day, here our Lives must be Intermingled as Time is in this world, with Speech and Silence, Dayes and nights. There our Glory shall be Exposed unto all. Here it cannot be understood. There it Shall be seen: but God Almightye most Highly Remembred. It is Inconvenient here to [be] Exposed unto many. Bright Be and Humble: that is Divine and Heavenly on the Inside.

66

Temperance in Expression is the Art a mong the Sons of Men. They suspect a Depth, and see Majesty in few words. We have millions of Things to utter and Declare which are Infinitly clear and Rich in them selves But must utter them by Drops; becaus they seem Dull and Dubious. O the misery of confined Man!

67

As my work of calling others is Greater then to Enjoy, So ought my Care in that work. O my God who Lovest the manner better then the Deed, Delineat in my Soul an Exquisite Ability, that I may Express it in my Life with Exquisit care.

68

Dead flies corrupt the Apothecaries oyntment, so doth a Little folly Him that is in Reputation for wisdom and Honor, A little flaw in a Precious Diamond maketh it Base. a small stain is Insufferable in the finest Lawn. a Little Poyson spoyleth the Expence of the Curious Dish. And a Light mistake rendereth the most Pleasing Person[s] Discours Ingratefull. O my God How many Thousand Imperfections weaknesses and Errors hav I committed?

69

In my Close Retirements I was some years as if no Body but I had been in the world. All the Heavens and the Earth are mine: mine aLone. And I had nothing to do but walk with God, as if there had been non other but He and I. When I came a-mong men I found them to be Superaded Treasures. and I am aLone Still: The Enjoyer of all. But have Greater work: To Glorifie God. O that I could do it, wisely, as I ought.

70

It is my shame and one of Actual and Infinit crimes: that I do not constantly Ascrib and Acknowledg unto Him the Glory. It is my Infinit Shame, and by confessing it I must Lie under it. but I will confess it that I may a voyd it; and Escape its causes. O my God pardon my vileness: And enable me with Infinit Desires Always to Thirst and Intend thy Glory.

71

I Shew thy Glory, in Discovering unto Men the Glory of thy Kingdom. but therin have Designed mine own. now O Lord thy Goodness hath overcome me. And I am obliged to Delight in thy Glory more then in mine. O Let me Annihilate my Selfe, and vindicat thy Glory. Bear all Reproaches for thy Sake, and forgetting my selfe Endeavor Always that thou maist be Gloryfied, men saved, and Jesus Satisfied. Thine Infinit God Head hath made that my Glory, Salvation, satisfaction. In the Deepest Highest and Best of manners.

·72

The Liberty of my Soul to pass over all the creatures in Heaven and Earth is my Joy and felicity. The Greatness of my Soul that Beholdeth the Ends of never Ending Eternity is my Joy and Felicity. The Swiftness of my Soul that can flie in an Instant from East to West is my joy and felicity. The Activity of my Soul that can never ceas from meditating and thinking is my Joy and Felicity. The Riches of my soul whose Interior affections are more Acceptable then the Heavens is my joy and felicity. The Excellency of my Soul whose sight is more Excellent then the Light and Day is my joy and Felicity. The keeness of my Soul, whose perceptiv Powers are So Distinctiv as well as Great is my joy and felicity, but especialy it is my Glory to use them well. not mine, but thine O Lord: who gainest Glory, by giving infinit

73

While every Soul is an Interior Temple of all Eternity, And all the Beings in the Eternal Diety are included in it, In evry Soul the fullness of the GodHead Dwelleth forever: as it doth in christ, in whom the fullness of the GodHead Dwelleth Bodily. God therefore in giving, in

evry Soul, giveth all Things and Eternity to me. in every Soul
Himselfe: the fullness of the Godhead in every Soul. How much therefore ought I to Labor after every Soul, Since in every Soul I gaine a
Temple, wherin the Fullness of the Godhead Dwelleth! But if the fullness of the Godhead be in every Soul forever to be enjoyd, oh what
Rooms, what endless Depths, what Glories are in mine! which cannot
onely See the fullness of God but see it a gaine in every Soul. And
compr[e]hend all those in whom the fullness of the Godhead
Dwelleth.

74

O my Lord did I Lov thee Perfectly, surely I Should be Infinitly
Greived when I offend Thee. For He that offendeth against Him that
Loveth infinitly before and resolveth to Lov Him Equaly afterward, is
infinitly Guilty tho He be forgiven. yea So much the more by How
much the more Gracious and kind that Lov is, which resolveth to
forgive. O my God I abhor my Selfe in Dust and Ashes, that I Love
Thee not more tenderly. And I pray thee giv me Such a Lov that I may
fear Thee becaus of thy Lov And watchfully hearafter take care to
please thee becaus I shall be forgiven. Above all things in Heaven and
earth Let me Dread to need forgivness, for to offend against infinit
Love is the greatest misery, shame and sin.

75

The least Slip of our Heart (out of the Devine presence) is Like the
fall of Angels, So is the Least Cessation wherin we forget to make God
our Supreme End. I ought therefore evermore in the Beginning of evry
Enterprize; to remember God, and aime at His Glory as my Supreme
End. When I forget Him I walk in Darkness, when I aim at my Self it
is in vain Glory. for He Lifteth up Himselfe above God that maketh
Himself his Last End. In every Conference therfore Discours and
enterprize I must actually remember His presence, and Direct my
Intentions to His Glory. Not to do it, not to do it is the Beginning of
Error and of all Calamity. for by forbearing to do this I wander In the
Dark, and become Subject to all Transgression. for from the very first
moment wherein a man doth otherwise He is Alienated from God,

made weak, Apt to be Led into all Temptations.

76

How much are We bound to Almighty God, for makeing provision of our Saviours merrits, to whom we may resort as to the Rock of Ages! And Since evry Slip is Like unto the Fall of Angels, How sweet and Refreshing is His Righteousness, How reviving His Death, How comfortable and Precious his Blood, which Continualy Covers our Imperfections; and Heals the Bruises and putrified Sores of our frequent falls! Oh what Zeal, and How much Ardor ought I to use in running unto Him, and Abiding under His Reviving Shaddow! Especialy Since by How much the more frequent my Transgression[s] are, by So much the more Rich and Gloryous his Satisfaction and Intercessions are. O my Saviour How Amiable art Thou, whom even Sins them selves Enrich and Beautyfie.

77

It is a Question moved by Some, that Desire to know wheather they are in the estate of Grace, what kind of sins are Consistant with it. unto which we Answer, No Sin Allowed, Any Sin Hated and Repented. Yet further, it is a Question what kind of works we may Delight in, Wrought by a Man in the Estat of Nature? Truly when Things are seen, we can Delight in non of His works. for we can Delight onely In [those] which God accepteth. And what are Those. Those which we do with all our Power. for God accepteth no works in which we use not all our might. nor in any such can we be satisfied, much Less Delighted. For it greiveth us to see a man use His power Carelessly for God Almighty. He that doth a Good work with all His Might shall certainly be Saved, unless he Apostatizeth from that work. we speak not here of outward Power, but Inward. He that stirreth up the Powers of His Soul, to intend God, Angels, and men with all His might, in evry work; Shall undoubtedly be Saved if He Apostatizeth not from that Intention. Which by Neglecting to Second that work with Like ones following certainly he doth. But He that useth all His power to do a Good work, and doth it with all His might is in the Estate of Grace? Truly so he is. for He that useth all his might is accepted with God, in any Estate. And to be in the Estate of Grace is non other then to be in the Estate of Gods favor and Acceptation. which Sheweth how Easy it is for any man in any moment to Step from the Estate of Nature into the Estate of Grace. for he that doth a Good work with all his might is in the very doing of it accepted of God, and so in the Estate of Grace. which any man may be, becaus any man may use all the Power which He hath. wherfore Cavil not, Dispute no more. But do Good works with all thy might, so shalt thou be in the Estate of Grace. but forbear to do them, or do them with Less then all thy might; and thou Shalt never be Sure thou art in that Estate.

78

Mans Humility and Gods Highness are wedded objects to each other. Let me see the Nothing out of which I was taken and I Shall See the Glory to which I am exalted. Thy Glory and my Lowness increas and perfect my Happiness. of both which while I am Sencible I Sencibly feel my Eternal Fulness. For as the Heavens a bove are in a Mirror seen, as far beneath them, as they are a bove, and both Conjoyned make an Intire Sphere, Seeming Divers but the very Same; So doth God and my nothing, both Apprehended. For while I see both I am infinitly Greater. An infinit Distance is between God and the Highest cherubim: an infinite Distance between Nothing and the Lowest Sand. Nothing Less then an infinit power being able out of Nothing to creat a Sand. while I contemplat the nothing out of which I was made, in the Bottom of my being I See his Glory. And at once possess the Zenith and the Nadir of his Eternal Sphere, the Heights and Depths of His Infinit fullness. And by How much the Lower the valley is out of which I am raised, by so much the Higher the joy is to which I am exalted. God at the Bottom being the same God, with Him that Reigneth in the Highest Throne. And my Happiness Greater to all Eternity, by how much the Less from Eternity it was. yea from all Eternity far Greater then if I had been from Everlasting. God and I are more Blessed in what whatsoever is. I more obliged to Lov his Goodness for makeing me out of Nothing: and He more Exalted, while I obliged. He more pleased by How much the more I am Delighted, and I more Blessed, while He is Pleased. From all Eternity to my First Conception I was Nothing, from my first Conception to all

Eternity I am a Being. From all Eternity my Being was with God Almighty. to all Eternity my Nothing will be before my Face. From all Eternity to all Eternity my nothing and my Being Endless and unmovable: and I in both infinitly Greater, the Joy of Angels and Men both infinitly Greater. that being Best which forever is. God seen all Activity Life and Power, in raising me from nothing to infinit Glory. Humility is the Bride and Queen of God: The Lowest foundation and the Highest Throne: The Earth removed and the Heavens seen: Gods fulness in Mans Emptiness Best Appearing.

79

He that will be Happie must see his wants that He might See his Treasures for his Treasures. For as pictures are made by a pleasant Admixture of Lights and shades so is Happines compleated by a fulness and variety of wants and Treasures. wants and Enjoyments go hand in hand. They infinitly agree while they seem to differ. For without want there Could be no Enjoyments, but all Redundancies and Superfluities, for which respect even want it selfe is a soveraign possession. From all Eternity God wanted us, or else we could not be Superadded to him. From all Eternity God included us, and therefore He could not at all want us, we Could not at all be Superadded to Him. we could not be superadded to him, could we not be made His Treasures, we could not be superadded to Him becaus we were in Him. From everlasting He was before us, from Everlasting He was within us, from everlasting He was beyond us, with us and without us, from everlasting Infinitly present, near and Distant, His Goodness wanted us and that is His Glory. It is the Glory of God that he loves to be Enjoyed. Who Loving to be enjoyd we are the Treasures of his Goodness, becaus its Recipients. Blessednes Naturaly Loveth to be seen, and is Like milk in a womans Breasts more Delightfull in being Distributed, then in Lying Still in its own Fountaine. It curdleth there and recoyling upon it selfe: in flowing from the mother it feedeth a nother and becometh usefull. Delightfull to the mother while it is usefull. But this in God is Incomprehensible. For as Fountaines are Flowing all into the Sea, at the Same time they are derived from them: and are all Extant, and surrounded at once within the Heavens, Soe all these Emanations of Delight are extant in God and at once enjoyed.

From everlasting we wanted on[e] to give us a Beginning and Therefore is God an Infinit Treasure, because He supplieth that necessity. Had all Things been from everlasting in them selves there had been neither place nor occasion for Gods Goodness. Had all things been from everlasting in Him, from everlasting we might all behold his Glory. And soe we shall. For becaus it is necessary to see our wants, before we can See and Possess our Treasures, our wants and Treasures Shall be forever present, casting a sweet Reflection upon each other, that we might Equally be Effected, and with both Delighted. But O the Abysses of Endless Eternity! O the Riches and Depths that are in it! Where even wants them selves Glitter in a fulness of Eternal Treasures. And are all present, tho all supplied, that they might the more be seen!

80

Goodness in God is infinitly Beautifull becaus infinitly usefull upon all occasions. For out of infinit evils, when once Committed, it ever Extracteth Greater Good. Had not man Sinned there had been neither Place nor roome for the Incarnation of God. Nor for those worlds of Delights, that are Shut up in the work of our Redemption. our new want accidentaly superadded by that Transgression, Jesus christ an Infinit Treasure. even the Sin of man makeing it possible that God should Superadd another infinit, an Infinity of Lov in the Death of our Saviour. So that from all Eternity it was convenient that Sin Should be, but from all Eternity it was convenient it should be against the commandment and will of God. being at the same time both forbidden and permited. That it was forbidden is infinit Delight: That it was permitted was infinit Delight: That it was forbidden and yet permitted Sheweth infinit Misteries in God Allmighty: Beauties in Eternity, Riches in his Kingdom. It was Forbidden with infinit Beauty, becaus the occations of Forbidding it were infinit. It was permitted with infinite Beauty becaus the Occations of permitting it were Infinit. And the Benefits of both Endless in Number value and Duration. Which therefore Blind men Cannot See becaus they are Apostates and Liv in clouds.

81

Sin was Forbidden with infinit Beauty, Becaus it was Evil, and God hated it: Hurtfull to man, and an Odious Spot in the Kingdom of Glory. The Beauty of Permitting it is Likewise infinite, becaus man that was forbidden was made Free, Enabled with a Power to Displeas God, that by chusing to please him he might become a Treasure. and the more soe by making Himselfe Delightfull. becaus also God did fore see how infinit Good might be brought out of that Evil. but that it Should be Permited and not forbidden, would have been an Evil infinit in God Almighty. From Eternity He willed that man Should be free and Sin if He would: but would not that man should sin, from all Eternity. He gave Him a Power to Disobey his will, but never would that He Should abuse his Power. It was not given for its own Sake, but that by useing it well we might Live in Glory. Sin with its Circumstances were all necessary: becaus from Everlasting and most Excellent. but then it was necessary in all its circumstances, of freedom, and Possibility not to be Committed. Yea in desires in God Almighty that it Should not be committed. Obligations and Rewards, Prohibitions and Punnishments Deterring us from Committing it. All these were necessary too, that it Should be Amiable to forbear, and ugly to do it. Sin being So, without sin in Eternity God made it self[-]made (by wisdom infinit an infinit Treasure Forbidden and Permitted at Same time[)].

82

God is a Fulness in all Extremes: Happieness a mistery in which contrarieties are coincident: And Glory an Abysse in which contradictions unite, and reconcile them selves. He is an Infinit Sphere, yet an infinit Centre. He is infinitly before us yet infinitly after us. we are Equal to Him, yet infinitly beneath Him. And more Blessed then if we had been from Everlasting. By obliging us to Lov Him more then our selves He hath [made] us Blessed as Himselfe is. By makeing us Blessed as Himselfe is He hath made us infinitly beneath Him. By makeing us each a Possessor of Eternity and the End of all Things He hath made us Like Himselfe. By makeing us Like Him hath exalted us to his Throne and by doing so made us his Peers. All Like Him, of whom it is said, Arise O sword and smite the man that is my Fellow. No Distance was convenient between God and us, but that of obligation. We are infinitly beneath Him, becaus infinitly obliged.

83

When I see a Little church Environed with Trees, how many Things are there which mine Eye discerneth not. The Labor of them which in Ancient Ages Builded it; the conversion of a Kingdom to God from Paganism, its Protection by Laws, its subjection to Kings, its Relation to Bishops, usefulness and convenience for the Entertainment of christians, The Divine Service, office of the ministery, Solemn Assemblies Prayses and Thanksgivings, for the sake of which it was permitted, is Governed, Standeth and Flourisheth. Perhaps when I Look upon it, it is Desolate and Empty almost Like an heap of Stones: non of these things appearing to the Eye, which nevertheless are the Spirituall Beauties which adorn and clothe it. The uses Relations services and Ends being the Spiritual and Invisible Things: that make any material to be of worth. He that cannot see Invisible cannot Enjoy nor valu Temples. But He that Seeth them may Esteem them all to be his own: and wonder at the Divine Bounty for giving them so Richly becaus were there non such, and he able to Erect them, for these End[s] it were very Amiable that Himselfe should Endow them. The Services are such that He should Delight in; and becaus so rejoyce in God for Preparing them to his Hands. Especialy I who have been nourished at universities in Beautifull Streets and famous colledges, and am sent thither From God Almighty the maker of Heaven and Earth, to teach Immortal Souls the way to Heaven, to sanctifie his Sabbaths, to instruct them in his Laws Given upon mount Sinay, and to shew them the Lov of a Glorious Saviour Slain upon mount Calvary: to Lead them by his Merits to Eternal Joys.

84

By such thoughts we come to know what things Invisible and spiritual are. The uses of Material[s], which he that cannot see can Enjoy Nothing. The services and Ends of Material Things are those which constitute all their Excellencies. And it is the Excellency of Man that

He is Able to Enjoy them. A Beast cannot see into those Ends for which Temples are Erected: and Therefore all churches appear unto them, but an heap of Stones. A carcase Seen whose Soul is a way. It is mans Soul and the Excellencies of it, that makes and apprehends all other Excell[e]ncies. For were it not able to see farther then a Beast can see, into the Depth of Things: Their Inward Beauty would Lie concealed, and be infinitly fewer and Less then they are. For to what purpose Should the world be made or Temples Stand, were not the soul able to Enjoy all Things? These Spiritual powers wherby we see the services of Things are Likwise Invisible and spiritual Things. So are our Thoughts and our Imaginations and affections, souls them selves and Holy Angels. but neither the Angels nor souls would be of any worth were it not for the uses Relations and Ends unto which they serve. He therefore is a Spiritual Man, that Seeth these, and Prizeth these. A waken thy soul and stir it up to feel and behold the services of things. For without the Sence of Invisible Things no Thing visible can be enjoyed. But of what value are those Souls that infuse the value of all beside!

85

Gold and silver were it all mine, after this world: would rust in my hands. Had I all the Riches of the Indies alone, it would be but Rubbish. An Idle spectacle of splendid Ruines. The sons of men are my Greatest Treasures for whose sake Riches are Esteemed. And by whose ministery Gold is actuated and wealth Enlivened Throughout the world. while it Adorneth Kingdoms with flourishing prosperity, and covereth the face of the Earth with Beauty: It is most mine as it is Animated by others, and serveth for the Highest and the Best Ends, as it ministereth to Men, and Serveth those whom I Love and of whom I am beloved. I eat not the Grass that Groweth for my cattle, yet it is mine, and Soe are all the corn feilds upon the whole Earth: becaus it sustaineth a more Noble Breed. Gold and Silver is Shining Grass: unto which they have imputed a fained value, but of Less then Corn and Grass in Eden. All these serve me as they Display the Glory of my fathers Kingdom, and Shew his Bounty and his Lov to men. But O the Riches of my Great Estate who have other Wealth beside these, even Endless Treasure. All the Corn oyl wine in the world is mine, the Best of Ends, in the Best of manners. How much ought I to rejoyce in God, who hath so Profoundly given all Things to me: and to rest Satisfied in my Enjoyment of them, Since it is in his Similitude!

87

Solomon tels us that the Heart of the wise is in the House of Mour[n]ing, but the Heart of fools is in the Hous of mirth. Since therefore it is better to goe to the House of Mourning then to the house of feasting, Let us go a little Travailing abroad, and visit the Houses of Dying Persons. Not of People near about us: for of those Perhaps we shall Learn but Little. but Let us goe rather over the mountains, and cross the seas and Penetrat the Bowels of other Nations, and there either in Tents or Citties, we shall find wise and Glorious Persons, whose manner of Life differeth much from ours, and from the Life of any about us. As haveing Greater Grandure, a more Divine Education, Celestial Company, Higher Preferment, Sage Experience, Ancient Presidents, nearness unto God. And first Let us go down into the House of Jacob, in Gen: 49. there we shall see Him upon his Sick Bed calling his children alltogeather, Speaking of Abraham and Isaac his Fathers and of the manner how they walked with God, of Gods Appearances, and of the Angel that redeemed him from all Evil: Blessing his twelve Sons, and foretelling their Happy Estate in the Kingdom of Canaan; his Mind reaching to after Generations, and beholding their Glory, while it was a far of[f]. Being filled with the spirit of Prophesie it was near unto him, even imediatly Present before his Eys. The Scepter of Judah, the Royal Dainties of Ashur, the Havens of Zebulun, the coming of Shilo, the Preisthood of Levye, and the Blessings of Joseph, were his Discours: as if he were the father of all the Earth, and the world his familie. No wals of a chamber could contain Him, but He maketh mention of Heaven above, and of the Earth beneath, and of Bless[ings] comming from the utmost bounds of the Everlasting Hils. And so Drawing up his feet into the Bed, he yeelded up the Ghost, and was Gathered to his People. Had we been in the chamber of Some Dying man a-mong us, we should have heard him talking of such a Meadow, and such a sum of money, such a Hous, and such Trunks of clothes, given to this and that and the other Son: while this mans soul was open and clear to all the Gloryes of

Heaven and Earth: his spirit was set upon Great Things. And haveing
his Ey open to see in clear Light the Joys of the Kingdom of Heaven,
in the midst of all, he crieth out, O Lord I have waited for thy
Salvation! Least He Should Seem Singular, Let us next go to the Hous
of Moses upon the Brink of Death, hear his speech and see His behaviour. He Assembles the 12 Tribes of Israel togeather, who were now
grown to an Host of 600000 Men; and having all the Heads of their
Families before Him, with venerable and Sacred care he Blesseth them
all. They may Seem to be more Peculiar objects of Jacobs care, becaus
they were his offspring; but they came not out of Moses Loins: yet his
Lov had naturalized and made them all His Bowels. as if therefore
they had been all his family, in a Sacred manner he Blessed their Tribes
before his death, makeing Mention of the Journeys of our Lord, who
Shined forth from Paran, and came with 10000 of his Saints; and of the
fiery Law, of the urim and Thummim, of the Precious Things of
Heaven, the Dew, [and] of [the] Deep that coucheth beneath, the
Precious fruits brought forth by the sun, and the Precious things Put
forth by the moon, the cheife Things of the Ancient Mountains, and
the Precious things of the lasting Hils: the precious Things of the Earth
and the fulness thereof, and the Good will of Him that Dwelleth in the
Bush. such Things agreed with the Grandure of his Holy Soul: and all
these did he see in a clear Light, the kingdom it Selfe being but a
Privat house, and Israel his faimily, no walls Could Limitt his affections, nor any chamber containe his Treasures. And Least he Should
think these Extraordinary and rare Examples, David Prayeth;
Remember me with the favour that thou bearest to thy People: O visit
me with thy Salvation. That I may See the Good of thy chosen, That I
may rejoyce in the Gladness of thy Nation, that I may Glory with thine
Inheritance. Every man being the End the Heir and Possessor of all
their Peace and joy and Glory. O my soul, why Shouldst thou not,
attain the Estate and Grandure of these Heavenly Persons.

88

Enter into his Gates with Thanksgiving and come into his courts
with Prais, be Thankfull unto Him and Bless his name. For he more
delighteth in Giving then men in receiving. And when He giveth, Like
a God, He giveth most Perfect wealth. Kingdoms and Ages which are

obscure unto fools (who Therefore Shall never stand in his Presence becaus they cannot enjoy them): But Treasures to the wise So Divine and Glorious, that as in wideness they are infinite, in value they are more, Too clear, too Sweet, too Great, too Good to be Esteemed. It is a hard thing to beleev such Things are ours: more hard to beleiv they are so Excellent. Yet are they so True So Real and Divine, that their Benefit is as Infinit, as their Face is visible: and He onely an Immortal King that Knows how to Enjoy them. God Almighty when He gave the Treasure[s] of God to man, gave them in Such a Sort, that non might enjoy them but He alone that Liveth Like a God, which is the Sole reason they are not understood. O my Soul for this oughtest Thou more Abundantly to Esteem them. For the Life of God is the Glory of thy Being. which therefore Men wonder to hear of, becaus they are Alienated from the Life of God.

89

Since God hath given all the Treasures in Heaven and Earth, it concerneth us much to heighten our Apprehensions that we may Possess his Treasures. It is of infinite Moment to have worthy Thoughts, and to Discern their value; It is Impossible to exceed in judgeing of their Excellency, our Duty to reach it: which Since it is so infinit, the helps are infinit, and infinitly Necessary that Enlarge the Soul, Strengthen the Apprehension, Quicken the Sence, Heighten the expectation, Actuat the Endeavor, and Enlighten the mind truly to Discover them. Is it Possible that the works of God should be inferior to the Best! And if they are the Best that Almighty Power could attaine, what mines of Excellencies must be hidden in them! what Secret seas, Fathomless Inward unexpected Oceans! Surely had not God known them to be infinitly Perfect He had never trusted us with a Power of Examining them. But they must be infinit. For his infinit Goodness wisdom and Power are Glorified in Preparing them, and indeed are enjoyed in them. Each one of which as if they had been Studied from all Eternity are fit to be seen to all Eternity. Those Things had need to be well don that being once don are to Last for ever. And that therefore if any man should ask me what God was doing before the world began? I would not Answer with Saint Austin: that He was makeing Hell for such Busy enquirers. But studying from Eternity to do all in the most Perfect manñer. For all things are so perfect that they [are] worthy to be Seen for ever, and are in very Deed, the Product of Eternal Study. The Heavens are exceeding High, but mans Soul wanteth wings to soar unto them, The Treasures of Eternity Exceeding Great but man wanteth Armes to Embrace and comprehend them, the value in every thing infinitly Deep, but man wanteth a Plummet to fathom them. yet is man the most Perfect creature. As Great as all, as Deep as all, the Proper offspring of Almighty Power.

90

That Almighty God Should ever make an Infinit Creature, is impossible to beleiv. Yet he hath made [the] best that can be, which cannot be Less, becaus Almighty power When wholy Exerted can never rest but in infinit Attainment. tis the highest the most excellent attainment, but if it hath made then the Best that can be, it hath made [it] infinite. Yea but can He not infinitly Proceed? yes. Then infinitly more perfect then the most Perfect may be made. He can make a Sand, a creature above that as Glorious as the Sun. Another a bove that as far as the Sun is above the Sand, And so Proceeding by finit Steps, for ever. But if He Pleas to Exert all His Power, And at one infinit Endeavor attain a creature that shall include them all: beyond that He can goe no further, becaus infinit Differences and Degrees of Excellency are at once attained. Hath He don this? yes. How Shall we know: Becaus He hath made a creature infinitly most Perfect. How Shall we Prove that: He hath made An Angel, a cherubim, a Man. A Man; is he So Perfect? yes. God hath don all in creating Him that He could Possibly do, and doing so hath given Himselfe to man. How shall we rest assured: He hath made his Imag. Is that so Great? yes. God Himselfe Cannot make a greater thing then His Image, It is impossible to Creat a God, but an Image of Him, He hath created. Could He creat a God, that God could be but his Son, his freind, his Bride, His Companion, the Image of Himselfe: and that man is. But Surely if God hath don all he can Man must be an Astonishing and Stupendious creature. What can he do ? he can See Eternity, and Possess infinity.

91

If God hath don for man the Best of all possible Things why then did He not at first make him in the Hypostatical union. For since it was Possible for a creature from the begining Personaly to be united to God, It seemeth as if Gods Lov were Defective in the Beginning, Since He did not for man that Best Thing Possible. O my soul His Lov was Perfect, The Hypostatical union was not Possible from the Begining. For Nothing is Possible that is not Agreeable with the Divine Wisdom. It is not Agreeable with the Divine wisdom to doe any thing Superfluous. Vain and Superfluous are both the Same. In the Estate of Innocen[c]y that man Should Personally be united to God was vain and superfluous. because there it was no need that God should die but onely be enjoyd. which then might easily and Perfectly be don by the Benefit and communion of Lov alone. The union of Lov is the compleatest union, and in it selfe the most Beatifique. the Hypostatical. were the union of Lov in the Hypostatical Removed, the union of Lov would be more Perfect then it. But the Hypostatical union is founded in Love. to wit in a Greater measure. For tho our Restitution to The union of Love [is] the End why Jesus christ the Son of God was Incarnat: Yet God so Loveth this End that He most infinitly Loveth the meanes by which it is attained. And the manhood more by which He gaineth it, then all the creatures in Heaven and Earth. becaus all the creatures both in Heaven and Earth He Loveth, by Him He gaineth. It was sin alone that mad the Hypostatical union Possible.

93

The union of Love is so Great an union that the 3 Persons in the Trinity are united in it. It is the union of God. And the two natures of our Saviour are united by it. It was the End which God both in the creation and Redeeming us Principaly Intended, His First and His Imediat Desire. His Last also. It is so Perfect, that God who did all Things Best in the first Begining [made] all other unions superfluous; by this we reign in the Throne of God, and are Pleasing to Him. The union of Souls is far Greater then the union of Soul and Body in the same Person. more Blessed, and more Delightfull. the Body is the Seat wherein the Soul Liveth: but anothers Soul the object of its joy. In this it acteth upon that: forgetteth the Body and rejoyceth to feel it: Is more allured to be Present with it, more busied and Exercised about it. cleaveth to it more Inseperably, Loveth it more Ardently, as a more worthy object. Dwelleth there with Greater Complacency; and is more Satisfied in that Blessed union: contemplateth its Beauty, feeleth its Activity, Is affected with its Life, allured by its Lov, clarified by its understanding, and Liveth in it. But the union of our Soul with God is the more Sublime. He being more us by the force of Love then our very selves. He liveth in us while we contemplat and Admire Him. Our Bodies are but dust in Comparison of Him, By seeing and Loveing Him we are Transformed into Him, become his Similitude, feel his Blessednes, Enjoy his Glory, possess his Treasures and become his own. Love maketh us to Dedicate our selves unto Him. That Monarch as soon as born ruleth all, Disposeth all, ordereth all our faculties and Powers, and maketh us to consecrat our selves to his will and pleasur, While on both sides it maketh the Lover infinitly Subject to [the] Person beloved, it maketh them both Supremely each others. We Lov him so much that we Magnifie and Adore Him, and annihilate our selves and all our delights to be Delightful to Him. The Beloved of God is a God unto Him: By his Infinit Goodness strangly Exalted. For whose Sake He beginneth all Things, to whose Benefit He refereth all Things, in order to whose Pleasure He Disposeth all Things. The Lover abandoneth Himselfe to the Disposeall of his Beloved, is absolutely his Subject, and infinitly Delighteth to be commanded by Him. which so Pleaseth us that we can take notice of nothing else, nor be Present with any thing in thought beside. This Therefore begetteth the most infinit union in the whole world. on the Bodies Side the union is imperfect, becaus that is Passive and Dead. nor can the Soul be united to it in the intention perfectly in ferver of the Inward thoughts, because it is incapable of so much Love, being an object much inferior and Less Excellent. The union of Souls is So Sublime that a spirit would forsake its Beloved Mansion and Permit it to Die, and Lie for ever in the Dust, to conserve its union with a nothers soul. which union is compleat on both Sides, Since both are alive, can see and Love.

94

Being so infinitly Beloved, our Falling into sin made Hypostatical union Possible: Gave God an occation, with out which He could never have Shewed more: his Love was so Great and Perfect in the Beginning. Sin gave Him an Advantage to Exalt us more: By Giving Him occation to make God a Man; And to Shew the Perfections of his Ancient Love in a new Light by a new Demonstration. The Infinit Excessivness of it was manifested by its continuances notwith-standing our sin. He that Loved us more then the Angels then: Loved us more before. The new sight of and sence of our Amiableness was objected before Him, in the Loss of Angels as well as Men. That there-fore a sheapherd Leaveth 99 sheep in the wilderness to seek one that He lost; becaus the sence of its value was Quickned by its absence; is no objection in this case. That Loss Quickning the sence of their value in the faln Angels as well as in us. He Loved us more then the Angels whom He Left in the same Estate, Redeeming us. But How could God become a man, without takeing an Humane Person? O my soul Admire the Perfection of thy union with God which all the Things in Eternity, Heaven and Earth Adorn, Heaven and Earth and Ages Beautifie. Yea which occationed the Son of God to be come a man! For a Peculiar End did He assume our Nature. And haveing made us every one Kings before, He made Jesus christ King of Heaven and Earth that we might Reign. But How can His Humanity be a Man, Yet not a Person? Consider O my soul when thou art seperat how thou wilt be a soul and not a Person. Thou art a Rational Being Distinct and Single, is not that sufficient to make a Person. No. Thou art Imperfect. Imperfect! in what my Soul? Thou lackest not a faculty: Thou canst know and Love Like an Angel, Comprehend Eternity, Exist and be, Admire and Adore, Sing Praises and be Enflamed as well as any cherubim. But a cherubim is not ordained to another Nature, nor is an Angel Related to a Body. Then this is thy Imperfection, Thou relatest to some other that Thou mayst be more Perfect. Being ordained to some Higher End; with out which Thou art imperfect. Much more imperfect is the Humanity of our Saviour, without its union to the Deitie. Their unity being from all Eternity ordained for some Higher End, which without their Individual Relation to each other Could never be attained.

95

The End for which our Saviour v as ordained of God to relate to the
Second Person in the Trinity is I'lain and Evident. God and Man
become one in Person that God and Man might be one in covenant.
The Humanity of our Saviour is a Perfect nature, not a Person, becaus
it relateth to the Deity. The soul of Man is a Perfect Nature, not a
person, becaus it relateth to its Earthl[y] Body. And if by reason of that
relation it be imperfect, that impe[r]fection is wholy founded upon
the will of God. But why shoul[d] the soul be made so to relate to the
Body? For what Soveraign End could that be ordained. certainly it is
far more Difficult to tell then why our Saviour relateth to his
GodHead. Separat Souls are Single Angels, relateing in Heaven to
Earthly Bodies, Able to Enjoy the celestial world, to see and Delight in
Spiritual Things as Angels do: to Lov the Divine Essence and to reign
in communion with God as do the Holy Cherubims. Why then should
they Pertaine unto Bodies, being So Divine and Perfect Beings, why
not made Single as the Angels are! why not absolute and Eternaly
separat? Surely for Some High and Lofty End. If not Equal to that for
which Jesus christ became a Man, yet like unto it, and the End of it. He
came that we might be restored to that End for which we were made:
to relate to Bodies. which was that there might [be] room and Place
among invisible Things for Material creatures, use and Benefit in a
Material world. It was Impossible that Heaven and Earth Should be
created did not our Souls relate to Bodies. were it not for us no Sun, no
Sea, no Star, no day, would in the Kingdom of God have either Place
or Being. Where no eye is, no Light is needfull. where no breath, no
Air, where no visible Body, no Dominion over Fowles and Fish and
Beasts. where no soul informing Such a Body, no such Body can at all
be usefull. To the Intent Therefore all the Glory of Divine Wisdom
Goodness and Power Seen and Exprest in visible Things, might be
commodious in all our Eys, our Souls were made to relate to Bodies,
That for the Benefits they receive even by there Bodies, in all the
Glories of the visible Heavens, they might returne the Sacrifices of
Prais and Thanksgiving, which no Bodie without a Soul is able to
Return. Man being thus made the Soveraign End of all visible and
Invisible Things. the centre of union wherein all the Fulness of
Godhead closeth. meet with the Angels to Enjoy By his Soul the

Eternity of God, with all the Invisible Treasures of his spiritual kingdom, and by his Body meet to Enjoy all the Materials of the created world. He Being the head of all the Creatures.

96

We no where read of men ministering to the Holy Angels: but we often read of Holy Angels Ministering to men. which were we not Blind and Seared Devils might make us understand. man is in this Glorious world Environed with Delights and Spiritual Exaltations, Ineffable Joys and celestial Treasures. But is in the midst of all a filthy Peece of Insensat Dirt, a careless Stupid and Repining Devil. Yea worse then they. not a Grave or a Dead carcase, but a Hell unto Himselfe. O then what sences ought we to Awaken, what Thunder to speak unto our Selves, what charmes to use, what strong Endeavors to A waken our Souls and a rise from the Dead, that we might Loath our Abominations, Lethergies, selves and begin to see with God our Treasures! O what veneration Joy Thanksgivings ought we to use. What Angels wings to Aspire after, that we may Escape the Lethargy Sloth and Dulness under which we are Accursed Dead and Buried!

97

When we hear or read of the Hypostatical union; Divine Lov, or the Passion of our Lord: These objects appeare as Divers, as the Eys are several, that behold the Same. The Things are open and obvious to all: but the Right Apprehension of them Inaccessible. To Some Eys they Seem False, to some Dubious and uncertain, to others Dim and to others Light and of Little value. To all the world distant and Sublime: to the most of all, Cold and unEffectual. onely to the wise and holy they appear what they ought. to me they appear infinitly Less, weaker and Inferior then what they are. others see them as things a far off, out of their Houses and concerns. I see them in my house my infinit Concern. Singly and Soly Pertaining to me, True, Real, near, certain, Infallible. I See them also as my joys Invaluable, Divine, and celestial. But O that I could see them with a Sad yet Great and Serious Eye, fain would I have a Stable, Sound, and venerable Esteem, a Profound and Reverend Apprehension of them, as they are indeed infinitly Deep

True and Serious. Is not His Blood Deep and Serious! are his Agonies Sighs and wounds Things to [be] Jested at! O the Deep and Dreadfull Abyss of his Humiliation! Let me my God see the Serious Profoundness of thine Eternal care, and while I Lament my Levity, Let me attain that fixed and Heavenly frame that may keep my Heart Close unto thee. O make [me] weighty in all my Deeds! and Let me be as Serious in enjoying my Treasures, as Jesus christ was in Redeeming Sinners! It is my tedious Shame that I am not Answerable to the Powerfull Bloodiness of his most Serious Passion.

98

O my God shall all the Things in Heaven and Earth be my Daily Treasures, and shall I be so much beloved of thee, and Shall I not Live as a son of God? O no more Shall Little Things take up my Life! Why Should Parlors and Jewels, Rents and clothes and monies, words and Injuries So Engage my Soul. Let the creation of the world and the Redemption of men, the Hypostatical union, and the Day of Judgment, the Laws of God and the Glory of His Lov, the Abundance of the Sea be converted unto me, and Eternal Joys in the Kingdom of Heaven be my Real weighty and [sub]Stantial Treasures. We are all undon by despiseing Great ones, and Regarding Little Things.

99

My Growth is Strange! at first, I onely knew
The Gates and streets mine Infancy did veiw
In those first walls. But Thence my nimble Ey
In Speedy Sort did to the mountaines flie
Command the feilds and make the Eden Mine
Which round about these Citty wals did shine,
Then other Citties at a Distance found
In unexpected Sort my Powers Crownd.
Then Seas, and Lands that were beyond the seas
New Kingdoms Distant did my spirit Pleas
Yea all the nations of the Peopled Earth
Became my joy my Melodie and mirth
My Light my wealth, The Skies those Higher Things

The Sun the Stars the Holy Angels Wings
All These Adornd at once my Heavenly sphere
And round about me did my Joys appear.
Can any more then these my Riches be!
Can any more Adorne Infinitly!
yes other Worlds! whose Ages stord with Joys
Kings sages Queens, new Hosts of Girls and Boys
That Standing in Misterious Sort behind
Each other, ravish and Delight the mind,
Nor ceas I yet, but in each Spirit See
All These, the world, my God, again to be
As in a sphere of Light, And these as mine
In every soul with new Delight did shine.
At this I stopt; and Thought no other Store
Could move my Soul his Glory to Adore
But when I these at once began to see
In every Soul more Plesant far to be
Then in them selves, Lands Ages Kingdoms there
More Rich more Bright more Glorious to appear
Being clad in thoughts, I scarsly could beleive
The Splendor of the wealth my God did give
A Greatness then my soul did seeme to gaine
That wholy was Divine and did remaine
Inlayd with Depths of Pleasure and Delight
That made the Greatness much more Infinit.

100

Holy Father Almighty and Everlasting God whose power is infinit
in creating all Things, and care most Great and Divine in upholding
them: O Magnifie thine Almighty Power, and Glorify thine Eternal
Love, by Doing for me as Thou Didst for Jesus christ when thou Didst
rais him from the Dead, and Seat Him at thine own Right Hand in the
Heavenly Places. creat in my soul a Life AnSwerable to all thy works!
Fill me with a Divine and Holy Sence, That I may be made Possessor
of thy Heavenly Treasures, Give me Continuall and Repeated
Meditations, Livly Praises and Powerfull Thanksgivings every Day. O
my God, I know I ask as Elisha did a hard thing, Yea much Harder

then the creation of worlds. For as much as Thou hadst rather make many worlds, then be Enforced to creat Apprehension in an unwilling soul: or to infuse affections into a careless Spirit. Not onely becaus it is always unwelcom to Thee to compel a free Agent, but becaus also Thoughts and affections are more Excellent Things then Material objects, and the fruits which thou requirest us to return for thy manyfold Blessings. Those Thou hast given us a Power to creat Like thee, that with the most Precious we might Delight and Pleas Thee. O work in me, for I Loath my Selfe, and confess I am a Rebel. my Heart is Rotten, and Daily Backsliding. But yet well as I can I offer it up unto Thee. O take it, and hear my Cry. creat in me a clean heart O Lord, and renew a Right Spirit within me! Give me those Sences Thoughts and Apprehensions which I pray for, for they are mine in Desire, and reall Endeavor. Let them be thine O Lord by creation in me: and therein Thou wilt shew Thy selfe more mercifull then Thou wast before in creating all Things for me. Thou art infinitly mercifull in Delaying the Time that those Thoughts might be mine, by which the world is so infinitly to be Enriched: I will therefore Endeavor to improve that Golden and Blessed oppertunity, and to Treasure up in store a Good foundation against the time to come in Good works, Thoughts, Endeavors, Resolutions. Thou art infinitly mercifull, in takeing the work into thine own Hand, when at last Thou dost work in us. in any of us. For they are but a few in whom Thou So workest. For when all thy Precepts and Endeavor fail, Least all our Advantages turn into Miseries, and thy mercies into Agravations: Thou workest in us of thy Good Pleasure and Bringest us to Glory. Wherefore all the Glory of every Holy work be to Thee O Lord Forevermore.

SELECT MEDITATIONS
THE FOURTH CENTURY

1

Had God created only one Image of Himselfe, and made it to behold his Eternal Godhead in so doing He had Given it Himself. For He had Loved it infinitly, and made it a Temple of all Eternity, and Glorified his Almighty Power Wisdom and Goodness in so Highly Exalting it. Yea He had made it to Live in union and communion with Himselfe for evermore. This seemeth True at the first appearance: And that therefore God is Superlativly Wonderfull in Giving and super-adding other Treasure. But in very Deed, had God only made one Image of himselfe, and no more, He had not Given Himselfe to that Image, nor could that Image have seen his Eternity, So Adorned and Beautified as now it is; nor have Beheld his Power wisdom and Goodness in exalting it to Happiness. For the Goodness of God is infinitly infinit in this respect, that it overfloweth unto Thousands And maketh every one Happy in all those upon whom His Goodness overfloweth, and every one of those my infinit Treasures whom it maketh Happy. His wisdom is seen by communicating his Goodness to so many Millions, Yet Recollecting all that Goodness, and makeing it the Treasure of every Soul: His Power is seen in Adorning and Beautifying Ages and Kingdoms. without these Eternity would be Empty, neither His Goodness seen nor His Power Enjoyed. He Giveth His Godhead, by Doing and Living in all His Glory, and makeing us the Recipients of it. Did not God do the same Things that He doth He would not be the Same God that He is.

2

The Foundation of all mans certainty, Hope and Glory: is His compr[e]hension. To which in all my Thoughts I have continual recours, as to a Strong Tower on every occasion. For by it is He a Divine and celestial creature. It is a Rasa Tabula Prepared in Him for the Drawing afterward of all the Pictures in Gods kingdom: An inward Theatre of all His Actions: An infinit Mirror of His Divine Glory: A concealed Centre of IIis Eternal Being: yea a Temple of His omnipresence, made so visible, and Powerfull in the Soul, that when we reflect upon it, it is impossible to avoyd it. on purpose we might be sure we are Eternal Creatures. The Love of God is written in it in characters of Light, as Legible as the Sun: For wheras Two things are necessary to our Happiness, the Possession of all Treasure in Communion with God, and the Imitation of Him, in all Amiable Actions toward all objects: in neither of the Two could we be Glorious without this Power of comprehension. which as an Empty Faculty is nevertheless a cause of infinit Delight, becaus it is a Pledge and ForeEarnest of Eternal Glory. And in the Kin[g]dom of Heaven where Things are Seen in Simple Light: will appear a Gift of infinit Wonder. Even considered in it selfe becaus it relateth and Standeth in order to all Enjoym[e]nts. The Infusion of it was an Effect of Infinit Lov, and the Possession of it maketh us infinit Creatures.

3

This Endless Comprehension of my Immortal Soul when I first saw it, so wholy Ravished and Transported my spirit, that for a fortnight after I could Scarsly Think or speak or write of any other Thing. But Like a man Doteing with Delight and Extasie, Talk of it Night and Day as if all the Joy of Heaven and Earth were Shut up in it. For in very Deed there I saw the Divine Image Relucent and shining, There I saw the foundation of mans Excellency, and that which made Him a Son of God. Nor ever shall I be able to forget its Glory. I can comprehend in my understanding the Magnitude of a Room, the wideness of the Hemisphere, and spaces Extant a bove the stars. The Heaven of Heavens are not able to contain me. For my Soul exceedeth all Limitations. It is so Like God Almighty, that it comprehendeth the Heavens as the Dust of a Ballance, Spanneth the world, seeth all Ages as one Day, Surmounteth the Heavens and Searcheth further. What Spaces are beyond the Heavens! which wheather Full or Empty, are Limited or Endless. If Full and Limited, there are spaces Empty beyond those, and spaces still beyond those. Nor is it Possible there should be any End of space, beyond which there will not still and evermore be space. so that I can Plainly see infinit Space, and am a creature Able to Enjoy Infinity. And if infinit Space then all the Treasure contained In them. For it Is as Easy to see the Things in a Cabinet as the Empty Cabinet: and every Thing contained in every Poynt of Space, as the point of Space in it Selfe Empty. This is my Joy, that in evry point of Space God wholy is, and wholy there by me to be Enjoyed. Being as infinitly Rich in working as in Essence. This Infinit space is a Thing So intimately known to the soul, that tis Impossible to remove it. It prevents the Information of all sence: and Endureth for Ever. It is the onely Primum, et necessario Cognitum in rerum natura. It is Impossible so much as once to unsuppose it. we may annihilate the Heavens and the Earth and suppose them gon. But the Space will remain behind, wherein they stood, and will be as necessarily seen, as the soul is, or as the Power of seeing it. Nor will it endure a Limitation, but as necessarily appear beyond all Extreames as appear at all.

4

Becaus God wholy is in every Moment, therefore all Eternity may be wholy Seen in every moment. And the very Reason why God is wholy every where, in every part and moment of time, is because his whole Eternity is at once Existent, and therefore obvious to every part and moment of Time. Since therefore His whole Eternity is at once Existent, All its Futurities and Præteritions are Existent in it, objected round about me, Present to my Ey, and fit to be Enjoyed. It Proceeding from the Perfection of the Nature of God that I am made his Son and united to Him. This very Thing is the Divine Light that Shews me to be his Bride, that maketh me his Image, Advanceth me to his Throne, giveth me Ability to Inherit all Things, maketh me his freind, enableth me to Live in communion with Him. All these being Links Depending upon the same chain, and streams issuing from this first Spring of our comprehension. In being able to see Infin[i]ty and Eternity we are the Divine Image, for by that we are Like God. in being So we are made his Sons, we are made his Heirs. every Son is his Fathers Image, and being Heirs shall Inherit all Things. Inheriting all Things Sit in his Throne, Raign as Kings, be Amiable as Brides, Live in communion with Him as freinds. Rejoyce as men, offer up the Sacrifice of Praise as Preists, Obey as Subjects, and do that which Himselfe Commandeth, Enjoy Him and all the Things in Heaven and Earth. O the Admired unity of Things So Different. Swavity and Delight is my Portion for ever! The Lines are faln out unto me in Pleasant Places, yea I have a Goodly Heritage.

5

God being Infinity Wholy Every Where, all Extreames fall in a Point, an infinit Contradiction in Materiall Things, but Surmounted in Him, whose Essence is Transcendent to all Imaginations. Infinity being wholy every where, is wholy present in the Soul of man. How can He be Desolate that may Confer with Infinity? Infinity being present in the Soul of man causeth the Extreame[s] of an Infinit Line to be there togeather both to Lye hid in the Same centre. And at once to be seen in the Inward mind. This is the Reason why a soul can see the East and west in the same moment. And the Thoughts So Swiftly flie in an Instant to objects infinitly from each other, but all in the soul, and to that Equaly present. But oh my Soul! Thou lover of Propriety, They are all within Thee. Present, and within Thee! How real then may be thy joys! All objects are Equaly nigh, being at once present in the soul of man. It is but to fix an Intention of the mind upon any of them, as they are lying there, and it is Exhibited to us. To Extend a Thought to such an object, and to Shine upon it with a Ray of affection, and it appeareth in us. Thoughts therefore Travill not abroad, nor make they Journeys infinit within. But with an Instant Intuition are imediatly present in their own Centre, with any object or Treasure there. Can behold there centre, it Being Indivisible, and therefore all Things in the same moment.

6

Over the Gate of Apollos oracle there was this Inscription. Know thy Selfe. As if by that alone we were Directed to the Treasuries of all understanding, to the Abisses and Depths of wisdom and Knowledge. For He that Knows the Powers of the Soul, Shall See Himselfe an infinit Creature. He that Knows their Extent number and value, Shall see Himselfe ordained to be a king, a king of Glory Attend[ed] with state, served with majesty, Possessor of Heaven and Earth, A Temple of Heaven, a Divine Receptacle of the Eternal Diety, a Temple more Heavenly then Heaven is, in all Things the Image and Seal of God. For as a Sealing Seal, and a Seal Sealed has the Same Liniaments cuts and Figures, so hath He the Similitude of all the Divine Attributes, in the most Sublime and Illustrious manner. Infinity, Life, understanding, Power, with whatso ever else in hope or capacity. nor will there ever be found one Attribute in God, but it will imediatly appear in the Soul of man, if the Soul be Seen in a clear Light. By which man is made to be unto God, what God is: a God, unto God, and all His creatures.

7

The Inclination of Love is ever infinit. It is its very Nature to Adore and Deifie its objects. God is to be Adored, as the Fountain of all Goodness, the President of our Joys, and the Author of our Glory, because he a lone hath Prepared all obligations Treasures and Rewards, is the onely Light and Support of our Being. But How God should Deifie us is an Infinit Question. An Infinit Question must have an Infinit Answer, for none other can solve it. He Deifieth us in makeing us the End of all His Doings. How much he Loveth us we may see by his Dying for us. O God! Shall we be for ever Blind? He that Abandon'd Himselfe to Death for us, in this Dark and Injurious world, is not Beleived to have Loved us Infinitly. Whom did He intend in makeing Heaven and Earth? Whose Happiness did He Purpose in creating Angels! What Benefit Could He Gain in makeing Men? To what use can an Eternal Spirit Put Gold and Silver and Pearl and wine and oyl? All these are the Treasure of his Goodness which intendeth us. We are the Magnified objects of his Soul. He Abandond Himselfe from all Eternity to our Happiness as much as He did for Dying for us. Is not his nature Love, His Measure Infinit? we are the Kings that Reign in his Bosom. We the Bride whom He Designeth to Please and Delight, we the End to which He referreth and Disposeth all Things. That His nature is so Perfect that while He doth this, Himselfe becometh the End of all Things, He most Pleaseth and Delighteth Himselfe, Doth Satisfie His own Desires, Glorifieth

Himselfe, and Gaineth Treasure. Is the wonderfull Perfection of the Divine Essence, whose Love to Himselfe and us are one. But us He setteth on his Right Hand: and in Loving us satisfieth and Delighteth HimSelfe most.

8

I wonder Greatly as I walk in the Light of his Holy Kingdom, that any Divines Dwelling there, Should think any of his Attributes incommunicable. Surely they forget that His will is Infinit. Is He not Infinitly communicativ. Is He not the more Good the more He is communicativ. It is the Glory of His Infinity that it is Infinitly Helpfull; Infinitly usefull; infinitly Delightfull. Two ways there are whereby He doth commun[i]cat His Incommunicable Attributes, His Infinity, His Eternity, His Almighty Power, his Soveraignty, &c. first by expressing them to Sight, and makeing them objects of our Enjoyment. Secondly by obliging us more to Lov Him then our very selves. the natural consequent of which is, to Delight in them more for being his, then for being ours. It being Impossible that they should be made ours, but they must be made more, more then ours by obliging us more to Lov their Possessor. He made His Infinity and Eternity ours by Employing both for our Advantage, His Soveraignty and Power, because it Pleased Him to use those in Exalting us to his Throne. But all these He implanted in us by being what He is, Love alone. By making us what we are, By Lov alone. Can there be any thing in Lov which it will not Dedicat to anothers Service! can infinit Lov Detain any Thing? I admire at this, that even the Stewards of His Kingdom Should not understand the Treasures they Dispence. And abhor our Darkness, who are soe far revolted from the Divine Image, that we [do] not even beleive its Perfections, when they are told us.

9

By making us to Lov, God hath made us the Best of all Possible beings, for the Best of all Possible Ends. Divine and Perfect Possessors of all His Glories. All Things are ours of Necessity that are His, and more then so. The very way is infinit as well as the Treasure. Can we See Infinity and Shall our Sight be Less: Lov can Extend its Beams through Eternity, and touch an object as imediatly near, that Seemeth Situated at an Infinit Distance. But O my Soul, when it hath once fixed its Thoughts upon it, it is Present with it: my Body is here, but my Love is preSent with my Joy and my Bride beyond the Seas. It is with God in Eden, it Delighteth In I Ilui I'iom everlactiny, liwlu ih lr Ih it Solfo Beloved from all Eternity, Extendeth and rejoyceth that God is with the Last and is with Him there. It is the Absolute Soveraign of Heaven and Earth: becaus it rejoyceth to See God Exhibit his Goodness wisdom and Power so Blessedly and Gloriously to all the world. By all His Proceedings is Infinitly Gratified Satisfied and Delighted. For while God satisfieth infinit Love, He satisfieth Lov in Him and us. O my God, Thou hast given us the Similitude of Thine Incommunicable Attributes.

10

There is nothing to be wished in all Eternity. every thing is So Perfect, that he hath done for us, more then we can Ask or think. It is better with us then if we had been from all Eternity. we have Such a world and such a kingdom that nothing can be desired. Calamities may be Improved. there is not a Supposition, but is actualy Exceeded, nor an Inclination, in the Soul of man, that is not infinitly Satisfied. Covetousness, Ambition, Lov of Propriety, Curiosity, Liberality, evry thing is Satisfied. Yea Tho contradiction Seem to meet in the Satisfaction. Covetousness is satisfied in the fulness of Treasure. Ambition, of Glory. The Love of Propriety whereby we desire to Draw all Riches to our Selves, is Delighted in our being made the End of all Things. Liberality in the mean time wherby we Desire to Communicat all, be pleased in the Communication of infinit Treasures to every Soul, of which we are the End, yet every one is the End. Why we are so: And we the End, to which their being So, is a gain referred. in the contemplation of such Things is our curiosity Pleasd, Repugnancies and mixtures of Impossibility and Beauty feeding that with infinit Surprizes. In every Soul we are again Enjoyed. In every Soul are Supreme and Soveraign. by Lov alone are made the soveraigns of Heaven and Earth, In every Person anew againe Inherit all Things.

11

Having Prepared in us an Interminable Sphere Like an infinit Temple remaining Empty, He would that we Should fill it with infinit Treasure: and gave us a Power to Enrich it with Thoughts as infinitly Excellent, as the Sphere was wide. There is not the Possibility of one Desire wherein his Bounty hath not Prevented us, having don more for us then we could find out How to Imagine. our curiosity could be Tickled with the Desire and Hope of making worlds. And would this pleas us? He hath Enabled us to make Delicat worlds as Great as these and infinitly Better. worlds in vive, and Spirituall worlds, worlds in thoughts, and Thoughts in worlds, or which is very comprehensiv, A WORLD of THOUGHTS. concerning whose Hidden Excellency the Eagle Ey hath not been conscious: nor his that seeth with no other Ey then Flesh. Till the Inward man begin to Appear a Real Selfe, Intelligable objects will seem Impertinent, weak chimeras. But they are as Real, as visible ones, and Truly more Excellent. Thoughts therefore are very fit to be understood, As being the very Real Thing for which the world was made. the onely meanes whereby we Enjoy felicity, more Immediatly nigh to the Divine Essence, more Dear to his will. the Soul Exprest, the Rule and fountain of all our Actions. The Light of Eternity, The Liveing Exemplar and Types of Things, the ornaments of the wise, and the onely Treasures of the Divine and Blessed.

12

Thoughts Penetrat the Soul Like Lightening, and are the onely Things that touch and Affect it, thoughts are the Life of the Inward man, and the onely Soul in every Action, The Rancor of a crime, or the Inward Beauty of an Holy Deed. without which all works are Empty carcases. one Broken Sigh, or contrite Groan is of more worth in the sight of God, then the seas and skies and all the Dead Materials of 10000 worlds. Thoughts constitut the cream of all Things, the very Flower Prime, and Top of Beings. Prayses, Thanksgivings, Pleasures, Joys and Triumphs, Hosannas and Delights, all Sweet and Amiable Resentments, Honours affections, with what Soever else that relates to the Intelligable world, Thoughts are either the Substance, or the Color of it. Since therefore For my Single Persons Sake, Thoughts Seated either in me or others are So Precious, that without them all the world would be a Dead and Desert wilderness, either without those by which I enjoy it, or without those that are Payd unto me: Thoughts are to God So rich and Precious for my Sake; and to me for every ones. The world is a thing of infinit value as it Proceeds from Him, but in returning to Him can be of none but by our Thoughts. As it obligeth us for his wisdome to Lov Him, for His Power to Admire Him, for His Goodness to Adore Him, it is an Incomparable Treasure. But never Effectuall, Till received by our Thoughts and Exprest within, nor at all Profitable, till it is so understood, as to be enjoy'd, and to be come the Ground of infinit Thankgivings.

13

God Hath don more for us then we could find out How to Imagine. All the world is in his Infinity, and His Infinity within us. yet hath He made the Soul Empty, as if there were noe Such Infinity within us, no such world, no God, no Being. nay not a Soul till we meditate upon it, to the Intent it might have a Power to Creat these Things and Seat them in it Selfe, as God did by Thinking creat all in Himselfe. They are there but are not seen till the understanding Shine upon them. That we can So Sudainly make and abolish Thoughts hath been an Argument hitherto and a ground of Contempt. But in it Selfe Sheweth the Exceedingness of our Power and Glory. for the Best and Highest things are Easy to us. The Angels that fell miscaried in a Thought. what therefore doth their volubility Shew, But that being infinitly Bound to the Eternal majesty, who infinitly desireth our Thoughts Should be alwayes Holy, we have infinit Libertie given us to Shew infinit Lov by infinit care. In which we are bound instantly to persist night and Day. To Erre in a moment is an infinit Crime, Apostasie, Damnation. But to be Amiable in all our Thoughts, is to be Divine and Glorious, in a Measure Transcendent to all Imagination.

14

God hath Glorified his wisdom and Power, by giving them to us. And hath given them to us in giving us a Power, to Produce Things into Being that altogeather Please Him as much a[s] those which he hath created. O the Jubilee! O the Care! O the Salvation Joy and Satisfaction that hence ariseth. I will Sacrifice my Selfe O my God unto Thee; And enrich Eternity with Holy Thoughts, Heavenly Joys, and Living Treasures. I will admire thy Goodness which by Giving all Things Prepareth a Power of Receiving more. And renouncing the world, Dedicate my Selfe to Liv in thy Bosom, where a lone I am Beloved, Exalted and magnified in an Infinit manner. From Thee to Thee, I came and Proceed in the Best of manners.

15

O Sing, O Soar, O faint, O pant and Breath!
O saint Rejoyce! O Lov Him here beneath.
Here Heaven is could we but See
Here, Gold! here Soveraignty!
All Thine!
For Thee my soul, for thee I shine.
O ye Eternal freinds they all are mine.

18

Here [an] Aphorism and there a Song: here a suplication and there a Thanksgiving. Thus do we bespangle our way to Heaven. Admiring that felicity should wean us from the world, Fill us with Grandure, Ravish us with complacency. make us to live in Communion with God, Exalt us to his Throne, Humble us for our Sins. Sweeten our Retirments, Season our Mirth, Sanctifie our Joys, fill our Lips with Prayses and Thanksgivings, Lie in the closset, appear in the church, strive in the world, make us a Treasure to the Sons of men. Calcine Evils, Enrich our Redemption, Enflame our Love, Animat our Studies, Quicken our Endeavors, Strenghthen us against temptation, and carry us above the fear of poverty. It doth all for it is the Queen of Heaven.

19

Felicity doth open controversies, and vanquisheth Devils.

20

What Shall I render unto Thee O God for my felicity. wherwith Shall I come before the Lord, and bow my selfe before the most High God? Shall I come before him with offrings, with calves of a year old? will the Lord be Pleased with Thousands of Rams, or tens of Thousands of Rivers of oyl: Shall I give my first born for my Tran[s]gression, the Fruit of my body for the Sin of my Soul? He hath Shewed Thee O man what is Good: And what doth the Lord require of Thee, but to do justly, and to Lov mercy, and to walk Humbly with Thy God? O Shew the Glory of thy Kingdom to thy Holy Catholique church. Let all thy Saints Bless Thee from Day to Day and Speak of Thy wonderous works. Let me Speak of the Glory of Thine Excellent Kingdom, and tell of thy Greatness. O Let Thy People in their Citties and villages See Thy Majesty. Let me Praise Thee night and Day O my God for ever and ever.

21

Vertue of old hath been counted So Generous and noble a Thing, that it hath not onely made men Gentlemen, But Gods too in the Account of the Heathen. This Reason Tully gives why Hercules and Æsculapias were reputed Gods, becaus while they lived they [were] Excellent and usefull men. How therefore may a man become Excellent and usefull while He Liveth? certainly by Meditating the welfare of all, by Endeavouring Daylie to heal mens Souls, by Adorning Himself with all kind of vertues, by Delighting alwayes in Doing Good, by Adorning God with continuall Praises and Daylie Thanksgiveings, By exposeing Himselfe to Dangers for orphans and widdows, by Suppressing the Lustre and violencies of Men, by Shewing all Examples of Justice Prudence Temperance and courage, By Expending his Estate for other mens Benefit, by Shining Brightly in His Possession of the world, by reducing men from the Paths of and wayes of misery and Endeavouring to bring them to Truth and Glory.

22

Knowledg is a rare Accomplishment, and they who undervalue it betray their want of it. For it hath no Enemy but Ignorance. Yet is it not a Star of the first magnitude nor the one Thing needfull. It hath many times the Honor to be as Saint John Baptist was to our Saviour, a P[r]æcursor to Goodness. Yet we must Say as He Did, That which comes after is Preferred before it. Grace and vertue must Carry us to Heaven. These are the fruites which in the Light of Knowledge must Grow upon the Ground of Gods Blessings. There is Somthing So Amiable in the nature of virtues, that they Please God more then the works of His own Hands; Are more necesSary, and more Imediatly near to our Eternal Happiness. Bare Knowledge gives no man a Title to Heavenly Joys: It is the Light onely in which they are Enjoyed. He that when He Seeth the Glory of God and of Heaven and Earth, Angels and men, would Enjoy the Same, must according to the Light of that Knowledge in which He Seeth, be Transformed into Goodness, and become the Similitude of God Almighty in His Thoughts Wayes and works and Perfections. For Goodness is the End which by Knowledge is attained. Goodness is the Object in which Knowledge Delighteth, Good is the Thing that maketh a man as God unto all. Heavenly Goodness Sublime and miraculous! for out of nothing we are created to be an Infinit Sphere of Delights and Pleasures, Fruits and Beauties, Delectable Things, feasts and Treasures to Angels and Men throughout all Kingdoms and Ages. which till we truly are we can never Enjoy them, for we Enjoy them most by being Delighted in. Goodness is the meanes whereby we Enrich and Enjoy all Things.

23

O The Beauty of truth: How Infinit the Amiableness of vertue: O How Excellent! vertue in truth is so Fathomlessly Good, that nothing more Discovers the Apostasie of mankind, then their Blind Defective, Dark Apprehensions of its Glorious Intrinsick Invisible Riches. every Body has a Soul to Save and therefore obliged to understand the way that Leads to that Salvation, and more then so, to walk in it: every Body has a world to Enjoy Enrich and Benefit, a Life to Beautifie; a God to Please, a neighbour to Advance, an Estate to preserve, a Body to regard, a Felicitie to Attain. And all these by Living vertuously are Atcheived. By this alone is Religion Actuated Exprest and Promoted. Oppression   Banished,   Rancor   sweetned,   wars   Annihilated,

Covetousness Abolished, Envy rooted out, Heathens Converted, Ath[e]ists convinced, the Angels pleased, and God Glorified. Oh How Great must that be, upon which the welfare of the world Dependeth! the Delights of Ages! the ornaments of Time! the Treasures of Eternity! the Glory of the Soul! the Answer of obligations! the fruition of Rewards! the fullfilling of Laws! the Perfection of the mind! the satisfaction of God in all his Designs, and the Pleasing of our Saviour, in the End of our Redemption! To Do all this is Put into our Hands. Now judge wheather Divine Lov hath not Deified us, and made us a God to God Almighty.

24

O Lord what an innumerable Abundance hast thou provided for thy Servants! I am Amazed at the Multitude of thy tender mercys, and confounded in my Selfe at the Infinity of thy Blessings and Transcendent Excellency of thy Treasures. The Heavens and the Earth and the Seas and all that is theirin; the Interior Beauties, Ample Regions and Sacred Riches of all Kind of vertues Practiced by men, the Examples and affections of all thy Servants, The Powers and faculties of our Immortall Souls; the Perfections of thy Blessedness and the Attributes of thine Essence: all these are Treasures of thy Bounty unto me. O Empower me a Son of God to be Possessor of them. And So to order my conversation aright that every thought and Action of my Life, may be a Substantial Prais returned unto Thee. By useing the faculties of my Soul aright let me receive and Admire and Love Thee for all these, Admire these for thy Sake and Thee for them; become a Blessing to the Sons of men in all my wayes; and by these attain that Strenght, which is Proportionable and Answerable to So great foundations. Thy ways in all Ages, The Solemnity and Triumphs and Thankesgivings of Kingdoms, The Saboths and Festivals and ordinances of thy church, these are Happy Delights, Glorious Treasures, Divine Ayds, Celestiall Benefits. O that I could Liv and walk a-mong them with a perpetual Sence! Brightly Shine in all their abundance, and Glorifie Thee the Giver of them. The Trees of Eden and the flowers there are Poverty to these. O Let me understand my joys and make [me] great enough to Possess thy Treasures.

25

The wideness of understanding must be Conversant among its fellows or else felicity Cannot be enjoyed. Tho we know things never So well we must actualy feel and Delight in their Goodness, or else they will be Lost. Strength and Brightness in the understanding, Life and Diligence in the Thoughts and Apprehensions, an Ardent Zeal and vigor in the affections must be always ready awake and Permanent, or else felicity cannot be enjoyed. O for a presence of Soul among Great Things! O for a Divine spirit Delighting ever to be enjoyed! O for a Quick and Peircing eye to see the Excellencyes in every Being! and a Faithfull Heart to render all their Due Esteeme! O For a sensible and Seraphick soul! It is the Excellency of a Nature that maketh it able so to Enjoy. The Satisfaction of Goodness being the Strongest Delight. It makes the very world a Heaven, to Consider how God hath disposed All Things. O for an Enflamed Heart to Lov Him, a constant spirit to cleav to Him, an Intuitiv Ey to see Him, an Humble Soul to Adore Him, a living Spirit, to feel His Presence, an Infinit Comprehension to receiv Him, An Angelical Life and mind to Imitate Him, An Elevated Being to Delight in him! His Nature is So Excellent that He enjoys all the Things in Heaven and Earth: and Himselfe alsoe, becaus He is Perfect Goodness and Delighteth in the Happieness of other Persons. The Benefit of which is, that He becomes the Treasure and the Joy of all, and therein most of all to HimSelfe a Treasure In all Ages, in Heaven and Earth infinitly Wide Rich and Glorious.

26

All Things are Treasures to God Almighty by their being So to us. Whose Lov is His Blessedness: Infinitly Perfect on every Side. For it is the work of Delight, The TreaSure of Angels, the Joy of men, the object of Glory Beneficial to God Himselfe, the enjoyment of His works, the way of Happiness, and the Enjoyment of ours, The Soul of His Gifts, the Delight of our soul, His Compleat sati[s]faction; who Delights to be enjoyed, and to see us Happy, to communicat Himselfe and to be ever Praised. From all Eternity He Possessed all Things: and Loves that we should See Him in His Possession. Becaus He is infinitly

Amiable, and Lov is the Light wherein His Attributes and Powers
Shine. Loving that we Should See Him, from all Eternity He saw us
see Him, who were in Eternity when we were out of it. He has a venerable and Glorious Nature, which maks these Things possible which
were impossible to ours. us in Him, with Him, and before Him, even
from all Eternity, while our selves were Nothing. And Certainly it will
Pleas us to see How Miraculously we were in Him from all Eternity,
not as if we were before these moments wherein we now Live: but
becaus these moments were before in Him without Beginning. And
we obliged and Delighted more then if we had been from Everlasting.
having an Ey also to See it So.

27

Infinit Joys in respect of wideness, Infinit Joys in respect of value,
Infinit Joys in respect of variety, Infinite Joys in respect of Fulness,
infinit Joys in respect of Duration, make a Soul infinitly Happy. He
that converseth with all these infinit Joys, is now in Heaven. With
which we can be present noe other way, then by thought alone.
Eternity is as near us now as ever it will be. So is the creation. the Lov
of christ and his Holy passion. A cause of Joy as any in the kingdom of
Heaven. How much then doth it Concern us to be Present with
Eternity that we might See Joys infinit in wideness; to See God in
every Being that we might see Joy infinit in value; To see all his Laws
works and wayes, Thoughts counsels Times Creatures Qualities oper-
ations &c. throughout all Eternity, that we might see Joys infinit in
variety; to see the Fulness of their uses varieties Relations Ends
Services &c. in Time and Eternitie; and to acquaint our Selves with our
Immortalitie, and our Interest in these Things, that we might see our
Immortality, and see Joys infinit in Duration, infinit in Fulness. O
Sence, what need of sence, sence to Enjoy them.

28

when we Say that all Treasures are in Gods Essence, what a
Dubious Speech do we Seem to utter? But when we say Gods Essence
is Eternity and that all Treasures are contain'd in Eternity, How Plain
and clear! Eternity is the Key, and the Divine Light of his Heavenly

Kingdom. Which being it Selfe well understood maketh us beside to understand all Things. O what Advantagious and Heavenly Things are clear Apprehensions! Distinctiv Thoughts and Bright Ideas, are the very soul of Heaven and face of Things, which no man can Enjoy in confused clouds. But if Treasures be in Gods Essence and Gods Essence be Eternity: then we are all in Gods Essence; and as soon as we Begin to Walk in Eternity may See how we were there from all Eternity or Everlasting, for we are there in all our modifications. So Long time without a Beginning, at such a Time Existing, Endureing for Ever. which very Thought disgested will Transform the world and make it Heaven. Being therefore contained in So Sacred a Repositorie as God[s] Bosom, How Carefull ought we to be of all our Actions that we defile not our Selves! for from all Eternity we were what we are, infinitly free to Act and doe, and tho we were, truly Shall be, doing either Good or Evil. For Those Goods and Evils which we do are in their moments there, but we in those moments the Authors of them, who might have done otherwise if our Selves would. The nothing which we were from Everlasting is in Eternity. our Present Being is in Eternity, our Estate that Shall be is in Eternity. In Reference to us there is a Past Present and to come; but in reference to Eternity all is Present.

29

God is Happy in Himselfe, and Happy in us. Happy in Eternity, Happy in Time, Happy in Heaven, Happy in Earth, and So Shall we. Happy in the creation, in the Redemption, in the day of Judgment, and soe Shall we. Happy in His works, Happy in his Laws, Happy in His wayes, Happy in his counsels, Happy in the Glory of his Eternal Kingdom; and so Shall we. who must of necessity be Transformed into his Divine Image, that we may thereby becom one with Him. Since therefore in all these courts and Treasures of Eternity our Happiness is found, we ought to Apply our Thought and mind of these Things. For these are those the Apostle Speaks of, when he Saith if ye then be risen with Christ Place your Affections upon those Things that are above. Above the Thoughts ways and Expectations of common men. Abov their Pleasures, above their Treasure, in value, Greatnes, Beauty, Duration, Truth, Sweetness, certainty, &c.

30

The Sun is a creature 1000 times more Glorious to the understanding then to the Ey. How Sweet and Amiable are the Seasons of the year: How Precious the Drops of rain which He bringeth out of his Treasuries? How Glorious and delightfull is it to see People in the Harvest Gathering in the Earth: But then all these must be Seen in their Circumstances. For else Like a Temple Stark naked to a Beast, they will be dead carcase Devoid of ornaments. mans Original and Rise from God, His Progress and Rest in God, Eternity about the world and the Glory about Him, the ministery of the Stars and His Dominion over the works of God must all be Seen, With the Invisible delights of Ages, Else the Harvest cannot be Esteemed. What makes the Ground where Troy stood So venerable, but the Remembrance of Priamus and its Ancient Glory? Its Light and Beauty in the Times of peace, Its wars and Towers, far more Adorn it Tho all Absent, then its Present Ruines. They are Absent from the Ey, Present to the understanding.

31

Gods Invincible and Eternal ways are Sublime profitable and infinit, but So high no Angels wing can Soar unto them. they will make a mans Soul faint and Sweat in endeavoring to comprehend them. But when they are Attained they are infinitly Rich and Amiable within, as well as infinitly Great and Sublime and Wide. Som of the Highest and most universal are Such as man would think Impossible, yet Such as that in them his infinit Goodness Wisdom and Power are Infinitly Magnified: our Happiness in them infinitly concernd, His Glory and our Happiness by them attained. What are they! you would fain Know. But will you not contemn them? As soon as you hear them you think you Should have known them from all Eternity, yet could no more find them then the Bottom of the Sea; or centre of the Earth. They were onely open before his Eys, before whose Face Hell is naked. but He revealed them to the Angels and to the Sons of men, becaus His Almighty Power was wholy uttered in Atcheiving them, and they are infinitly Glorious. And some are these.

1. He giveth unto one all Things, wholy to be enjoyd

2. He giveth one Thing to all, by each wholy to be enjoyed

3. He maketh the Enjoyers to enrich the Enjoyment.

These Three have an infinit Influence upon all the Things in Heaven and Earth, Enrich the Angels, Amaze the cherubims, are the Song of both, And them Selves Treasures to the Sons of men. but Forgotten by the Fall, when we were all Astonied, and ever Since either held in Ignorance, or Despised being Known.

32

Other ways Dependent upon these and exceeding curious are

1. That every man Should be obliged infinitly.

2. That evry man should be the End of all Things

3. That evry man should be to all a Treasure.

4. That every man should be as God unto all

5. That evry man should be Blessed in all

6. That every man should be the freind of God.

7. That in evry thing there Should be an infinit Treasure

All in all conspiring and meeting There.

unto which we might adde. That every Thing might best be enjoyed in its Place: the consequence of which is infinit Complacency, the Interminable compleatness of mans Happiness, Gods giveing Himselfe wholy to evry Person, every Thing in all its Services Uses and Relations, every mans Treasure Tho ever So remote. The Beauty and Perfection of Gods Kingdom, wherein He walketh with every man Singly Solely and wholy.

33

The reason why God would make a visible world is Deep and Fathomless: Why not every Sand an Angel, a mote a cherubim? Then had there been no Sun, nor Sea, nor star. nor had those cherubims then been Happy. Excellent Beings capable of varieties Multitudes Depths of Treasures unfullfilled. The ear is a more noble Being then the Harp or Organ. yet were there no organ there would be no melodie, Angels ears hear the melodie, which Gods Goodness Wisdom and Power maketh in the visible and created world, which is the Divine organ of all Eternity. cherubims Eys are Ravished with the Beauty of his

Kingdom here. The Lips [of] Seraphims Drink in the flouds of Hony and oyl, that flow in all His Rivers here beneath: Anoynt them with Glory, Supply their Lamps, renew their Flames, and Fill them with Gladness there, onely men are gon out of his kingdom by Alienating their minds and wandering Desires.

34

The Atheist is a Prodigious miracle in this world, a walking carcase in the Land of the Living, a monstrous Lump of Darkness in the Light of Glory, a Prisoner onely to visible Things, a Beast walking in the Kingdom of Heaven. Dead to Invisible, What Demonstrations would He have of a God: or why is He Dissatisfied! Is He Dissatisfied becaus God is not Seen with Bodily Eys! God is invisible. nor is it Possible He Should be a Body nor at all convenient. For being infinit, were He a Body, there would be no Place for any Thing besides. being Invisible there is Room for all Things. But He might assume a Body. must that Body Shew his infinit Presence! Then must it fill all the Spaces of all worlds. The same Inconvenience arising a[s] before. He that would have God to be visible, Disliketh not the manner wherein He revealeth Himselfe, but the nature of God: that He is such a God as He is. He that would have God pretend a Body that He might Shew Himselfe in a visible manner would have God to Delude the world with a Shew of Glory which is not his. But he may tell us that Body is non of His, yet by that reveal His Glory. What Kind of Body wouldst thou have it to be! an infinit Bulk would exclude thee to stand and behold it. suppose it therfore a Body Like Air wherby we may Stand and See a visible Glory at a certain Distance, Which by reason of its wonderfull and Amiable Appearance Ravisheth the Beholders, that not by its Infinitness, but Glory might Convince us. This Glory could not be uniforme, for the Sun is the most Glorious for uniforme Beauty in the whol world, yet if the whole world were one sun, it would not be So Glorious as now it is. Let us Therefore suppose this Glorious Appearance, not to be a Bright uniform Splendor, but an admirable variety of Glorious objects Conspiring togeather in unconceivable manner: and composing a Thing of the Greatest Glory that visibility is capable of. When all is don this Glory being Permanent, and but a Thing seen, would at Last Grow Common, and as Little be regarded as the world is. Why therefore may not the World be made to be that Body and so Esteemed? All that we can conceive is Inferior to it, and Less Effectual to Discover a Diety.

God in Assuming the world for His Body, hath out don all that the Atheist can wish or desire. He Hath told us Plainly it is non of his, and yet it Exhibiteth Him, more then it is Possible any other should do. It offereth to our Ey not onely the Image of his Infinitness in the unsearchable Immensity of its Extent and presence: but of His Eternity in the Ages and Generations. we come into it and there is noe End we can discern of it. It was before us as if it had been from everlasting. We goe out of it and Leav it behind us. It Sheweth its Glory in the magnificence of his Beauty: His wisdom in His wonderfull order; His Goodness in His Amiable Convenience; His Lov in our Dominion of it. A Dead Bulk of Eternal matter would be an unprofitable Token of Gods Presence: an inconvenient Trifle, an unsearchable wall, and fall indeed unspeakably short of that which is. But this Sheweth his Life and Being: and in that His GodHead. A Dead carcase hath the Lineaments of a man: but Speech alone and motion Discover the Presence of a Soul. A Quiet Body (tho infinit and Eternal) would never shew the Being of a God, but the motion of the Sun, and the flowing of the streames, the vegitation of the Plants and the Life of Beasts, the Ascents of vapors, and carrying Seas into the Skies, and the falling of raign, the Alternat chang of night and Day, the moving winds, and unchangable Seasons of the Delightfull year, shew a Living and Eternal Deity ruling all, in such a manner that no Language can Speak his Glory, Thus hath God revealed Himselfe in a Body more Abundantly without, he hath done it also within

35

Had He made a Body infinit in Bulk, tho it had been from everlasting, it would have been to no Purpose, there being non to observe, or find it out. To make therefore an Infinit Sight, a creature that should see infinit Space, was to communicate Himselfe in a nother manner then it was Possible else He Should be revealed in. Thou carriest Him in Thee by a Sence and Knowledge infinitly Greater then any thing else but Himselfe Could make. An infinit Body might have been made in vain without an Observer. To make an observer the Greatest

Difficulty. A Sencless Bulk is not that to which, or by which God can reveal HimSelfe: But an inward Spirit, that Can See Eternity Tho it be no Bulk, and infinit Space tho not a Body; This is a Miracle infinit Like God, infinitly Excellent for infinit causes. For it can Admit All Things, See all Things, Enjoy all Things. Enrich all Things, Be a Blessing, Prize and be Thankfull. Return an Answer, Lov and be Active as a Freind of God. Tis impossible for any one to be a Stranger to God that knows Himselfe. And wheras Gods Essence is Such a Being that Admits all Things, and Such a Temple that Holds all and upholds them; This is such that it can be a Lord of them, a Spectator of their Beauties, and a Temple of them too. In makeing which God hath most discovered Himselfe. For He hath shewed the Profitableness of his Infinity, which being wholy here Excludeth nothing and yet Enableth an Invisible Spirit, to see Infinity it selfe and Enjoy all Things.

36

To Enlarg the Certainty whereby we beleiv that there is a God, doth Enlighten and Beautify the Soul that walks in Communion with Him. To be frequent therefore in the contemplation of his Goodness is exceeding Profitable to the Soul of man. In which the similitude of His Infinitness Goodness and Power are sublime and Endless. His Life wisdom Blessedness and Glory are there Exprest. which are all seen in the Amiable Discharge of one Duty. A Lov Answerable to all the Things in Heaven and Earth, wisdom in seeing and Knowing their Nature, Holiness in Prizing their Sacred value, Blessedness in the Possession of their infinit Treasures, Glory in appearing the Possessor of them, and in pleasing God by that Amiable Action. of all which Infinity of Comprehension is the root and Ground. For by that comes to Pass that we can behave our Selves wisely Holily and Justly towards every Being in Heaven and Earth. O that my [soul] Could always feel what it Selfe is; and Liv for ever even every moment the Life of God.

37

Wheather Angels or men are the most Glorious creatures is a needless Question, by reason of the Greatness of the Love between us. But to Quicken man by reason of His Dulness, and in order to his Gratitude very Convenient. The visible world is a wonder in Eternity, made imediately for the sons of men, not for the Angels. men have a Power to beget their Similitude, which is Greater then to creat a whole world. to beget a Lord or a king of it is Greater then to make it. The Soul is within, All that [an] Angel hath or is. the Body Superaded Shall be Like unto Jesus a Temple of God for ever more: As the Soul is Like his. And if Angels seeme to have a Higher Prerogative for that in their first Estate they were nearer unto God, man being a creature so Divine, by his Depression was Exalted: to be an object of Greater Compassion and Endearment, exposed to a more Dangerous Estate that He might be more Acceptable and welcome unto Glory. whose works also were more Delightfull, being wrought in the Shade of a weak Estate, being more nigh to God by How much He Seemed more Inferior and Remote. All which Things were wrought for the Sake of Angels, to whom God also bestowed the visible world. While they as Spectators behold His Goodness wisdom and Power manifested in it. But man is the Angel of Angels themSelves: And the onely means by which they enjoy it. for without us the world to cherubims would be unprofitable. we are the crown in whom they enjoy it. For whose Sake it was made that we might be the freinds and joy of Angels. Who Since the Treasuries of Divine wisdom and Goodness and Power are their Delights, are a Blessing to all those Heavenly Hosts, becaus the occation of these Delights. And therein more Glorious then in possessing. All because it is a Greater Blessednes to be a Blessing. more Blessed then the Angels are, for as much as to be a Blessing is Greater then to receive. With all the Things in Heaven and earth are the Angels enriched by our meanes. Abraham was the Blessing of all Ages, we of Angels.

38

O with what a Love thou Lovest me! who hast created Heaven and Earth for me, Redeemed me by the Bloud of thy Son, Purchased all mankind to be my Treasures, Advanced me by thy Holy Laws to the Throne of God, Beautified all Ages with thy ways for me, made me thy Sole and Peculiar freind, Intended me in all Things just as thy Selfe, made me Like Jesus Christ the Head and End of all Thy creatures, Given me a Nature So Excellent, that neither cherubim nor seraphim, nor any creature infinitly Higher, exceeding the Being which thy Divinity made me. In me thou hast included all Possible Infinites, and attained the utmost of all Attainables. O my God in all this Greatness which I have Borrowed of thee and in all my Glory I Fall down before I hee, and Annihilateing my Selfe Adore thy Glory

39

O my God I am abundantly Satisfied with the Fatness of [thy] Hous; Thou hast made me to drink of the Rivers of thy Pleasures. my Honor and Happieness is Greater then I can Conceive. And the multitude of the Treasures wherewith Thou hast Enriched me are innumerable and Endless. I will now Liv as a son of God in communion with Thee: And above all these Things Delight in thy Glory. Being Enabled by thy Benefits So infinitly to Lov Thee, I will Liv a bove them all, Admiring the Lov which I see in them, abov them. All Exterior works will I Performe to Please Thee: but by Delighting in thy Love will be united to Thee. Thy Lov to me Shall Dwell within me, Return againe, be Lov unto Thee, Transform my Soul, and make us one. O my Father and the Bridgroom of my Soul, all these are Treasures, and thy Palace wonderfull, but thy Person is the Joy and Happines of my Soul, which exceedeth them all. Other Persons are made Amiable by Lov. Thy Person is Lov: the Fountaine of all Beauty Amiableness and Delight. O Let me be fast united unto Thee that nothing may Divert me from Contemplating thy Lov. Let me turn a way from the Thought of clothes, Rents, Houses, monies, Injuries, with all the Inferior Little Things which engage inferior and Feeble minds, and Liv above the Doubts of all Apostates in the Actual Fruition of thy Goodness Wisdom and Power. All which Thou hast magnified in every Being in Heaven and Earth to Shew me thy Love. but thy Lov it Selfe is the GodHead which I Adore; the fountain and the End of all thy Benefits: fully manifested in all its Operations: in them and in it Selfe ever to be enjoyed. O make me feel How infinitly I am Beloved, and Let me be the Rest of my Soul for ever.

40

That I am Beloved of God the Eternal King, and that He hath manifested his Lov in all Places of his Dominion, That he hath made me the Best of all Possible creatures, exalted me to his Throne, and every where united me to his Eternal Essence, is my continuall meditation Joy and Satisfaction. Being Beloved of a King So wise, of a Lord So Great, of a monarch so mighty, of a Prince and freind so Glorious and Blessed, Let me now in all Actions Learn to Please. Let me take courage to be High and Amiable in His Kingdom. Time to Sing, and Celebrat his Praises, Eas and Rest in the Possession of His Treasures; Begining with Him, Let me Learn to behav my Selfe well towards all Things. And to offer up those Sweet odors in Grace and vertue that are Acceptable to Him. Let me trust in Him, Relie upon Him, fear and Honor Him, Rejoyce abundantly that I have a God to Lov So Great and Good. He cannot chuse, but tender me as the Apple of his Ey. Having don all these Things for me, He will Keep me as his Bride, from all evill, Rejoyce over me, and make me Reign in every Bosom Thuoughout all worlds. He will Reign in every Heart for my Advantage, Ruling and Disposing all their Thoughts. onely Let me Delight to Please Him, He will bring me to Honor, His Gentleness shall make me Great, God is mine if I but Prize the Things which He Hath done for me.

41

Being Redeemed by the Bloud of His Eternal Son, I must behave my selfe Amiably towards Him also. Adore His majesty and Prize his Lov, in Doing which I shall return unto Him. Be Faithfull to the Death as His Redeemed Freind, in all Things Imitate Him, Die for Him.

42

Being made a Temple of the Holy Ghost I must obey His Dictates, cherish His Inspirations, Retire into the Solitude of my own Heart to hear his Admonitions, keep my vessel all ways Pure, and Take Heed that I send Him not a way Greived.

43

The Holy Ghost is the third Person in the Trinity Proceeding from the Father and the Son, one in Essence with God Almighty. God is Lov. The Lov of the father Giving his Son, the Lov of the Son in giving Himselfe, being manifested to us Proceedeth from them both: And is ever more one Lov, which being Seen is the Holy Ghost Dwelling in us. While this Light Shineth in us we are Temples of the Holy Ghost, With what Reverence and zeal ought we to Prize the Benefit of this infinit Light: and no more to Let it Extinguish then the Jews did the Lamp in the Tabernacle of God. For in this Light alone are we Honourable, Divine Persons, and of an Excellent spirit. This Lov is that alone which Sanctifieth: for it maketh the Soul Divine and Noble, maketh it a king, infuseth the most Divin Heroick Principles, Elevateth the Thought and refineth the affections. This Lov seen is or Begetteth Lov within us. All whose Dictates are the Sacred inspirations of the Holy Ghost. He that followeth what Lov inspires, and ever doth what the Lov of God doth Purely Dictate, Walks by a never Erring and Blessed Rule, contemns Himselfe for the weal of others, Promotes the Benefit of mankind, Doth all Things Honorable, and Sacrificeth Himselfe to Gods Glory.

44

The Holy Catholick church is the Bride of God, which He tends and sheilds and Loves and Governs in this world. a bout which all His Actions and Thoughts are conversant, that she may be exalted, that She may be Beautified. In all Times Ages and Generations He was alwayes Loving her, He made her the End of all His Doings, and The[e] a Temple and Bridgroom of her. Thou must needs be Desolat if Thou do not Lov her: for God Himselfe cannot be without Her. Prize her therefore and Rejoyce in Her. Love God and Delight in Him for Being Gracious to Her. He will bring Her into His Kingdom with the Joyfull Acclamations of Innumerable Angels Attending upon Him.

45

Toward the Holy Angels Let thy affections burn in the Divine Image. Rejoyce that they were made to minister unto Thee. In all their Embasies, in all Ages, in all their Attendance upon the Bride of God, in all their Praises and Thanksgivings in the Heavens They minister unto Thee. Delight in God for His Goodness and Wisdom and Lov unto them. But infinitly Rejoyce that mankind, and Thou a-mong them, art made a Blessing to the Holy Angels. Survey their Joys, and Imitate their Perfections. See How they Enjoy God in His Goodness unto all. See How they Enjoy this visible world. they have neither Ey, nor Tongue, nor Ear, need neither Light nor meate, nor Day: Yet having an Intelligence they enjoy it all. Enjoy it by their Lov and Delight in Man, without whom the world would be to them, yea to God also, an unprofitable Wilderness.

46

All Kingdoms and all Ages Shall see Thee Eternaly, And thou even the very Thoughts of all persons in all Kingdoms and all Ages. clothe thy Selfe with Beauty that Thou mayst be a Delight unto them. Lov them Intirely. And in every Action Design their Happiness. Prepare to Enjoy them. And night and Day in evry place think thy selfe a mong them. For So Thou art and shalt be Eternaly.

47

Towards Forrein Nations be always venerable. Pitty Those that Lye yet in Darkness. Long and Pray For Pagan Kingdoms, That their Eys may be Opened, and they may Delight thy Soul by Building Temples unto Jesus christ. Behave thy selfe in all their Eys, as if upon thy Actions of shame or vertue all the Glory of Religion did Depend. Greiv at the Prophaness and at the Idolatry of christians, that offendeth Turks and Hindereth Infidels.

48

Let the Joy and Splendor of the citties wherin Thou Livest; the flourishing of the villages, the Beauty of thy Kingdom, ravish thy soul. Rejoyce in the order peace and majesty of its magestrates and ministers. O Pray for the Peace of Jerusalem, They Shall prosper that Lov Thee.

49

Let the Heavens and the Earth appear before Thee in all their Glory. Let the Sun and stars minister unto Thee in Serving all Ages. Esteem the world the wonder of Eternity, the Hous of God thy Great Inheritance, the Temple of His Glory. Rejoyce in it as a Mirror wherin the Angels See his Glory, Let it minister unto Thee in all its Influences, as it serveth this and every Kingdom.

50

Be venerable to thy Selfe, and Let thy Person be Sacred in thine one Esteem. O Prize thy selfe as thy God prizeth Thee. And becaus he serveth thee Infinitly, in Tendering thy Selfe Rejoyce to Pleas Him. Thou who art His Freind, and Sole Heir of Heaven and Earth: Admire His wisdom that could make every one Sole, and becaus thou art more then Sole infinitly, Infinitly more regard thy Happiness and welfare then if Thou wert Sole, becaus thou art to keep thy selfe as a Sacred Treasure unto many Thousand others: That are Heirs of the world, and in Thee to Inherit the Similitude of God, and in that Treasure beyond all Imagination. Then Shall men speak well of Thee, when Thou dost well to thy Selfe. Keep thy selfe from Blots Fals and wounds. And remember that every Sin is an Infinit Poyson: that the Laws of God are the Laws of Lov, commanding onely those Things that are Sweet and Beneficiall, wherin thy Happiness and Honor are concerned.

51

Look upon His Service as Perfect freedom. And rejoyce that Thou art instituted in a Life fraught with Divine Employments. Lov to be a Blessing and Joy unto all: feel thy Enjoyments. Sing Praises for them.

52

It is no small matter to Dwell in community or in a congregation, and to convers there without complaint, and to Persevere Faithfully in it untill Death. Blessed is He that hath there Lived well, And Ended

Happily. They are as so many Gods if we respect the Grandure and Power of their Soul: and wheather Innocent or miserable it is a weighty thing to be conversant a mong them and not to Erre. Innocent no man is in this world. much Less a Congregation. If there were we ought to be Spotless, and that is weighty, to revere their censure, to be Amiable in their Eys, to enjoy their Persons, to hold them Sacred, to be the Sons of God, to enjoy their Glory: Promote His, Establish our own. To walk as Gods would be then our Duty, which would be no Small Inferior Thing. But if they were miserable as the most are, to be filled with great comp[a]ssion, to retain the Sence of the Eternal Diety. to Lov them as the Saviour of the world doth, not to follow their Opinion, not to be Provoked by their censure, not to approve ones selfe to them, not to give them occation of evill Speech, not to be swayed by their example, are Difficult Things, and He that passeth Thorrow all thes Bryers well, and is in e[v]ry moment prudent shall be more beautifull then if he had never sinned nor been a mong them.

53

Towards thy neighbor thou must behave thy Selfe with as much candor and sweetness as if He were an unspotted Angel. Becaus He is the Redeemed of christ, made and called to Inherit all Things, an object of compassion. yea by How much the Greater His Glory is and He knows it not, by so much the more is He to be Lamented, Aided and Pittyed. Therefore to the works of men Shouldst thou always bear an E[n]flamed Lov, and Zealously thirst after His Eternal Happieness. Suffer thy Selfe to be Injured for His Greater Benefits, and to improve all the wrongs and Injuries He doth, to His Best Advantage: which is the Salvation of His Soul. O that my Heart might be made a Stepping Stone for any ones Ascent into the Kingdom of Heaven.

54

Remember the Estate that Thou art in, and consider all wayes that the world is Corrupted. Wonder not therefore that men do not their Duty: but rather, How Thou art permitted to Breath a-mong them. Expect not to find any Good among them, but all Disorder and Perversness and Confusion. And if Thou find any Better then thy Soul

Expected, Let it be thy Amazement and Joy, and with Great Admiration ascribe all to thy Redeemers Love. If they Discharge not theirs, remember thou what is Thy Duty: to imitate Christ: and Discharg it faithfully. By the Benefit of His Love, these Disorders were Put into thy Hand, and given to Thee as Infinit Treasures. which Thou by wisdom must more improve then Adam could the Soyl and flowers in Eden. As being objects of thy care, and fair occation of Enriching thy Soul [with all] Kind of vertues.

55

Consider, and well understand, that Among invisible Things vertues are the fairest, being therefore made the way of Rewards, and the End of Things, becaus they are the Interiour Treasures of the Soul, and wholsome Beings, wherewith we Delight our selves and Enrich Eternity. Till men are acquainted with Invis[i]ble Things, it is exceeding wonderfull vertues Should be So Glorious. But when we know them, we see manifestly they are the onely Beings whose Influence Blesseth the Life of man, Enricheth the world, and Atcheiveth Happiness. Those Things may be Spoken of them which no Ey ever Saw, and which have not yet been uttered by man. They Satisfie the Soul becaus they Ex[   ] its Thirst of Glory, clothe a man with Beauty before all Ages, make Him the Treasure and the Joy of Angels, becaus He voluntarily doth those Things, And it is their Joy to see Him doing those Things, That crown Gods works, Satisfie Gods Desire, Compleat His Happiness. The world would be in vain were it not for vertues: for by them it is enjoyed. without these it would be a Den of Theeves, and a Caos of Confusion.

56

Begin with wisdom. wisdom is the Light in which Happiness is Enjoyed, by which our safety is Established, and our Life Adorned. It is that which guides us to our Soveraign End, Discovers the value of all our Treasures, shews us our Interest and Propriety in them: Teaches us the Glory of Pleasing God, Forewarns us of Dangers, makes us to see the Fulness of the Earth, and the Blessedness of His Kingdom. It is that which Directs us in all Arduous Affaires, makes us to Aime at the Best of Ends, and Helps us to Atcheiv them. It renders us Amiable in the Eys of others, and is in all respects Better then Rubies. It is the very Possession of felicity, one with Righteousness and true Holiness Divinity and Blessedness. Happy are they that are not troubled with the false Apprehension of Things. A clear Sight and Bright Knowledge is much, but wisdom more. For to Know all Things and not to Prize them is the Greatest Folly in the whole world, to Do them truly, and enjoy them all is the Highest wisdom. Wisdom includes Knowledg, and the Improvment of it. It is Impossible for one to be wise, that does not Effectually Discharge His Duty. Therefore does wisdom contain the Residue, and is by Eminence every vertue.

57

Prudence is a choys Selection of the means: wisdom Exercised in Particular Things, Removing obstacles, Improving Evils, Laying Hold of oppertunities, finding Advantages, shunning Extreams, Attaining the mean, and walking warily in it when it is Found. O that I could hold this celestial vertue, which hath So much Place here upon Earth, as if it had none in Heaven. The truth is there will be Little need of Prudence there among all Stable and Permanent Things, which will Shine there as Eternal Objects to perfect wisdom. But here upon Earth a-mong such Lubricities, variety of Dispositions Apprehensions and occurrences, Prudence is a Thing so Eminent and Illustrous: that it will Shine in Heaven for the Sake of the Benefit it did on Earth, and be far more Bright then the morning Star. Will you know How God Almighty made this vertue: By giving us a Power to see Advantages, and a Liberty to improve them. or which is the very same, By Commanding us to be considerat, and Leaving us to our selves. By which He did for us a most Glorious Thing: For He Enabled us as Gods by our own vertue to Rule the world, and to Please Him, with Admirable Deeds, While He as a Spectator Delighted in them. Of all vertues in the whole world this is that which I most want. Since there-fore it is so Delightfull: and of Daily use in evry occurrence, Let me Labor more Industriously for it, clothe my selfe more Continualy with it. It is of universal Benefit in Finding vertues, nay in Framing composing creating them. For this alone Applies the Rule, and Discerns the Golden mean where vertue Lieth, So that if I will enrich the world or my Selfe with Actions, Prudence must be my Companion, Light and shadow. Once more becaus I am exceeding Dull in Appr[e]hending this vertue (Through the Real Splendor of this celestial world, and the Standing Rules and objects there); becaus none but this and Pride are incident continualy, non that I want so infinitly as this and Humility: once more remember, that through Imprudence, in not Bounding and Methodizing Things, Thou hast seemed vicious,

58

Courage is a vertue of Little use in our First Estate, but of infinit Since. For in Innocence it was Exercised with infinit Ease in the Propelling of Temptations, and nothing more then an Habitual Resolution to forsake all Things for the Lov we owe to So infinit a Benefactor. But now it is a vertue a-mong Stronger Assaults, more frequent and more continual, in a time also wherin we are more weak. And Therefore needs to be assured with Greater Strenght. And so it is. It is Aided with the Death of Jesus christ, whose Love and Example Should more Enflame us then all the Gloryes of Heaven and Earth. When is courage but in the Time of fighting. Eternal Torments which we hope to Escape, Everlasting Enjoyments which we hope to Attain, and the infinit Glory of an Assured victory are her Magizines. And Gods Assistances her onely Second. Where Courage is High, and Heroick indeed Enemies and battles are her Jubilee and Delight notwithstanding she can enjoy her enjoyments. It is a Masculine vertue that is Lord of the world, calamities are its Trophies, oppositions Her Jubilee, She Thrives by Difficulties, And is ever Triumphant in all Distresses. Yet without Prudence to Moderate and Guide it, this Amazon and virago is but a Bruit: tho without it no man at all Dares at all to be vertuous. Courage is that which Animates and Actuates every vertue, Plucks of[f] the vizzar from evry Bugbear and make a Laughing Stock of every Danger. In which I Long to be more Compleat: For the truth is it makes every Thing a Joy, and the Earth Heaven.

59

Justice is that vertue by which we render unto all Their Due. And of infinit use from the First moment even to the End in Heaven. For it is at once the Payment and Enlargment of our Selves in the Fruition of our Blessedness. The Enlargment of our selves because the Extention of our Selves unto all objects, the Payment of our Selves because we owe our Selves to all Beings. which we Accomplish in Rendering a Due Esteem. The Primativ Soul of spiritual Justice; the Root and Fountain of all the Particular Acts wherin Justice can Express it selfe. without which we retain the precious and Expend the vile: and Lose what we Retain. For all vertue is of that Nature that it is Lost by Retaining, becaus by being retained it is not Permitted to Come into Being. All Justice without rendering a Due Esteem is an Empty Carcase. But that Justice of Esteeming Duly by way of Eminence includeth all. And causeth all, and causeth all. when we render unto God His Due Esteem, we are Just to Him, Render Him that which is most Pleasing, value His Essence according to its worth, Rejoyce in the Benefits we receive of Him, Sacrifice our Being in Homage to Him. For in rendering to Him a Due Esteem we offer up our selves in that Esteem: and becaus He is infinit, Prizing infinitly we are Loth to Lose Him, Love to Enjoy Him, and for that cause Delight to Pleas Him. Render Him his Due, Obedience, Thanksgiving. And which is the whole of both and soul of both a Genuin Lov, infinit and Pure. Justice extendeth to other Things. We are just to men when we render unto men their Due Esteem. For by valuing them truly we Lov them according to the Excellency of the Goodness that was infused into their Natures. And Dedicat our selves to Serve them becaus they are So much honoured by God. nay we do Justice to God by serving them Whom He Loveth, for we owe Him that Duty. And when we lov them as we ought we shall Prize them as our Selves: Liv in them, Tender them with Care, Render them a Due regard in Str[i]ving alwayes to Promote their Happiness, be Exalted in them, and Delight always in their Glory. Justice is a vertue of vast Enlargments; and so Great that no Age, nor world can hold it. It extendeth our affections and Due Esteem to Angels, cherubims and men, men of evry Age Kingdom and Generation, Patriarchs Prophets Apostles &c. who are all by being Prized, Embraced and Enjoyed. we Transfer our selves into them whom we Prize as our selves, and are Seated there, are there affected, feel and receiv, do the work of nature and Delight, are by them received. But Justice Extendeth further. Inanimat creatures are capable of it. We ought to do Right to the Sun and Sea and Stars, to the skie the Earth Beasts and Trees. to value the Services which they already do us, which are by being Prized all Enjoyed. To them also do we giv our selvos (in Pondering their Excellencies) and in them to God Almighty. Justice is a Kind of Bartering of ware, a commutativ vertue Exercised in giving and receiving, to the Common Benefit and Good of all. we are Enlarged in the Sun while we are there Esteeming it, becaus each of them are our Second Selves in God Almighty, becaus He is more. And in all this is the work of Blessedness, becaus it is our Interest both to giv and receiv, to be a Blessing and to Inherit all.

60

Temperance is the Execution of what Prudence Advised. It relateth not onely to meats and Drinks, but to all our Behaviours Passions and Desires. It settles them Effectualy in the Golden mean. There is a Temperance in Gesture Speech and Lov. In the right Temparament and Proportion of which, the Health and Harmonie of our Life consisteth.

Sit modus in Rebus, modus est Pulcerrima virtus

A lesson which becaus boys are taught to season their minds at first with vertue, they Despise when they are men: and for most Part when they are Exceeding old, need go to school againe to Learn the Practice.

All musick sawces Feasts Delights and Pleasures.
Games Dancing Arts, consist in Governd measures.
much more do words and Passions of the mind,
In Temperance their Sacred Beauty Find.

61

These 4 Cardinal vertues ought evermore to be united into one. Courage in Attempting, Prudence in Directing, Temperance in Proportionating and justice in Resolving to Pay evry Thing its Due. They are all Exercised in the Light of wisdom, and founded in Love: Lov is the Ground of courage that fuels and Inspires it, Lov is the Light of Prudence, becaus it actuates and makes it tender, makes it wakefull watchfull cautious, Lov is the very Soul that Animates and Distributes Justice, and the very Debt it Selfe which Justice Pays, even a Lov Proportiond to the merit of its cause. Lov is the Hand and Rule of Temperance. for it must be Pleased, which it cannot be but by Hitting right for the welfare of its Beloved. Acts of Justice and Courage them selves are Things beloved, and so are mens Persons And a mong these Justice must Excite us to every vertue.

62

Beside these moral the[re] are Theological vertues. Faith Righteousness Holiness and Humility. Faith is the First and the Basis of all. which hath its use and Being only a mong Sinners Since the Fall. That Knowledge wherby Adam in Innocency foresaw His Happiness and the Rewards in Heaven, was rather Sight, and a certain Sence in Reason then formal faith. So was that wherby He beleived Sin was Death. For He saw it Intuitivly. But in beleiving that Death Should follow upon His Eating the forbidden fruit He Exercised faith. And yet even there also God Haveing forbidden it Him, His reason told Him it must be so. But since the fall without faith it is impossible to Pleas God, it was impossible to be vertuous, for till God Discovered His new Lov we could not be wise: which Lov we must see before we can be Blessed. As Long as we Apprehend God implacable in His Hatred towards us, we must of necessity hate Him. Before we can Love Him, we must beleiv He Loveth us. That Jesus Christ is the Redeemer of the world we must needs beleive before we can enjoy Him, that there are Eternal Joys, and that we have Liberty to gain them, before we can be Discreet or vertuous. So that unto Sinners even faith it self is the mother of wisdom, the Light of vertues: and in its own nature necessary to the Attainment of Eternal Joys. It includeth the Begining of every Grace, and is of infinit value a mong the sons of men. How wonderfull is it that Sin Should be the Parent of so Amiable a vertue. Lov includeth all other vertues. This Preventeth it and is the foundation of it. but what Horrible Confusion do they make who remove that Lov which Preventeth this; the Lov of God which is the object of it. They Lock men up in the chains of Darkness, take a way their Glory, Exhibit God in a False Mirror and in the Dungeon of this world encreas their misery. This faith is a vertue that Glitters in obscure Darkness, Like a King in Gold, Invested and Shining in Sun Beams.

63

Righteousness is but another Denomination of Justice and is a vertue to be Exercised in all worlds. Justice seems to be Exercised in
giving, this in receiving: both in either. Its Etymology is light wisdom,
its operation the work of Right Reason, Its office the Answer of all
obligations, and the fruition of all Treasures. Its Excellency consisteth
in the fulfilling of all Laws, its Reward is the Goodness of what it
Prizeth. It is never Perfectly attained, till all Things are infinitly rich
and ours. For that they are ours is Part of their Goodness. And this
Part we Rob them of, by not beleiving it. All Things in Heaven and
Earth are ours which when we have Courage to beleive and wisdom
to perceiv, we hav Great need of Temperance and Power to Govern
ourSelves, of Prudence to Direct and Justice to Regard the Grandure
of others that are as Great as we.

64

Holiness is more then Righteousness is. It [is] the Zeal wherewith
we render unto Things their Sacred value, The infinit care Intention
and Fervor where with we Discharge our Duty, whoe are so violently
Addicted to Discharge it in evry part and tittle of it, that even for
whole worlds we should not Omitt it in the Least Degree. And this
I[n]tension and vehemency of Lov, how far soever beside the
Substance of Things it may Seem, yet is it the onely thing that
Sanctifieth our Duty, the onely Grace that maketh it Acceptable. The
very Holiness of God is the infinit Intension and Greatness of his Lov,
which maketh all Things Easy, Himselfe infinitly Delightfull unto us,
and us unto Him.

65

Farewell ye Rarities!
Yee Palaces, ye Kingly Jewels and Delights!
Mysterious Peeces, wonders, which the Eys
of mortals feed Passing all Exquisites
I Joys have found
new Joys which here in Earth Surround

Surpassing these as far as all the Skies
Surpass a Sand while these alone I Prize.

2

Rare vertues are the Gems
The Rarities the Feasts the Pleasant Theams
The wondrous Towers and the Diadems
The unseen flouds of Bliss the Hidden Streams.
The onely Things
Fitt to Transport the Greatest Kings
To rais misterious Raptures, and Dispence
The Joys of Heaven, by their Influence

66

Humility is the Shade of Refreshment, the Habitation of Tranquility, the Ground of Contentment, and the Basis of every vertue. it is a certain seasoning of felicity, that give[s] a Relish, and Diviner Tast to all our Joys. It is the Light in which we see them. And the Advantagious valley in which we stand to behold them. A Strange Illustrious Jewel, that fils no room, yet hath infinit Regions. within Its Borders we may Traveil Through Infinity: And see all wonders in that Cool Hidden Day more sweetly ours. nay without Humility it is Impossible to see them. for we must first stoop down to the Lowly Estate out of which we were taken before we can Discern them. Till we see our nothing, we cannot understand the value of our Being: Till we see our wants, we cannot see the Benefit of our Treasures. It is a Pleasant Thing to See How Amiably Humility behaves its selfe in all Estates. In the Estate of Innocency, mans Humility was to retain a sence of the nothing out of which He was made, and to be Ravished with just wonder at the Greatness of Gods [   ] in creating so Glorious a world for Him that was nothing. but more to see Himselfe made so Glorious a Being, and yet more to see Divine wisdom so infinitly Adorning Gods Eternal Kingdom for his Dust and Ashes. In the Estate of misery Restored to Grace, It does not think Basely of it Selfe as it came out of Gods hands, but Admiring to see its selfe restored to its former Glory, is Deeply sencible of its unworthiness by Sin, and Laments his Baseness that being so Glorious, Lives So infinitly beneath Himselfe! He retains a sence that now He is restored from an Estate worse then nothing, and infinitly values the Redeeming Lov of Him that did it. Being Redeemed, for evry Sin committed Since, it is more Deeply Humble. every such unworthyness opening a New Territory of Humble Resentments boyond event in which while the Soul walketh it is more Profoundly Enlarged to Possess its Joys, not as if the room of his Soul were Encreased, for that is impossible, But room Equally Great is Laid upon room, as couler upon couler in a Double Die. wherin the Same Joy stands over and over, and the Same God in all His Mercies appear[s] again with a nother Glory. It is sencible of the Rebellion out of which it was taken, when it was first Sanctified. And for every Sin committed after that sweet and violent Act of God, Its Illumination and Grace infused, is Double Greived. In the Kingdom of Heaven at one Intuition it beholdeth it Selfe continually in all these Depths of nothing and unworthyness, and Sees it[s] mercies Enriched with Answerable Proportions. High at first, Infinitly Infinit, and the Latter Greater. All which Enflame it abundantly with Divine Lov. And makeing it Sencible of its wants and Depths, feel it with Pleasure and Admiration at its Heights and Treasures.

67

O that I could keep a Lively Sence of my extraction out of nothing and Exaltation to Glory in the Kingdom of Innocence, of my Apostasie From His Throne and Devolving my Selfe into Abyss of misery. of my Restitution by the Bloud of Jesus, and Guilt infinit in Despising it! of my Rebellion against the Lov of God and His Absolute Grace in my Sanctification. the Horrible Sin of my Backsliding afterward! The many Inspirations and Holy Motions which from my childhood upwards He inspired into me. all which I have Layd wast and neglected wholy. And whereas to Deny those Parts and Abilities that one hath is not Humility but a faigned Modesty, O that I could be Sencible whence I received them, how unworthy I am of them, how I have abused them. How many Thousand Degrees and Perfections there are that I have not attained. how many Excellent Persons there are gone before me. And in all my Behaviour toward all the world be more meek and Lowly then if I had never received those few Degrees and measures that I have!

68

The Reality of Invisible Beings is Admirably in the Real Efficacy and almost visible Influence of Divine vertues. What Plain helps and Aids are vertues every one to each other! Humility Fecilitates every Grace, Strenghtens all vertue and makes it Easy. It Heightens Gratitude by a Sence of our unworthiness of the Benefit we receiv. It increaseth Faith becaus it maketh a man, being Sencible of His own weakness, willing to resigne Himselfe to Divine Authority. It rooteth in meekness, becaus it maketh a man Despise Himselfe, as one that hath been an Enemie Greater then the Greatest. It enduceth Patience as knowing we have Deserved Greater Calamities. It is invirond with Peaceableness, and Perpetual Quiet, becaus it neither moves others, nor is it Selfe moved with restless Provocations. It begetteth Contentment even in the meanest Estate becaus we are unworthy of Common Blessings. It Inspireth Courage, becaus it Always contemnes it Selfe, and Dares go Down into the Grave becaus Lower before. He that can be as Low as His Enemies would have Him, that Aspires not the Preferment of this world, nor is covetuous of Riches, may be as bold as a Lion, becaus He is uncap[a]ble of being Hurt or Injured. He is alwayes safe becaus He never Exasperates; and ever cheerfull, becaus always obliging in Preferring others before Himselfe. This Discovers the Prudence and wisdom that Lieth in Humilitie, which is always Receptiv of clear Light, and ever Amiable in all its Behaviours. Civility and Taciturnity attending all its motions, as its Shaddow doth the Body in a Sunny Day. Since Therefore every vertue So naturaly riseth out of Humility, How much ought I to Prize Humility, which is the motiv of vertue in Such a manner.

1

The Living waters that revive
A fainting mind
And keeps a Thirsty Soul alive
Is Hidden in the Find
They Stream beneath and Flow in Thee
The Spring of Health is Sweet Humility.

2

When Pride hath Like a Soultry Day
Parcht up my Bones
When Glowing Beams upon me ray
And tu[rn]d my Breath to Groans
I pant and gasp and fainting Flie
To Drench my Soul in Cool Humilitie.

3

O there new Life I Sweetly gain
It doth refresh from all its Pain
my very Soul
And cleans my Dying Flesh
The well of Life, the mine of Wealth
The Spring of Beauty and the Queen of Health

4

Narcissus Like the Queen of Bliss
Therin Her Face
Doth represented See: It is
Her Sacred Dwelling Place.
At once it is a Glorious King
A Queen, [a] Grace, a well, Tis evry Thing

5

It Rules the world tho't Lies beneath
[   ] all Subdue.
Flies Highest when it Scars doth Breath:
And all beneath it veiw
All Secret Wealth: and Joy doth See.
The onely Ey, Light, Days Humility.

6

upon its Banks all vertues Grow
Like Lovely Flowers
While Living waters in it Flow
To recreat our Powers.
All vertues nourisht there do Thrive
There there the Dying Soul is Kept alive.

Another

1

Humility! O Radient Queen
That most art crownd
And most in Glory then art Seen
When Sitting on the Ground
Shew me thy Beauties and Display
The Lovly Splendor of Eternal Day.

2

Sitting in Dust in Sables clad
Thou dost Display
A Beauty that is Bright tho Sad.
Thine Eys through teares do ray
Thy Peircing Beames even melt the Bones
Nay God Himselfe cannot resist the Groans.

3

upon the Ground above the Skie
She ever sits
Most Lowly, and yet tis most High.
Dispercing Benefits
From Heaven above it ever reigns:
And over all, tho weak, a Queen remains.

NOTES

References to Traherne's works are to the following:

Christian Ethicks   *Christian Ethicks* (London, 1675)
Church's Year Book   Bodleian, MS Eng. th. e. 51
Commentaries of Heaven   British Library, MS Add. 63054
Early Notebook   Bodleian, MS Lat. misc. f. 45
Margoliouth   *Centuries, Poems, and Thanksgivings*, ed.
                             H. M. Margoliouth, 2 vols (Oxford, 1958)
Marks   *Christian Ethicks*, ed. Carol L. Marks and
                             George Robert Guffey (Ithaca, New York,
                             1968)
The Ceremonial Law   Folger Shakespeare Library, MS V. a. 70

INTRODUCTION

1   The discovery of the manuscript was announced in James M.
    Osborn, 'A New Traherne Manuscript', *TLS*, 8 October 1964, p.
    928. For a description of the manuscript, see Peter Beal, *Index of
    English Literary Manuscripts, Volume II: 1625–1700*, Part 2 (London,
    1993), 478, 481–82.
2   See Beal, *Index of English Literary Manuscripts*, II.2, 479–82 for brief
    notices of these other hands. *The Ceremonial Law*, fol. 1r, also shows
    another person commenting on Traherne's unfinished work.
3   *Commentaries of Heaven*, 'Affairs', fol. 48r.1. For accounts of this
    manuscript, see Allan Pritchard, 'Traherne's *Commentaries of
    Heaven*', *UTQ*, 53 (1983), 1–35; and Julia J. Smith, 'Traherne from
    his Unpublished Manuscripts', in A. M. Allchin, Anne Ridler and
    Julia Smith, *Profitable Wonders: Aspects of Thomas Traherne* (Oxford:
    Amate Press, 1989), pp. 38–56.
4   Osborn, 'A New Traherne Manuscript', p. 928, suggests that *Select*

Meditations is addressed to a woman, but this is based on a misreading of the words 'know ledg' (I.93) as 'know lady'. For the possible identity of the friends whom Traherne apostrophizes, see note on II.38.

5 James M. Osborn, 'Thomas Traherne: Revelations in Meditation', in *The Author in His Work: Essays on a Problem in Criticism*, ed. Louis L. Martz and Aubrey Williams (New Haven and London, 1978), pp. 213–28 (pp. 216–17); Malcolm M. Day, *Thomas Traherne* (Boston, Mass., 1982), p. 131; Sharon C. Seelig, 'The Origins of Ecstasy: Traherne's "Select Meditations"', *ELR*, 9 (1979), 419–31 (p. 419); Louis L. Martz, *The Paradise Within: Studies in Vaughan, Traherne, and Milton* (New Haven and London, 1964), p. 209.

6 Osborn, 'A New Traherne Manuscript', p. 928. The similarities between *Select Meditations* and the *Centuries* are emphasized by Day, *Thomas Traherne*, pp. 131–36; and Martz, *The Paradise Within*, pp. 207–08, 211. Differences are emphasized by Seelig, 'The Origins of Ecstasy'; and Stanley Stewart, 'Two Types of Traherne *Centuries*', *John Donne Journal*, 1 (1982), 81–100.

7 Traherne did know some of Quarles's writing. See Anne Ridler, 'Traherne: Some Wrong Attributions', *RES*, n.s. 18 (1967), 48–49.

8 For similarities between *Christian Ethicks* and Traherne's discussion of the virtues in *Select Meditations*, see the Introduction and Commentary to *Christian Ethicks*, ed. Carol L. Marks and George Robert Guffey (Ithaca, New York, 1968).

9 Day, *Thomas Traherne*, p. 136; cf. Margaret Bottrall, *The Prayers of Thomas Traherne* (Cambridge: privately printed, 1988), p. 22.

10 Churchwardens' Presentment, quoted in Beal, *Index of English Literary Manuscripts*, II.2, 483.

11 Margoliouth, I, p. xxxii; 'A Thanksgiving and Prayer for the NATION', l. 217.

12 cf. *Centuries*, III.2 and 3. Day, *Thomas Traherne*, pp. 134–35, and Osborn, 'Revelations in Meditation', p. 219, comment on these similarities.

13 Stewart, 'Two Types of Traherne *Centuries*', pp. 87–99.

14 *The Register of the Visitors of the University of Oxford, From A.D. 1647 to A.D. 1658*, ed. Montagu Burrows, Camden Society, new series, 29 (1881), p. 338, note; Margoliouth, I, p. xxiv; A. G. Matthews, *Calamy Revised* (Oxford, 1934), for Traherne's ejected sponsors;

Beal, *Index of English Literary Manuscripts*, II.2, 483.
15 For a detailed discussion of Traherne's attitude towards this issue, see Julia J. Smith, 'Attitudes towards Conformity and Nonconformity in Thomas Traherne', *Bunyan Studies*, 1 (1988), 26–35.
16 See notes on III.4 and IV.51 for liturgy; and on I.82 and II.21 for Psalms; Margoliouth, II, 409.
17 For Traherne's response to contemporary politics see Julia J. Smith, 'Thomas Traherne and the Restoration', *The Seventeenth Century*, 3 (1988), 203–22.
18 Nabil I. Matar, 'Prophetic Traherne: "A Thanksgiving and Prayer for the *Nation*"', *JEGP*, 81 (1982), 16–29.
19 Christopher Hill, *The English Bible and the Seventeenth-Century Revolution* (London, 1993), pp. 351–55, 419–20; Richard Douglas Jordan, 'Thomas Traherne and the Art of Meditation', *JHI*, 46 (1985), 381–403 (p. 397); Barbara K. Lewalski, *Protestant Poetics and the Seventeenth-Century Religious Lyric* (Princeton, 1979), pp. 53, 175.
20 Seelig, 'The Origins of Ecstasy', pp. 422–26.
21 'Prophetic Traherne', p. 16.
22 *Commentaries of Heaven*, 'Acquaintance', fol. 29v.2.

TEXT

The language and imagery of many of the meditations are strongly biblical. I have given biblical references only where the quotation is extended, or where an awareness of the allusion is necessary to understanding the passage. This is particularly important where Traherne uses biblical language for political commentary.

Traherne generally quotes from memory, and his quotations are rarely accurate. I have noted variations from the Authorized Version only where they seem to reflect a knowledge of the Book of Common Prayer, a knowledge which again has political significance.

Title *Select* Choice, of special value or excellence. The manuscript contains no evidence to support the suggestion that 'Select' implies that these meditations were chosen out of a larger number.

The First Century

The first part of the manuscript is missing. It now begins on p. 45 with the end of meditation 81, and the heading 'The First Century' has therefore been supplied.

81. The incomplete sentence with which the manuscript opens has been omitted. It reads 'prepared, and feed within me in communion with Thee.'

l. 2. *leavi[ng]*   MS damaged.

82. This and the following four meditations (83–86) on the state of the nation make extensive use of the Old Testament as a medium for political comment. The chief quotations in I.82 in order of occurrence are Psalms 106.5; 128.3; 105.22; 74.19; Jeremiah 8.4–5; Isaiah 63.7; Jeremiah 25.11; Psalms 25.6; 104.33. A number of the quotations from the Psalms contain words which may be derived from the BCP, rather than the AV.

The following words are affected by damage to the page edge, editorial additions being indicated by square brackets:

l. 2. Thro[ne]; l. 3. th[ee]; l. 4. a[nd]; l. 5. bese[ec]h; l. 6. th[y]; l. 8. How muc[h]; ll. 11–12. End of all Thin[gs]; l. 14. purse[s]; l. 15. th[y] Glory; l.28. [be].

l. 23. *Riches*   Substituted above the line for 'Treasures', which however has not been deleted.

ll. 30–31.   Blanks indicate whole words missing because of damage to MS.

83. Biblical quotations include James 1.17; Isaiah 5.25 (AV marginal reading); Psalm 2.9; Ezekiel 22.24; Psalms 28.5; 25.6; Lamentations 2.1; Isaiah 65.2; Psalm 80.3; 1 John 3.17.

l. 25. *thou hast*   MS reads 'thou Thou hast'.

84. Biblical quotations include Hosea 12.10; Isaiah 1.3; 1.2; Jeremiah 15.6; 3.14.

The following words are affected by damage to the page edge, editorial additions being indicated by square brackets:

l. 6. [the] Riches; l. 7. from Generat[ion]; l. 14. Similitud[s]; l. 16. knowet[h]; l. 17. m[y]; l. 19. f[or]; l. 21. mor[e]; l. 23. wi[ll]; l. 24. o[f]; l. 27. an[d] Serv; l. 30. Inte[r]ceding; l. 31. strengt[h]; l. 37. [Tr]easures; l. 42. [sq]weez.

85. Biblical quotations include Jeremiah 23.11, 15; 9.3; Isaiah 5.12; Jeremiah 5.9; Ephesians 6.12; Isaiah 64.9–12.

ll. 11–12. Square brackets indicate damage to MS.

l 17 *my* This word has been heavily overwritten, and could possibly read 'any'.

ll. 27–30. Square brackets indicate damage to MS.

86. ll. 1–2. *Once more ... Ashes!* Genesis 18.27, 30; significantly Traherne pleads for England in the words of Abraham pleading for Sodom.

l. 8. *Extend peace* Isaiah 66.12.

87. All square brackets indicate damage to MS.

l. 20. *Comprehensiv* A significant choice of word in view of Traherne's commitment to comprehension within a national church rather than the toleration of nonconformists outside it.

88. l. 5. *Sons of Core* Korah and his followers (Numbers 16) protested against the spiritual leadership of Moses and Aaron, and were swallowed up by the earth as a punishment; they were frequently used in Restoration sermons as a warning to nonconformists.

l. 13. *fire* This word has been heavily overwritten, and the reading is conjectural.

l. 16. *goeth* MS reads 'gotheth'.

89. l. 7. *Bodies [   ]* MS leaves a blank.

stanza 2. This stanza lacks its final line, although no space is left for it in the MS. It should rhyme with the fourth line, 'flie', and perhaps should repeat the first line of stanza three.

90. l. 5. *Elas* Ela: 'the highest note in the Gamut' (OED).

l. 37. *cleeping* Calling, shouting.

l. 38. *them* MS reads 'then'.

91. All square brackets indicate damage to MS.

l. 10. *Sun That* MS reads 'Sun to That'.

l. 16. *Devine* MS reads 'Devivin'.

l. 19. *Such peircing* MS reads 'Such Such peircing'.

ll. 22–23. *were made* MS reads 'where made'.

93. l. 9. *Thousands of Rams* Micah 6.7.

l. 11. *Botleth up our Tears* Psalm 56.8; cf. *Christian Ethicks*, p. 512.

l. 15. *wherei[n]* MS damaged.

l. 22. *Joy of Angels* cf. Luke 15.10.

l. 25. *immitted*   Let in, admitted.

l. 26. *Elivates*   Raises in the form of vapour, evaporates.

ll. 26–33.   All square brackets indicate damage to MS.

l. 27. *refines and carries*   MS reads 'refine and carry'.

l. 34. *reflected is*   MS reads 'reflected are'.

l. 36. *Groans unutterable*   Romans 8.26.

l. 42. *o[f]*   MS damaged.

94.   l. 8. *[t]o*   MS damaged.

ll. 15–16. *for the evening ... Day*   Genesis 1.5.

l. 19. *the womb of the Morning*   Psalm 110.3.

95–100.   Mutilation of the MS means that the end of meditation 95, the whole of 96–99, and the beginning of 100 are missing.

95.   The incomplete sentence at the end of this meditation has been omitted. It reads 'That we Should at once be in Ten Thousand Operations, yet not know it nor'.

l. 3. *Some 5000 years agoe*   A traditional figure for the age of the world.

ll. 10–11. *Trees in a walk*   cf. *Centuries*, V.8, where Traherne expresses a very similar idea with the image of a moving ship.

l. 12. *the*   MS reads 'the The'.

The Second Century

Heading   *Meditations*   MS reads 'Meditatins'.

2–4.   All square brackets indicate damage to MS.

7.   l. 1. *to glory*   This originally read 'a gain', and has been imperfectly altered.

11.   ll. 2–3. *Thick Darkness ... the people.*   Isaiah 60.2.

l. 5. *magnifiing*   MS reads 'magnifinig'.

14.   l. 5. *All Things ... for Good*   Romans 8.28.

l. 6. *mor[e]*   MS damaged.

l. 8. *Orient*   Brilliant; precious.

15.   l. 2. *Golden wedge of Ophir*   Isaiah 13.12.

16.   l. 9. *see by*   MS reads 'see in by'.

l. 10. *Instauration*   Restoration.

17.   While most of the imagery in this apocalyptic poem is drawn from the Old Testament prophets, it also had contemporary significance. Many royalist writers had spoken of the dragons which inhabited the chaos of the Commonwealth, and the turtle dove, traditionally a symbol of the church or the people of Israel, was also used as a symbol of Charles II. Traherne's poem, however, sees the salvation of the English church not in political means, but in the call to repentance.

The turtle dove is derived from Psalm 74.19; the dragons have many biblical sources. The poem freely combines biblical images from many passages including: Malachi 1.3; Isaiah 13.10, 21–22; Revelation 8.7–8; Jeremiah 9.10–11; Ezekiel 30.12; Joel 1.20; Amos 8.9; Psalm 59.6; Jeremiah 14.6.

l. 28. *Cares [   ]* MS leaves a blank; the metre requires a word of two syllables.

l. 36. *lik Dragons* The brain of a dragon was reputed to contain a precious stone (draconites).

l. 39. *like Adders Blind* Proverbially adders are deaf (Psalm 58.4).

l. 58. *Like an Angel burn* The cherubim (or more often the seraphim) were portrayed as burning with ardent love for God.

18. ll. 9–10. Square brackets indicate damage to MS.

l. 12. *My Lovly Heritag* Jeremiah 12.8.

ll. 18–19. *in the land ... of the Lord.* Isaiah 26.10.

19. ll. 1–2. *The Heavens ... his Glory.* Psalm 97.6.

l. 6. *n[o]* MS damaged.

21. ll. 5–6. *the Earth yeeld ... his Blessing* Psalm 67.6; a conflation of the AV and the BCP.

24. l. 3. *Abysses* MS reads 'Abyssess'.

l. 4. *Borders of Eternity* MS reads 'Borders of Eterinty'.

25. l. 2. *Sacr[i]fice* MS damaged.

l. 2. *Complacency* Delight, enjoyment.

26–27. All square brackets indicate damage to MS.

26. ll. 6–7. *I have Said ... princes* Psalm 82.6–7.

30. cf. *Commentaries*, 'Human Abilitie', fols 6v.2–7r.1, on the superiority of enjoying to creating.

l. 8. *Demonstration* MS reads 'Dismonstration'.

31. The whole of this meditation is written in Traherne's hand.

33. l. 2. *that he may be a Treasure.* Added partly above the line, in Traherne's hand.

ll. 3–4. *is that, the satisfaction ... made all.* Written in Traherne's hand.

34. MS reads '(X34X)', suggesting that either the number or the meditation was to be omitted.

ll. 8–22. All square brackets indicate damage to MS.

l. 9. *an Abominable Branch* Isaiah 14.19.

l. 11. *the Book of thy Remembrance* Malachi 3.16.

l. 15. *the Sun of Righteousness* Malachi 4.2.

l. 16. *Holy Ghost ... overshadow me* Luke 1.35.

l. 28. *by thy* MS reads 'by the thy'.

35. l. 8. *prodigie* Monster.

36. l. 1. *a prisoner; a Malefactor* Zechariah 9.11; Luke 23.39–43.

38. ll. 1–2. *O my T. G. O my S. H.* The identity of T. G. is not known, but possibilities which have been suggested are Thomas Good (1609–78), prebendary of Hereford from 1660 and Master of Balliol from 1672, who certainly knew Traherne at the time of his death; Theophilus Gale (1628–78), whose writings were well known to Traherne; and Thomas Geers (c.1643–1700) of Bridge Sollers, about three miles from Traherne's parish of Credenhill.

It has been assumed that S. H. must be the devotional writer Susanna Hopton (1627–1709). However, in spite of Gladys Wade's enthusiastic description of Susanna's spiritual friendship with Traherne (*Thomas Traherne* (Princeton, 1944), pp. 79–80, 87–88), it is not known whether she knew him personally, or only through his manuscripts and the fact that her niece and god-daughter Susanna Blount married Traherne's brother Philip in 1670. Judgement on the identity of S. H. must therefore remain suspended.

On T. G. and S. H. see Martz, *The Paradise Within*, p. 210; Osborn, 'A New Traherne Manuscript', p. 928; Osborn, 'Revelations in Meditation', p. 225; Julia J. Smith, 'Susanna Hopton: A Biographical Account', *N&Q*, 236 (1991), 165–72.

l. 2. *O my Brother!* Philip Traherne (1640–1723), who was living in London by December 1663, became chaplain to the Levant Company in Smyrna in 1670 and subsequently minister of Wimborne Minster in Dorset. He was responsible for preserving Traherne's 'Poems of Felicity'. See Julia J. Smith, 'Thomas and Philip Traherne', *N&Q*, 231 (1986), 25–31.

39. l. 6. *manne[r]* MS damaged.

40. l. 2. *Appendencies* Appendages.

41. The scribe did not include a meditation 41.

45. l. 4. *each other*   MS reads 'each others'.

l. 5. *Resentments*   Feelings.

l. 7. *Exterminated*   Driven from.

46. ll. 1–4. *Blessed is ... Shall prosper.*   Psalm 1.1–3.

ll. 4–5. *the Rivers ... of our God*   Psalm 46.4.

ll. 7–8. *Through the S[c]ent ... bud forth*   Job 14.9.

48. l. 4. *Debateing*   Diminishing.

l. 5. *Displeasant*   Displeasing, unpleasant.

49. l. 3. *Which plato moved*   *Euthyphro*, 12A. The question is actually whether that which is holy is loved by the gods because it is holy, or whether it is holy because it is loved by the gods.

52. l. 2. *creature[s]*   MS damaged.

l. 4. *by our*   MS reads 'by of our', perhaps in the original text, 'by reason of our'.

58. ll. 4–5. *and be Ravished*   MS reads 'I be Ravished'.

59 and 60.   In the MS these two meditations were written in reverse order. 59 was then annotated 'this is 60' and 60 'this is 59'.

63.   The scribe did not include a meditation 63.

64. l. 10. *possesses*   MS reads 'possessess'.

l. 19. *Strange Dæmon*   Marks (p. 350) compares *Centuries*, IV.67 and *Christian Ethicks*, p. 311, which call love 'the Great Dæmon of the World', a phrase derived from Plato, *Symposium*, 202E.

ll. 19–20. *the Spring of all our affections*   A commonplace (e.g. Aquinas, *Summa Theologiae*, 1a.2ae.25, art.2), which is also found in *Christian Ethicks*, p. 72 (Marks, p. 321).

67–71.   Mutilation of the MS means that the end of meditation 67, the whole of 68, 69 and 70, and the beginning of 71 are missing.

67. l. 5. *will Gird Himselfe*   Luke 12.37.

l. 8. *never*   Inserted above a caret; only the 'n' is clearly legible.

l. 16. *thou require*   MS reads 'thou Thou require'.

l. 17. *wash thy feet*   John 13.5.

l. 18. *New wine*   Mark 14.25.

l. 30.   The last sentence of this meditation is incomplete.

72. l. 1. *Shadows in the water*   The title of one of Traherne's best-known poems, but there are no other close verbal similarities between the meditation and the poem.

73–75.   Mutilation of the MS means that the end of meditation 73, the whole of 74, and the beginning of 75 are missing.

73. l. 5. *Angels minister* MS reads 'Angels Minister and'; the end of the sentence is missing.

75–77. These three meditations (and presumably the missing 74) follow the pattern of the characteristically Protestant doctrine of Christ's threefold mediatorial office as prophet, priest and king.

77. l. 3. *Phænix* The phoenix, which immolated itself on a nest of spices, and rose up again from the ashes, was an emblem of the Resurrection; cf. *Centuries*, IV.61.

79. l. 1. *To see ... Living* Psalm 27.13.

l. 10. *satisfactio[n]* MS damaged.

80. A cento of verses from Deuteronomy 28.1–8 and Leviticus 26.3–8 in which God promises blessings to the Israelites if they keep his commandments; implicit in the meditation are the corresponding judgements threatened if they do not.

l. 2. *out of Egypt* Traherne shared the Royalist view of the Restoration as a parallel to the arrival of the Israelites in the promised land; for radicals it represented a return to Egypt.

81. l. 3. *possess the Double* Isaiah 61.7.

l. 5. *Marrow* The pulp of a fruit, goodness.

l. 11. *Multitudes* MS reads 'Multiudes', with the second 't' added immediately above the second 'u'.

82. ll. 6–7. *the valley of the Shaddow; the light of the living* Psalms 23.4; 56.13.

l. 14. *the same Pillar* Exodus 14.19–20; cf. *The Ceremonial Law*, fol. 10v.

84. l. 2. *Efflagitated* Eagerly demanded; cf. III.48, l.10 from foot.

l. 10. *that is* Heavily altered from 'these are'.

85. The scribe did not include a meditation 85.

86. l. 16. *I pant after Thee* Psalm 42.1.

87. ll. 22–27. *Yet it doth Illuminate ... Actuates all.* cf. *Centuries*, II.8; 'Thanksgivings for the Glory of God's Works', ll. 354–72; *Commentaries*, 'Accident', fol. 20r.2.

l. 23. *Disgesteth* Parallel form of 'digest'; 'to mature, or bring to a state of perfection, especially by the action of heat' (OED).

88. l. 9. *Illustrious* MS reads 'Illustruous'.

89. l. 6. *one of them* Written over 'each to me'.

ll. 8–9. *To me* 'To' altered from 'for'.

ll. 17–18. *lifteth up ... Gates* Psalm 24.9.

90. l. 6. *us* Untidily altered from 'it'.

91. l. 3. *His footstool* Isaiah 66.1.

l. 5. *Riches of His* MS reads 'Riches of of His'.

92. The following insertions above carets are made in Traherne's hand: l. 3. 'his' in 'his Thoughts'; l. 5. 'Im' of 'Immateriall'; ll. 8–9. 'when it is perfect as it ought to be'.

l. 6. *an Indivisible Atom without Bulk* A very similar description is applied to angels in the *Church's Year Book*, fol. 90r. Traherne expounds his idiosyncratic theory that the atom is incorporeal and without bulk in *Commentaries*, 'Atom', fols 169v.2–170r.1.

93. l. 8. *conamen* Endeavour.

l. 8. *All Act* i.e. all his powers wholly exerted, pure actuality (cf. *Centuries*, III.63–64 and *Commentaries*, fol. 30r.2; 30v.2). The words 'All Act' are inserted into a blank space in Traherne's hand.

l. 10. *Infinity here* 'here' inserted above a caret in Traherne's hand.

94. The MS contains two meditations headed 94.

94a. l. 7. *have* MS reads 'has'.

l. 8. *i[t]* MS damaged.

94b. l. 3. *from* This word, added above the line and probably in Traherne's hand, is not entirely legible, but may read 'frō'.

l. 4. *person* The 'p' seems to have been written by the scribe, and the remainder of the word filled in by Traherne.

l. 5. *external* MS reads 'exterternal'.

96. l. 2. *Ages* Heavily altered from 'Angels'.

l. 4. *either* Added above a caret in Traherne's hand.

l. 7. *sacred* Added above the line in Traherne's hand.

l. 15. *Distresses* MS reads 'Distressess'.

97. l. 8. *resent* Feel, be sensible of.

ll. 12–13. *and all ... Abolished.* Written in Traherne's hand.

98. l. 6. *boyl on a Grediron* The fate of St Lawrence.

99. l. 3. *Guid* MS reads 'Giud'.

l. 6. *contiguous* Closely associated.

100. l. 1. *created* Added above a caret in Traherne's hand.

l. 14. *weep in my secret Places* Jeremiah 13.17.

The Third Century

1. All square brackets indicate damage to MS.

l. 4. *Elizian feilds* The abode of the blessed in Greek mythology.

l. 4. *Lethe* One of the rivers of Hades, which caused those who drank it to forget the past.

3. ll. 9–10. *I might have* 'I' and 'have' are added above carets in Traherne's hand.

4. ll. 9–10. *Heaven ... Glory* From the *Te Deum* (BCP, Morning Prayer).

l. 10. *to awake* 'to' is added above the line in Traherne's hand.

5. cf. *Centuries*, II.87.

ll. 4–5. *of Beauty* These words have been heavily altered from '& Activity'.

l. 6. *he* Added above a caret in Traherne's hand.

l. 7. *Conflux* Flowing together. The word is partially altered to 'Influx', and it is not clear which word was meant to stand.

l. 8. *in our selves to* Added above a caret in Traherne's hand.

6. l. 18. *they are* MS reads 'they are they are'.

7. l. 3. *no Hyperbolie* A characteristic idea of Traherne's; cf. *Centuries*, II.52; *Commentaries*, 'Attendance', fol. 179v.1.

9. The following words are added above carets in Traherne's hand: l. 4. 'been' in 'been noe'; l. 5. 'hav'; l. 12. 'he'.

l. 15. *Adspectable* Able to be seen; pleasing to look at (not in OED).

l. 23. *the fulness ... Bodily* Colossians 2.9.

l. 25. *most [great] and Peculiar* The scribe missed a word here at the beginning of a new page.

l. 27. *is the wonder* MS reads 'the is wonder', 'the' being inserted above the line in the wrong place, and in Traherne's hand.

10. l. 5. *are most* MS reads 'are are most'.

l. 7. *hats and knees* Hat duty was under threat from the Quakers. Charles II permitted Quaker deputations, who would doff their hats only for God, to keep them on in his presence.

l. 9. *Tinsell* Glittering, gaudy.

l. 11. *were made* 'were' is added above a caret in Traherne's hand.

l. 21. *this were somwhat* Added above a caret in Traherne's hand.

l. 23. *Elements without* 'out' is added above a caret in Traherne's hand.

ll. 23–24. *restrain the Inordinat vulgar* Traherne shared the growing awareness in the Restoration of the social utility of ceremony. **11.** The origin of kingly authority, on which Traherne reflects here, was a very pertinent subject at the Restoration. In seeing kingship as a consequence of the Fall, he rejects patriarchalism, and in *Commentaries* he was to go further, clearly expressing the social contract theory in Hobbesian terms ('The Authority of Kings', fol. 187r).

l. 2. *other* Each other (OED, B8).

12. l. 7. *stable* Heavily altered from 'standing'; the 'ing' has not been crossed out.

13. ll. 3–5. *For the Lov ... many Sorrows.* 1 Timothy 6.10.

l. 6. *sophisticat* Adulterated, impure; artificial. 'Sophisticat' in l. 8 below is used with the additional sense of 'deprived of primitive simplicity'.

l. 15. *Diogenes* I have not been able to trace this remark either in Diogenes Laertius or in any classical account of Diogenes the Cynic. It might perhaps originate from one of the many Renaissance works in which invented speeches were put into the mouth of Diogenes the Cynic; equally it would not be untypical of Traherne to have given an incorrect reference.

ll. 16–18. *That the World ... Deitie.* Written in Traherne's hand.

15. l. 10. *therein* MS reads 'theirein'.

l. 12. *flies; frogs* Two of the plagues of Egypt (Exodus 8).

16. l. 1. *Plato* In his *Republic*, Book VI, 507. Traherne gives a shorter version of this in *Christian Ethicks*, p. 64.

l. 22. *figure* Shape, form.

l. 36. *his understanding* 'his' substituted above the line for 'the', which has not been crossed out.

17. Preachers of all persuasions in the early 1660s shared Traherne's concern at the profanity and moral degeneracy of the nation both under the Commonwealth and after the Restoration.

ll. 1–3. *He hath Shewed ... known them.* Psalm 147.19–20.

l. 13. *kept wreaks* Played pranks, behaved riotously.

18. l. 10. Mutilation of the MS means that the central part of this meditation is missing. Before the ellipsis, an incomplete reference to 'Platoes Lines' has been omitted, and after it some fragments of Psalm

89.15.

ll. 11–14. *In thy Name ... our King.* Psalm 89.16–18.

l 11. *[shall they]* These words are damaged in the MS, but the reading is confirmed by Psalm 89.16.

19. It is possible, because of mutilation of the MS, that a few lines may be missing from the end of this meditation.

ll. 1–2. *The Earth ... the fullness thereof.* Psalm 24.1.

20. Mutilation of the MS means that the first part of this meditation is missing. Some fragments of quotations from Revelation 21.2 and 5.13 have been omitted. The remainder of the meditation, with the exception of the concluding passage about the carter, is mainly a cento of biblical quotations including: Revelation 14.6; Isaiah 11.6; Revelation 1.20; 2.1; Psalms 147.4; 135.7; 104.3, 13; 65.10; 147.8–9; Jeremiah 5.22; Psalms 65.13; 82.1; Proverbs 31.9; Psalm 147.3; 2 Chronicles 16.9; Proverbs 15.3; Psalm 139.3–4; Matthew 10.29–30; Isaiah 54.16; 28.26, 29.

l. 5. *Golden candlesticks* Revelation 2.1. The golden candlestick of the tabernacle (Exodus 25.31) was seen as a symbol of the presence of God with the national church, and the fear that it might be removed (Revelation 2.5) was widespread in Restoration sermons; cf. *Select Meditations*, III.23.

l. 20. *Assemblie* MS reads 'Asssemblie'.

21. l. 10. *it reacheth* 'it' added above the line in Traherne's hand.

l. 12. *fear* MS reads 'rear'.

l. 17. *Adorning Quires; conserving Universities* Both politically significant acts: during the Civil Wars and Commonwealth many of the treasures which adorned the choirs (chancels) of cathedrals and churches had been plundered or destroyed, and the traditional role of the universities had been under threat from radical reformers who opposed a learned ministry.

l. 18. *Sending* MS reads 'Sending Sending'.

l. 23. *Reverance* Heavily written over another word now illegible.

22. The scribe did not include a meditation 22.

23. ll. 18–20. *Then had the churches rest ... were multiplied.* Acts 9.31.

24. l. 12. *Angel of Light* 2 Corinthians 11.14.

l. 17. *Pill of[f]* Strip off, peel.

25. l. 3. *right in his own Eys* Judges 17.6, 'In those days there was no king in Israel, but every man did that which was right in his own eyes'. After 1660 this text was repeatedly applied both to the Commonwealth, and to the potential chaos of Restoration nonconformity.

ll. 11–12. *they walked   Joyfull bound*   Psalm 89.15.

l. 13. *Almighty*   MS reads 'Alimghty'.

l. 15. *nursing parents*   Isaiah 49.23.

l. 19. *Independent*   The Independents (congregationalists) are the only Restoration nonconformist group named by Traherne in *Select Meditations*. Influential under Cromwell, they rejected the interference of the secular magistrate in religion, the point on which Traherne takes issue with them here.

l. 23. *unLawfull*   'un' is added above a caret in Traherne's hand.

26. l. 1. *Little foxes*   Canticles 2.15.

l. 18. *I was born*   No record of the date or place of Traherne's birth has yet been found, but according to Anthony Wood his father was a shoemaker of Hereford (Margoliouth, I, p. xxiii).

29. cf. *Centuries*, III.2 and 3.

l. 10. *moveing*   The central letters of this word have been altered and are unclear.

30. l. 2. *De Ente, De forma materiali, D[e] Quid-ditate*   Of being, of material form, of quiddity (that which makes a thing what it is); typical scholastic themes for disputation in the exercises for a degree.

l. 5. *chaffering*   Bargaining, haggling.

l. 6. *Hæcceities*   'Thisnesses', used disparagingly of scholastic terminology. MS reads 'Hæccieties'.

l. 7. *Roaring Boys*   Riotous fellows.

l. 19. *a Prodigal*   Luke 15.11–32; cf. *Centuries*, III.14.

31. The following are added above carets in Traherne's hand: l. 3. 'are'; l. 5. 'able' of 'Profitable'.

l. 3. *neither Angels nor cherubims*   cf. *Centuries*, III.27, 28 and 32.

l. 7. *Instructions*   Marks (p. xxxii) sees these 'Instructions' as 'a putative embryo' of *Christian Ethicks*.

31. 1. l. 7. *be thine*   MS reads 'by thine'.

31. 2. cf. *Christian Ethicks*, p. 103.

31. 8. l. 1. *thy Treasures*   MS reads 'thy Thy Treasures'.

31. 9. l. 5. *Like Abraham Heir of the world*   Genesis 15.3–7.

31. 10. l.1. *the; of Lov; his*   Added above carets in Traherne's hand.

31. concluding section. l. 11. *Pismires*   Ants.

31. concluding section. l. 16. *infiniteness* MS reads 'infintieness', with the third 'i' inserted above the line in the wrong place.

32–36. Mutilation of the MS means that the end of meditation 32, the whole of 33, 34, and 35, and the beginning of 36 are missing.

36. l. 1. 'is' has been omitted from the beginning of the incomplete sentence which now opens the meditation.

ll. 21–22. *Legal Righteousness* Righteousness derived from obedience to the law (rather than the imputed righteousness of Christ).

37. l. 23. *Should* Originally written 'Shall', and only partially altered.

38. l. 2. *The Answer* From here to the end the meditation is in Traherne's hand.

39. The scribe did not include a meditation 39.

42. l. 4. *Jesurun waxed fat* Deuteronomy 32.15.

l. 8. *concealed* MS reads 'con- concealed'.

43. l. 15. *which Image they tell us* There were a great variety of traditional interpretations as to what the image of God (Genesis 1.26) consisted in; this one is derived from Ephesians 4.24.

46. l. 16. *thirsted* Longed for.

47. l. 8. *midst of our* MS reads 'midsts of our'.

48. 7. l. 2. *concernment* MS reads 'con concernment'.

concluding section. ll. 11–12. *Like Arches Threatning Heaven and earth* Perhaps a reminiscence of the tower of Babel (Genesis 11.4).

49. l. 6. *a fountain of Gardens* Canticles 4.15.

l. 15. *Impertinent* Irrelevant, not to the point.

l. 15. *compared to a vine* e.g. Isaiah 5; John 15.

50. l. 7. *not* Added above a caret in Traherne's hand.

l. 11. *Desire* MS reads 'Desires'.

l. 22. *unprofitable* A very faint 's' has been added to 'unprofitable' in a lighter ink, but this seems to be an error.

l. 22. *Cyphers* Literally, arithmetical symbols for 'nought'; nonentities, people who merely fill a place.

l. 23. *yeild* Heavily and imperfectly altered from another word.

ll. 31–32. *And our ... of all.* Written in Traherne's hand.

51. l. 2. *Exigences* Difficulties, extremities.

l. 3. *Loss* Added above a caret in Traherne's hand.

l. 7. *His [   ]* This word has been so heavily altered that it cannot be read.

52. l. 2. *De futuritione Mali* Of the future existence of evil ('future' in relation to God's creation of an unfallen world)

l. 6. *facillima suprema* Translated by Traherne in the next sentence but one.

ll. 8–9. *Deus faciendo ... volens Malum.* Translated in the next sentence.

l. 35. *Emergencies* Arisings, occurrences.

53. l. 8. *studiing* MS reads 'studinig'.

l. 14. *brought to vertues* An expanded version of this discussion of the virtues which pertain to each estate is found in *Christian Ethicks,* chapter IV (Marks, p. 317).

l. 21. *magazines* Stores, munitions.

l. 30. *Bloud of Jesus* MS reads 'Bloud and of Jesus'.

l. 34. *It repented God* Genesis 6.6.

l. 35. *Infinit* MS reads 'Infinitly'.

54. l. 18. *Realty* Reality; royalty.

55. l. 2. *Enammel* Adorn, 'to impart an additional splendour to what is already beautiful' (OED).

57. Meditation 57 begins a new page in the MS, most of which is left blank, as though the meditation were incomplete.

58. Two meditations are assigned this number in the MS.

58a. l. 13. The MS leaves a blank for this line, which must rhyme with l. 11.

58b. ll. 1–2. *the Things included in Religion* A list of the fundamentals of Christianity, which Traherne shared with the Latitudinarians. As the end of the meditation makes clear, 'the Articles of o[u]r faith' refers to the Apostles' Creed.

l. 20. *God the father creating* cf. BCP Catechism.

60. ll. 2–4. *a Thin vail; which vail was rent* Exodus 26.33; Matthew 27.51.

61. l. 2. *who [   ] and Bring* MS leaves a blank. Lines 1–4 are loosely based on Deuteronomy 30.12–14, but this does not supply the missing word.

l. 6. *a [   ] Dul* MS leaves a blank.

62. l. 7. *Let in their cisterns* Put in their basins or water vessels.

64. l. 4. *Liv* MS reads 'Liv Liv'.

l. 7. *can* MS reads 'can can'.

65. l. 1. *Inspection*   Insight, perception.

l. 9. *With David*   Psalm 34.2.

l. 16. *a Bird of Paradice*   It was believed that the bird of paradise had no feet, and so never touched the earth.

l. 25. *Silere Tibi, Laus est.*   It is your glory to be silent.

68. l. 1. *Dead flies corrupt*   Ecclesiastes 10.1; cf. *Christian Ethicks*, p. 171.

l. 7. *weaknesses*   MS reads 'weaknessess'.

72. l. 12. *giving infinit*   A word may be missing at the end of the meditation.

73. ll. 3–4. *in whom ... Dwelleth Bodily*   Colossians 2.9.

77. l. 1. *a Question moved by Some*   A characteristic question asked by Puritans seeking assurance of salvation.

l. 1. *Desire*   MS reads 'Desires'.

l. 14. *intend*   Fix the mind on, attend to.

l. 17. *Like ones*   MS reads 'Likes ones'.

78. Marks (p. 360) compares the first part of this meditation with *Christian Ethicks*, pp. 407–08.

79. l. 3. *Admixture*   Mingling; cf. *Centuries*, I.41, where a similar image is used.

l. 17. *we are the*   MS reads 'we are the we are the'.

ll. 23–24. *as Fountaines ... derived from them*   cf. 'The Circulation', ll. 59–60. It was generally believed that the origin of rivers and springs lay in the circulation of waters between them and the sea.

81. This meditation is not numbered in the MS.

82. l. 12. *Arise O sword*   Zechariah 13.7.

83. l. 20. *nourished at universities*   Traherne was admitted as a commoner at Brasenose College, Oxford, 1 March 1653; B.A. 13 October 1656; M.A. 6 November 1661; B.D. 11 December 1669 (Margoliouth, I, pp. xxiii–xxiv).

ll. 23–25. *mount Sinay; mount Calvary*   Exodus 19–20; Luke 23.33.

84. l. 2. *Material[s]*   Things made of matter, corporeal objects; cf. III.95, l. 38.

86. The MS contains the heading 86, followed by a blank space of just over a page, but there is no entry.

87. l. 1. *Solomon tels us*   Ecclesiastes 7.4, 2.

l. 2. *Mour[n]ing*   MS originally read 'the Lord', imperfectly overwritten.

l. 12. *Presidents* Exemplars (precedents).

l. 17. *their Happy* MS reads 'his their Happy'.

l. 29. *Some Dying man* Traherne's own will, delivered orally as he was dying, disposes of a small sum of money, his 'best Hatt', his clothes and his books (Margoliouth, I, p. xxvi).

l. 32. *this mans* MS reads 'thus mans'.

ll. 36–37. *Hous of Moses* Deuteronomy 33.

l. 57. *David Prayeth* Psalm 106.4–5.

88. ll. 1–2. *Enter into his Gates ... Bless his name.* Psalm 100.4.

89. l. 20. *Saint Austin* This was a popular anecdote in the seventeenth century, but Traherne, like many other authors, misrepresents Augustine, who actually rejects the answer attributed to him here (*Confessions*, XI.xii).

90. ll. 4–5. *tis the highest ... attainment, but* Added in a hand which is neither Traherne's nor that of the scribe, but which is also responsible for 'A Prayer for Ash wednesday' and 'A Meditation' on pp. 229–32 of the MS.

l. 17. *Possibly* MS reads 'Possible'.

91. The number of this meditation has been altered from 92 to 91. The scribe did not include a meditation 92.

l. 2. *Hypostatical union* The union of divine and human natures in the person of Jesus Christ.

l. 18. *to The union* These words have been heavily altered from 'be founded'.

93. l. 32. *in order to* For the sake of, for the purpose of (OED, 'order', sb., 28); cf. IV.2, l. 19, and IV.37, l. 3.

94. l. 10. *objected* Presented.

l. 11. *a sheapherd Leaveth 99 sheep* Luke 15.4.

95. ll. 6–8. Square brackets indicate damage to MS.

96. l. 1. *men ministering* MS reads 'men ministery'.

l. 3. *Seared* Dried up, incapable of feeling.

97. l. 1. *Hypostatical* MS reads 'Hopostatical'.

l. 4. *Inaccessible* MS reads 'Imaccessible'.

l. 18. *Humiliation* MS heavily and imperfectly altered from another word, now illegible.

98. l. 9. *are all* MS reads 'are all are all'.

100. l. 1. *Almighty* MS reads 'Alimighty'.

ll. 5–6. *rais him ... Heavenly Places* Ephesians 1.20.

l. 10. *as Elisha did*   2 Kings 2.10.
ll. 21–22. *creat in me ... within me!*   Psalm 51.10.
ll. 29–30. *in store ... Good works*   1 Timothy 6.18–19.

The Fourth Century

Heading   *Fourth*   MS reads 'Forth'.
1.   l. 21. *Godhead*   MS reads 'Goodhead'.
2.   l. 4. *Rasa Tabula*   Blank tablet. In using this expression, Traherne apparently rejects the belief of the Cambridge Platonists in innate ideas implanted in the mind prior to sensory experience, and anticipates the empiricism of Locke (cf. *Centuries*, I.1). In IV.3 below, however, he makes an exception for one innate idea, that of infinite space.
3.   Martz suggests that this is the experience implied in *Centuries*, III.59–60 (*The Paradise Within*, p. 210).
l. 2. *fortnight*   MS reads 'fortinght'.
l. 6. *Relucent*   Bright, refulgent.
l. 12. *Almighty*   MS reads 'Alimghty'.
l. 13. *Dust of a Ballance*   Isaiah 40.12 and 15; cf. *Centuries*, I.19.
l. 27. *prevents the Information of all sence*   Precedes all sense impressions (and is therefore an innate idea).
l. 28. *Primum ... rerum natura*   The same phrase is used in a meditation on infinite space in *Centuries*, II.81, and there translated as 'Of all Things the only first and most Necessarily Known'.
4.   l. 6. *Præteritions*   Things past.
l. 23. *The Lines are faln out*   Psalm 16.6.
5.   l. 11. *Propriety*   Possession, ownership.
6.   ll. 1–2. *Know thy Selfe*   e.g. Xenophon, *Memorabilia*, IV.ii.24. The saying was proverbial in the seventeenth century.
7.   l. 3. *President*   Exemplar; original.
l. 12. *intend*   Have as the object of his attention.
8.   l. 2. *his Attributes*   Traherne expounds his rejection of the traditional distinction between the communicable and incommunicable attributes of God in *Commentaries*, 'Attribute', fol. 181v.1–2.
11.   l. 9. *in vive*   ?In living semblance, life-like.
12.   l. 8. *Top*   Cream; pinnacle.
l. 11. *Color*   Appearance, character.

13. 1. 12. *volubility* Versatility; changeableness.

1. 15. *instantly* Urgently, persistently.

14. 1. 2. *in giving* 'in' is substituted above the line for 'by', which however has not been deleted

16 and **17.** The scribe did not include meditations 16 and 17.

18. 1. 8. *Calcine* Burn to ashes, consume.

20. This meditation consists almost entirely of quotations from Micah 6.6–8 and Psalm 145.5–6, 10–11 (with phrases from both AV and BCP).

1. 11. *Thine Excellent* MS reads 'Thy Thine Excellent'.

21. 1. 3. *Tully* Cicero, *De Officiis*, III.v.25; and *De Legibus*, II.viii.19.

1. 6. *Meditating* Studying; designing. MS reads 'Meditation'.

1. 10. *Thanksgiveings* MS reads 'Thanksgivenigs'.

1. 11. *Lustre* External splendour (OED, sb.[1], 4c).

1. 13. *Expending his Estate* Traherne himself was said by an anonymous acquaintance to have been 'Charitable to the Poor almost beyond his ability' (Margoliouth, I, p. xxxii).

1. 13. *Shining* MS reads 'Shinining'.

1. 14. *reducing* Bringing back.

22. 1. 2. *no Enemy but Ignorance* A proverbial saying, also quoted by Traherne in Latin in the Early Notebook, p. 75.

1. 3. *the one Thing needfull* Luke 10.42.

11. 5–6. *That which comes after* John 1.15.

1. 23. *Kingdoms* MS reads 'Kinkdoms'.

24. 1. 19. *are Happy* MS reads 'are and Happy'; the scribe has probably omitted a word.

26. 1. 18. *Beginning* MS reads 'Begininng'.

28. 1. 2. *Dubious* Ambiguous, obscure.

29. 1. 10. *the Apostle Speaks of* Colossians 3.1–2.

30. 1. 2. *then to the* MS reads 'then the to', with 'to' inserted above a caret in the wrong place.

1. 13. *Priamus* The last king of Troy.

31. 1. 15. *Almighty* MS reads 'Alimghty'.

1. 23. *Astonied* Stunned, paralysed.

33. 1. 6. *no organ* MS reads 'an organ'.

34–35. Traherne's atheists, who ask why God is not 'an infinit Bulk', are materialists who like Hobbes denied the existence of any substances which did not have extension and corporeality; cf.

Centuries, II.19–20 and *Commentaries*, fol. 163v.2.

34. l. 18. *an*   MS reads 'and'.

l. 39. *Eternity*   MS reads 'Etcternity'.

l. 40. *we can*   MS reads 'we can we can'.

l. 57. *within*   MS reads 'within and'; there are apparently some words missing at the end of the meditation.

35. l. 4. *manner*   MS originally read 'way', imperfectly altered to 'manner'.

37. l. 3. *in order to his Gratitude*   For the purpose of bringing about his gratitude.

l. 20. *means*   MS reads 'mea- means'.

l. 28. *Greater*   MS originally read 'better', imperfectly altered to 'Greater'.

l. 30. *Abraham was the Blessing*   Genesis 22.17–18.

38. l. 9. *made me*   MS reads 'made made me'.

39. ll. 1–2. *abundantly Satisfied ... Rivers of thy Pleasures.*   Psalm 36.8.

43. ll. 1–2. *Proceeding ... the Son*   An article of the Nicene Creed.

ll. 2–6. *God is Lov*   Traherne also reflects on the Trinity of Love, ultimately derived from Augustine (*De Trinitate*, XV.vi, vii), in *Select Meditations*, II.72; *Centuries*, II.39–46; and *Christian Ethicks*, p. 200.

ll. 8–9. *the Lamp in the Tabernacle*   Exodus 27.20.

47. l. 1. *venerable*   Worthy of being respected or revered.

48. l. 3. *majesty*   Heavily altered from 'Glory'.

ll. 4–5. *O Pray ... that Lov Thee.*   Psalm 122.6.

50. ll. 1–2. *one Esteem*   A variant spelling of 'own'.

51. l. 1. *His Service as Perfect freedom*   Collect for Peace (BCP, Morning Prayer).

52. ll. 1–4. *It is ... Ended Happily.* From Thomas à Kempis, *The Imitation of Christ*, I.XVII.1. Interestingly, Traherne quotes from a Catholic translation; Protestant versions, very popular in seventeenth-century England, omit this passage on the religious life. Traherne also refers to the *Imitation* in *Centuries*, I.7.

l. 5. *Innocent*   MS reads 'Innocence'.

l. 15. *approve*   Recommend, justify.

55–68. The remainder of *Select Meditations* is, like *Christian Ethicks*, concerned with the virtues. IV.56 discusses wisdom, which is not classified, although in *Christian Ethicks*, chapter III Traherne classes it as both an intellectual and a 'divine' virtue. 57–61 discuss the four cardinal or moral virtues derived from classical philosophy. prudence, justice, temperance, and fortitude. Traherne had made notes on these in the Early Notebook (pp. 17–19) from Eustachius à Sancto Paulo, *Ethica*, in *Summa philosophiae quadripartita* (Paris, 1609), and also discusses them at length in *Christian Ethicks* (chapters XIII; XX–XXIII). 62–68 discuss four virtues which Traherne calls theological: faith, righteousness, holiness, and humility, only one of which is among the three virtues traditionally classed as theological (faith, hope, and charity). These too are discussed in *Christian Ethicks* (chapters X; XII; XV; XXVI), but Traherne reverts in the later work to the traditional theological virtues, classifying righteousness and holiness as 'divine' virtues, and humility as 'Christian' (pp. 26–27).

In spite of the similarity of structure between *Christian Ethicks* and this section of *Select Meditations*, parallels are not very close, as Traherne treats the virtues from different perspectives in the two works.

55. l. 11. *they Ex[   ]* The MS leaves a blank here.

57. l. 9. *Lubricities* Instabilities, elusiveness.

ll. 14–15. *By Commanding us to be considerat* Possibly modelled on Augustine's 'Dilige et quod vis fac' (Love and do what you will), *In Epistolam Primam Joannis Tractatus*, VII.8.

l. 32. There are probably some words missing at the end of this meditation, as a gap is left in the MS before 58.

58. l. 3. *Propelling* Driving away.

l. 18. *Distresses* MS reads 'Distressess'.

l. 19. *Bruit* Noise, clamour.

59. l. 1. *Justice is that vertue* This Aristotelian definition of justice was copied by Traherne into the Early Notebook, p. 17, from Eustachius's *Summa philosophiae*, and is also used in *Christian Ethicks*, p. 183.

l. 44. *commutativ* MS reads 'communitativ'. Traherne had made notes from Eustachius on the distinction between distributive and commutative justice in the Early Notebook, p. 18.

60. l. 1. *Temperance is the Execution* cf. *Christian Ethicks*, p. 323 (sig. Aa1r).

l. 1. *It relateth* cf. *Christian Ethicks*, p. 326 (sig. Aa2v).

l. 7. *Sit modus* Let there be a mean in all things, the mean is the fairest virtue. A sententia, the first part of which is derived from

Horace, *Satires*, I.i.106.

l. 11. *All musick* This poem also appears, with identical wording, in *Christian Ethicks*, p. 326 (sig. Aa2v).

62. l. 13. *As Long as we Apprehend God implacable* Marks (p. 341) compares *Christian Ethicks*, pp. 209–10.

l. 23. *Preventeth* Precedes.

l. 24. *they make* MS reads 'they they make'.

63. l. 4. *Right Reason* Conscience.

l. 7. *never* MS reads 'ne- never'.

64. l. 2. *Intention*; l. 6. *I[n]tension* Intensity, depth.

66. Marks (p. 359) thinks that this whole meditation bears a 'strong likeness' to *Christian Ethicks*, chapter XXVI, on humility.

l. 16. *Gods [   ]* MS leaves a blank.

67. l. 3. *His Throne* MS reads 'Him Throne'.

l. 3. *Devolving* Overturning.

68. First poem, l. 4. *the Find* OED does not illuminate the meaning of this; possibly there is a scribal error, but a rhyme for 'mind' is required.

l. 10. *tu[rn]d* MS leaves a blank; 'tun'd' is another possibility.

l. 19. *Narcissus Like* Narcissus, who pined away for love of his own image reflected in a fountain, is perhaps not the most suitable image for a poem on humility.

l. 25. *tho't* MS reads 'tho$^{t\prime}$'.

l. 26. *[   ] all* MS leaves a blank, which requires a word of one syllable.

l. 27. *Scars* ?Fears (OED, 'scare', sb.^{2}, 1), or just possibly derision, insults (OED, 'scare', sb.^{1}).

Fyfield*Books*

Two millennia of essential classics
The extensive FyfieldBooks list includes

For more information, including a full list of Fyfield*Books* and a contents list for each title, and details of how to order the books, visit the Carcanet website at www.carcanet.co.uk or email info@carcanet.co.uk